C000241314

Pete Selby, Andy Healing & Louise Ward

Welcome

This is not an official history of pop music.

Neither is it a high-brow book with lofty opinion and analysis.

However, it **is** a glorious pick 'n' mix assortment of pop memories, of record sleeves and long forgotten logos, of big hits and one-hit wonders, of personal favourites and terrible novelties, and of global superstars and fleeting local heroes.

What are captured here are moments in time.

88 moments over the past 31 years to be precise.

They have provided the soundtrack to your school days, to summer holidays past, to long-ago Christmases and distant Easters. They were there when you were young, they're still with you now, and they'll be with you for many years to come.

This book is for you, your Mum, your Dad, your brother, your sister, your children.

It is the complete history of **NOW That's What I Call Music** the greatest compilation series the world has ever seen.

We hope you enjoy it.

Contents

All statistics in this book relate to the eighty-eight editions of the main NOW series.

A Brief History Of *NOW*

The genesis of *NOW* is a fascinating story in itself. We caught up with Virgin supremo Richard Branson, who shared some thoughts about the beginnings of the series and how he feels now, looking back at the many years of success.

Multi-artist compilation albums had been in the marketplace long before the 1980s pop explosion. Classic label primers such as *Motown Chartbusters* were already rubbing shoulders in Our Price with the more opportunistic hit and miss assemblages from specialist record companies like Ronco and K-Tel.

'Virgin Records had a roster of incredible artists and numerous number one records at this time. We wanted to release an album solely dedicated to the best-selling records we had released and create an album everyone had to get their hands on. Music fans wanted a compilation album of our best records so we gave it to them. It was also another platform for our artists to sell their music through.

A lot of our artists loved the idea for *NOW* as we promised to only publish their songs in full. Rival compilation albums tended to edit and shorten song lengths in order to fit them all onto one tape. We decided to use two records or tapes, giving us the freedom to publish our artists' tracks in full, which they appreciated.'

The idea for a hit-stuffed, premium-quality compilation album was conceived at the Virgin Records office in 1983. Originally the brainchild of Virgin Records executives Stephen Navin and Jon Webster, the concept was presented to Simon Draper, who was Richard Branson's cousin and Head of A&R at Virgin Records. Over at rival record label EMI, MD Peter Jamieson was hatching a similar plan but, impressed with Virgin's ideas, music and enthusiasm, he agreed to a joint venture partnership utilising the very best of both labels' rich, chart blitzing repertoire.

'Luckily we managed to win him over with our music, ideas and passion. He agreed to the partnership and came to my houseboat, *Duende, in* Little Venice, to finalise the deal.

Partnering with EMI gave *NOW!* an advantage over the other compilation brands because we had access to so many great artists and singles other albums didn't have access to.'

Although hopes were high, those involved weren't necessarily anticipating decades of chart dominance and a high-quality hardback book celebrating the series thirty years on.

'There weren't grand aspirations for the *NOW!* brand. We all thought we were on to a winner, otherwise we wouldn't have pressed ahead with it, however I'd be lying if we thought it would turn into what it has today.'

Rival record labels were soon forming alliances to set up their own 'hits' albums, a challenge that Branson relished:

'In business if someone attempts to copy what you're doing then you know you're onto something good, I always tend to take that sort of thing as a compliment.'

There is, however, something else to clear up. How did a cartoon representation of a pig come to adorn the early sleeves, and who thought up that distinctive name?

Rewind a few years and Branson had taken a particular interest in the Dodo bric-a-brac shop on Portobello Road, a stone's throw from his Virgin HQ. One day, during a brief respite from bashfully attempting to woo the sales assistant*, he came across an old 1920s poster ad for Danish bacon featuring a pig listening to a singing chicken. It was captioned 'NOW, That's what I call music'.

He thought it would be perfect for Simon Draper and the poster was hung behind his cousin's desk at the Virgin Records office. There it stayed without comment until the image caught Jamieson's eye as the executives started to thrash out their plans for the nascent compilation album.

Now. That's what I call Music

'The instant Peter Jamieson saw the picture above Simon Draper's desk the name was decided. There was no other name on the table. *NOW! That's What I Call Music* summed up what we were trying to do perfectly!'

The poster had not only provided a unique visual mascot but, more importantly, the slogan offered the perfect solution for what to call their album. It was a powerful and meaningful statement in its own right and when abbreviated to *NOW* gave the ultimate contemporary message.

And as for what happened next? Well, the first *NOW* spent five weeks at the top of the album chart and, deemed a barnstorming success and Christmas bestseller, prompted a follow up edition a few months later. Followed by another. And another. And another. You get the picture.

Over thirty years and nearly ninety volumes later, much has changed in the world, in the music we listen to, and the way we get to hear it.

'It's true that the market has been transformed from the one that Virgin Records first operated in, however the reasons that people decide to purchase a *NOW* record remain the same. Each year there is a collection of songs which everyone in the country becomes familiar with. They'll be played on the radio, at parties, on nights out, in the office and at festivals. Those songs will represent a whole host of emotions and memories for people, so as well as a collection of great songs, it's those memories which people get when they listen to a *NOW* album. Whether you buy vinyl or stream, it doesn't change a thing in that sense.'

A final word from the man who was there at the start of it all. We wondered whether there was a performer Richard Branson had particularly admired, of the thousands that have appeared over the years.

'There are so many brilliant artists that have appeared on *NOW* that I couldn't possibly choose. I recall Mike Oldfield's 'Moonlight Shadow' was on the first *NOW* record. To see Mike continue to experience success is fantastic. After all, Virgin could have been a very different story if it wasn't for the success of *Tubular Bells*.'

NOW still sits at the centre of pop music, collecting today's hits and recording them for posterity, as it has eighty-eight times throughout its lifespan.

This book traces that history.

**Perseverance paid off – Joan and Richard have been together ever since.*

Double Album
30 GREAT TRACKS
including 11 Number Ones

Madness · Culture Club · Kajagoogoo · Duran Duran
UB40 · Phil Collins · Paul Young · Tracey Ullman · Limahl · Genesis
Rod Stewart · Howard Jones · Simple Minds · The Cure · and many more . . .

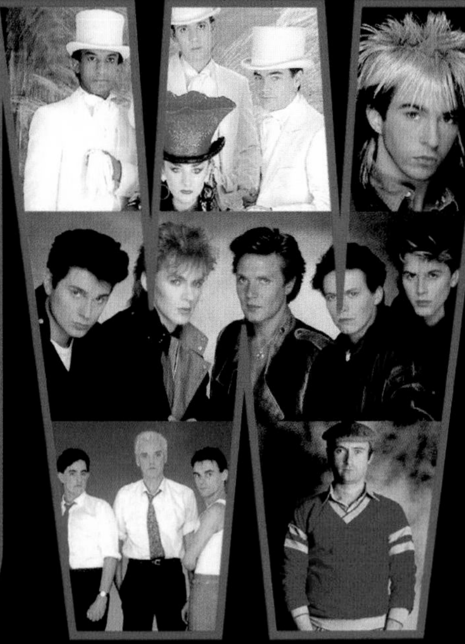

That's What I Call Music

RELEASED 28 NOVEMBER 1983

ALSO HAPPENING IN NOVEMBER 1983

- Protests greeted the arrival of the first American cruise missiles at Greenham Common
- £26 million of gold and diamonds was stolen in the Brinks-MAT robbery at Heathrow – this would be worth £75 million today
- The most-wanted toys were My Little Pony and He-Man and the Masters of the Universe
- *Return of the Jedi* and *Flashdance* were the year's top-grossing films
- This year's books included *Hollywood Wives* (Jackie Collins) and *The Witches* (Roald Dahl)
- Christmas No.1 was 'Only You' **(The Flying Pickets)**

TRACKLISTING NOW 1

Record 1 Side 1

1 You Can't Hurry Love **Phil Collins**
2 Is There Something I Should Know **Duran Duran**
3 Red Red Wine **UB40**
4 Only For Love **Limahl**
5 Temptation **Heaven 17**
6 Give It Up **KC and the Sunshine Band**
7 Double Dutch **Malcolm McLaren**
8 Total Eclipse Of The Heart **Bonnie Tyler**

Record 1 Side 2

1 Karma Chameleon **Culture Club**
2 The Safety Dance **Men Without Hats**
3 Too Shy **Kajagoogoo**
4 Moonlight Shadow **Mike Oldfield**
5 Down Under **Men At Work**
6 (Hey You) The Rock Steady Crew **Rock Steady Crew**
7 Baby Jane **Rod Stewart**
8 Wherever I Lay My Hat (That's My Home) **Paul Young**

Record 2 Side 1

1 Candy Girl **New Edition**
2 Big Apple **Kajagoogoo**
3 Let's Stay Together **Tina Turner**
4 (Keep Feeling) Fascination **The Human League**
5 New Song **Howard Jones**
6 Please Don't Make Me Cry **UB40**
7 Tonight, I Celebrate My Love **Peabo Bryson & Roberta Flack**

Record 2 Side 2

1 They Don't Know **Tracey Ullman**
2 Kissing With Confidence **Will Powers**
3 That's All **Genesis**
4 The Lovecats **The Cure**
5 Waterfront **Simple Minds**
6 The Sun And The Rain **Madness**
7 Victims **Culture Club**

▶ **Phil Collins** appeared as a solo artist another twelve times, awarding him the second highest tally of appearances for a UK male solo artist. A re-released 'In the Air Tonight' on *NOW 68* is his most recent entry.

▶ 'They Don't Know' hit maker **Tracey Ullman** voiced the very first TV ad for *NOW*. She appeared only once more on the second volume with 'My Guy'. **Paul McCartney** (seven *NOW* appearances between *NOW 2* and *NOW 67*) made a cameo appearance in the accompanying video.

▶ **UB40** appeared more than any other artist across the first ten albums – seven times in total, including twice on this volume.

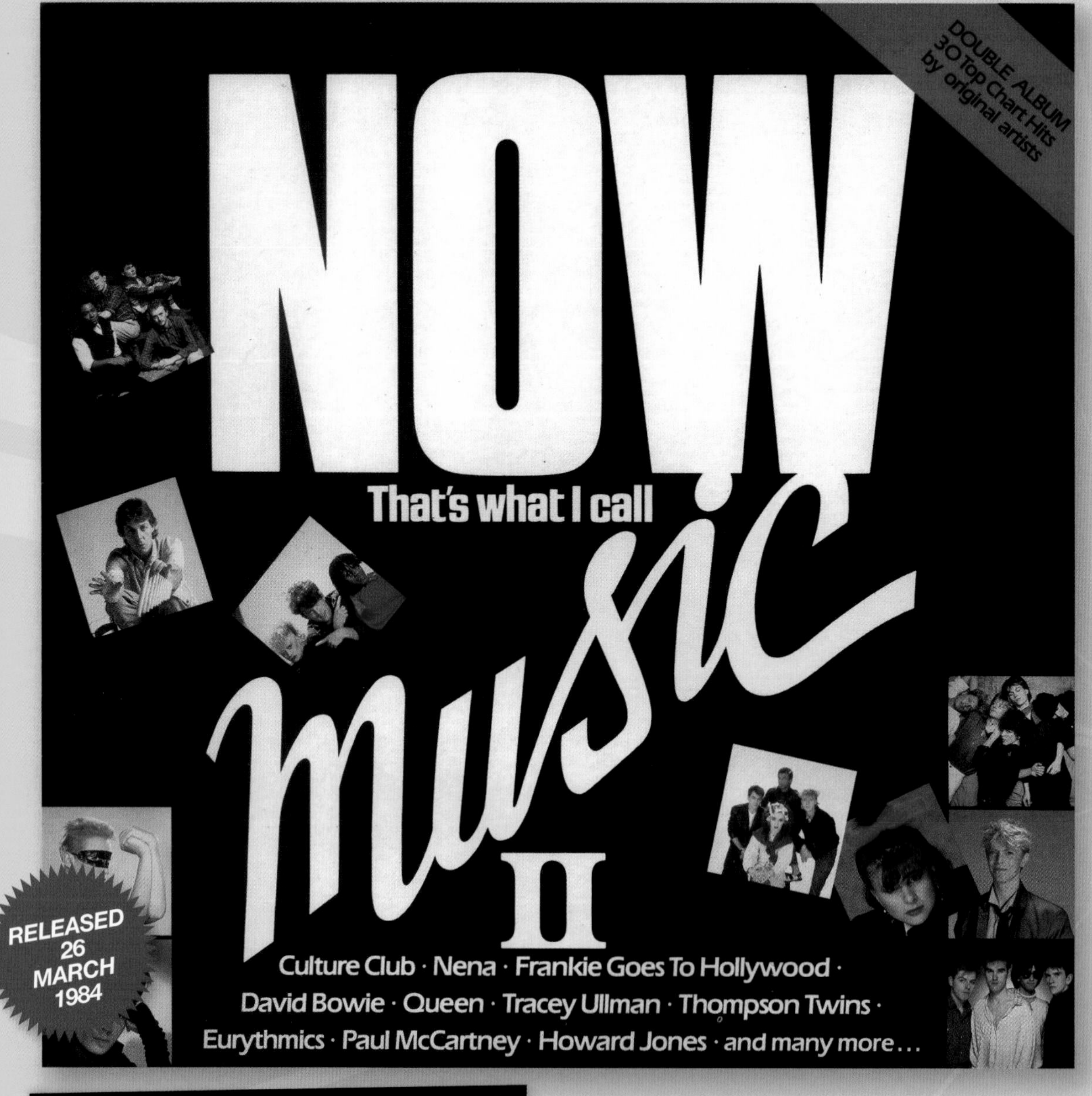

ALSO HAPPENING IN MARCH 1984

- A nationwide miners' strike began, lasting for almost a year
- **Michael Jackson** won a record eight Grammy awards, including seven for *Thriller*
- **Sting** parted ways with **The Police**
- The Apple Mac computer was released
- Torvill and Dean won gold at the Sarajevo Winter Olympics, becoming the highest-scoring figure skaters of all time
- *Starlight Express* opened in London, with music by Andrew Lloyd Webber and choreography by Arlene Phillips
- In the cinema: *Police Academy*, *Splash* and *Romancing the Stone*

TRACKLISTING NOW 2

Record 1 Side 1

1 Radio Ga Ga **Queen**
2 Wouldn't It Be Good **Nik Kershaw**
3 Hold Me Now **Thompson Twins**
4 Get Out Of Your Lazy Bed **Matt Bianco**
5 More, More, More **Carmel**
6 Michael Caine **Madness**
7 Only You **The Flying Pickets**

Record 1 Side 2

1 99 Red Balloons **Nena**
2 Girls Just Wanna Have Fun **Cyndi Lauper**
3 My Guy **Tracey Ullman**
4 Breakin' Down (Sugar Samba) **Julia & Company**
5 Break My Stride **Matthew Wilder**
6 That's Livin' Alright **Joe Fagin**
7 I Gave You My Heart (Didn't I) **Hot Chocolate**
8 Bird Of Paradise **Snowy White**

Record 2 Side 1

1 Relax **Frankie Goes to Hollywood**
2 Here Comes The Rain Again **Eurythmics**
3 What Is Love? **Howard Jones**
4 What Difference Does It Make **The Smiths**
5 (Feels Like) Heaven **Fiction Factory**
6 The Politics Of Dancing **Re-Flex**
7 Hyperactive! **Thomas Dolby**
8 Wishful Thinking **China Crisis**

Record 2 Side 2

1 Modern Love **David Bowie**
2 It's A Miracle **Culture Club**
3 Undercover Of The Night **The Rolling Stones**
4 Wonderland **Big Country**
5 Run Runaway **Slade**
6 New Moon On Monday **Duran Duran**
7 Pipes Of Peace **Paul McCartney**

▶ This was the only *NOW* to feature **The Smiths,** however **Morrissey** appeared again three times as a solo artist once the band had split. Guitarist Johnny Marr also showed up later as a member of **Electronic** on *NOW 22*. **Mark Ronson** featuring **Daniel Merriweather** covered the Smiths song 'Stop Me' on *NOW 67*.

▶ It's one of only two occasions a Roman numeral was used in the title – if that had continued we'd have been talking about *NOW LXXXVIII* by the end of this book.

▶ **Frankie Goes To Hollywood** sold 2 million copies of 'Relax'. The single spent most of 1984 in the charts, and even climbed back up to No.2 during the summer, outsold only by the next Frankie release 'Two Tribes' (*NOW 3*).

ALSO HAPPENING IN JULY 1984

- The Summer Olympics took place in Los Angeles and were boycotted by the Soviet Union. Notable events included Carl Lewis winning four gold medals, and British golds for Daley Thompson and Sebastian Coe
- In the cinema: *Indiana Jones and the Temple of Doom*, *Ghostbusters*, *Gremlins* and *The Karate Kid*
- **The Red Hot Chilli Peppers** released their self-titled debut album. There were also albums from **Bruce Springsteen** (*Born in the USA*) and **Prince** – *Purple Rain* went on to sell 20 million copies

TRACKLISTING NOW 3

Record 1 Side 1

1 The Reflex **Duran Duran**
2 I Won't Let The Sun Go Down On Me **Nik Kershaw**
3 Thinking Of You **Sister Sledge**
4 Locomotion **Orchestral Manoeuvres in the Dark**
5 Dancing With Tears In My Eyes **Ultravox**
6 Pearl In The Shell **Howard Jones**
7 Don't Tell Me **Blancmange**
8 Against All Odds (Take A Look At Me Now) **Phil Collins**

Record 1 Side 2

1 Two Tribes **Frankie Goes to Hollywood**
2 White Lines (Don't Don't Do It) **Grandmaster Flash & The Furious Five**
3 Nelson Mandela **The Special AKA**
4 Love Wars **Womack & Womack**
5 You're The Best Thing **The Style Council**
6 One Love/People Get Ready **Bob Marley & The Wailers**
7 Smalltown Boy **Bronski Beat**

Record 2 Side 1

1 I Want To Break Free **Queen**
2 Time After Time **Cyndi Lauper**
3 Love Resurrection **Alison Moyet**
4 Young At Heart **The Bluebells**
5 Robert De Niro's Waiting **Bananarama**
6 Dr Mabuse **Propaganda**
7 What's Love Got To Do With It **Tina Turner**
8 When You're Young And In Love **The Flying Pickets**

Record 2 Side 2

1 Wake Me Up Before You Go-Go **Wham!**
2 You Take Me Up **Thompson Twins**
3 It's Raining Men **The Weather Girls**
4 Dance Me Up **Gary Glitter**
5 Susanna **The Art Company**
6 One Better Day **Madness**
7 Red Guitar **David Sylvian**

▶ This was the first use of the pig and 'classic 80s' logo on the front sleeve. Whilst the series is inextricably linked with the pig, he only appeared on two further volumes.

▶ **Bob Marley** landed his first of three posthumous appearances. 'One Love' reached No.5 in April ahead of his bestselling *Legend* compilation. His son **Damian 'Jr Gong' Marley** kept the family business ticking over on *NOW 62*.

▶ It was **George Michael**'s debut appearance in the *NOW* series. He went on to feature another ten times as a solo artist or collaborator, but only once more with **Wham!**

ALSO HAPPENING IN NOVEMBER 1984

- The famine in Ethiopia came to public attention after Michael Buerk's harrowing reports on BBC News. **Band Aid** record 'Do They Know It's Christmas?' which sold over 1 million copies in its first week of release and stayed at No.1 for five weeks
- 1984's top selling toys and games included Care Bears and Trivial Pursuit
- *A Nightmare on Elm Street*, *The Terminator* and *Beverly Hills Cop* were all released
- Top albums in 1984 included *Welcome to the Pleasuredome* **(Frankie Goes to Hollywood)** and *Like a Virgin* **(Madonna)**

TRACKLISTING NOW 4

Record 1 Side 1

1 No More Lonely Nights **Paul McCartney**
2 Together In Electric Dreams **Philip Oakey & Giorgio Moroder**
3 Why? **Bronski Beat**
4 The Neverending Story **Limahl**
5 Warning Sign **Nick Heyward**
6 Missing You **John Waite**
7 Farewell My Summer Love **Michael Jackson**
8 Hello **Lionel Richie**

Record 1 Side 2

1 The War Song **Culture Club**
2 Passengers **Elton John**
3 Too Late For Goodbyes **Julian Lennon**
4 Shout To The Top **The Style Council**
5 Doctor! Doctor! **Thompson Twins**
6 Sunset Now **Heaven 17**
7 Respect Yourself **The Kane Gang**
8 Private Dancer **Tina Turner**

Record 2 Side 1

1 It's A Hard Life **Queen**
2 The Wanderer **Status Quo**
3 East Of Eden **Big Country**
4 Pride (In The Name Of Love) **U2**
5 Listen To Your Father **Feargal Sharkey**
6 Tesla Girls **Orchestral Manoeuvres in the Dark**
7 The Second Time **Kim Wilde**
8 Human Racing **Nik Kershaw**

Record 2 Side 2

1 Ghostbusters **Ray Parker Jr**
2 If It Happens Again **UB40**
3 Jump (For My Love) **The Pointer Sisters**
4 Hot Water **Level 42**
5 Sexcrime (Nineteen Eighty-Four) **Eurythmics**
6 Somebody's Watching Me **Rockwell**
7 Madam Butterfly (Un Bel Di Vedremo) **Malcolm McLaren**
8 Gotta Get You Home Tonight **Eugene Wilde**

▶ This was the first *NOW* to feature as many as thirty-two tracks. That's eight per side of vinyl or cassette.

▶ 'Farewell My Summer Love' was **Michael Jackson**'s only credited appearance in the *NOW* series until his reappearance on *NOW 88.* It was recorded in 1973 and re-promoted by his old label in the wake of the success of the *Thriller* album. Elsewhere on this album, incognito, he sings the chorus of **Rockwell**'s 'Somebody's Watching Me'.

▶ It was also the first *NOW* appearance for **Elton John**. He last turned up on *NOW 73* as a featured artist with **Ironik** and **Chipmunk** on 'Tiny Dancer (Hold Me Closer)', and has featured nine other times in between.

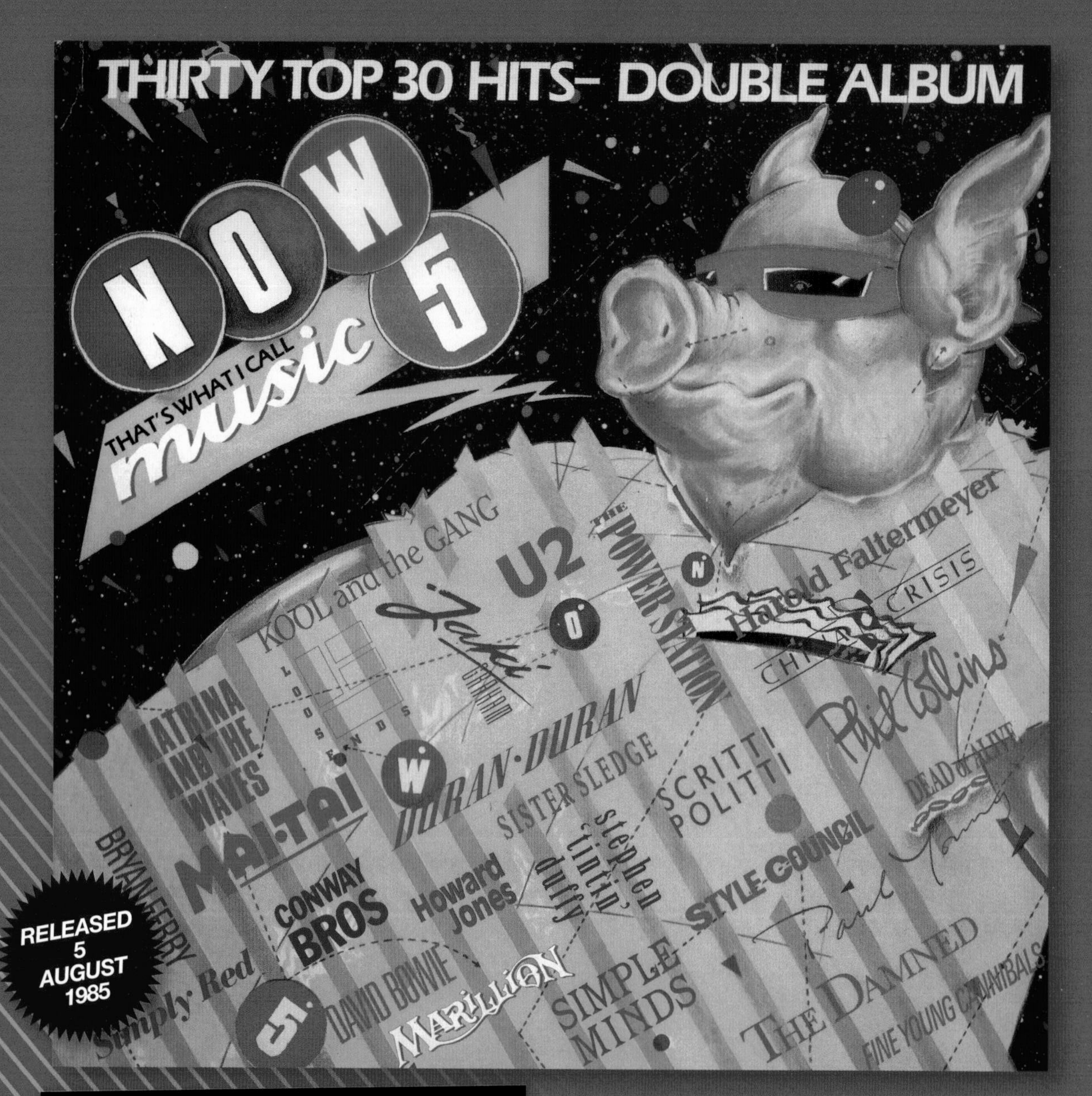

ALSO HAPPENING IN AUGUST 1985

- **Michael Jackson** bought the publishing rights to most Beatles songs for $47million
- The wreck of the *Titanic* was found
- Live Aid concerts raised £150 million for Africa
- The *Super Mario Brothers* game was released in Europe. Over 40 million copies were sold in total and until 2008 it remained the bestselling video game of all time
- This year's top films included *Weird Science*, *Pee-Wee's Big Adventure* and *Year of the Dragon*
- *Bullseye* and *Danger Mouse* were hits on TV, and the BBC's new soap *EastEnders* grew in popularity

TRACKLISTING NOW 5

Record 1 Side 1

1 A View To A Kill **Duran Duran**
2 The Word Girl **Scritti Politti**
3 Axel F **Harold Faltermeyer**
4 Johnny Come Home **Fine Young Cannibals**
5 In Too Deep **Dead Or Alive**
6 Icing On The Cake **Stephen 'Tin Tin' Duffy**
7 Cherish **Kool & The Gang**
8 Every Time You Go Away **Paul Young**

Record 1 Side 2

1 Kayleigh **Marillion**
2 Slave To Love **Bryan Ferry**
3 This Is Not America **David Bowie & The Pat Metheny Group**
4 Don't You (Forget About Me) **Simple Minds**
5 Get It On (Bang A Gong) **The Power Station**
6 Black Man Ray **China Crisis**
7 One More Night **Phil Collins**

Record 2 Side 1

1 Frankie **Sister Sledge**
2 History **Mai Tai**
3 Money's Too Tight (To Mention) **Simply Red**
4 Feel So Real **Steve Arrington**
5 Round And Around **Jaki Graham**
6 Turn It Up **The Conway Brothers**
7 Magic Touch **Loose Ends**
8 N-N-Nineteen Not Out **The Commentators**

Record 2 Side 2

1 The Unforgettable Fire **U2**
2 Walls Come Tumbling Down **The Style Council**
3 Walking On Sunshine **Katrina and The Waves**
4 Out In The Fields **Gary Moore and Phil Lynott**
5 The Shadow Of Love **The Damned**
6 Life In One Day **Howard Jones**
7 Love Don't Live Here Anymore **Jimmy Nail**

▶ The third and final TV ad to feature a voiceover from actor Brian Glover, signing off with the request to 'Make it Pig!'

▶ 'A View To A Kill' marked the first of only four James Bond theme inclusions. 'Licence To Kill' (*NOW 15*), 'GoldenEye' (*NOW 32*) and 'Tomorrow Never Dies' (*NOW 39*) made up the quartet. **Moby**'s 'James Bond theme' (as featured in '*Tomorrow Never Dies*') also appears on *NOW 38*.

▶ **Harold Faltermeyer** made his sole appearance as a performer with 'Axel F' but contributed to *NOW 18* producing **Pet Shop Boys**' 'So Hard'. 'Axel F' re-appeared on *NOW 30* and *NOW 61* covered by **Clock** and **Crazy Frog** respectively.

MOST FEATURED ARTISTS

ROBBIE WILLIAMS
29

BOYZONE
15

CALVIN HARRIS
17

SUGABABES
19

MCFLY
15

DAVID GUETTA
16

THE BLACK EYED PEAS
15

RIHANNA
25

BRITNEY SPEARS
19

GIRLS ALOUD
21

KATY PERRY
15

KYLIE MINOGUE
23

U2
19

Credited appearances only.

31
UK TOP TEN SINGLES

7
UNCREDITED VOCAL CONTRIBUTIONS
Four with Take That
One with Helping Haiti
One with Justice Collective
One with 1 Giant Leap

29
CREDITED APPEARANCES

ROBBIE WILLIAMS

The artist with the most *NOW* appearances of all.
We salute him.

5
DUETS
Kylie Minogue
Nicole Kidman
Pet Shop Boys
Gary Barlow
Dizzee Rascal

17
BRIT AWARDS

OLDEST SONGS

Recordings from before 1980 that appeared on *NOW*

1957

Jackie Wilson
'Reet Petite'
NOW 9

1958

Nina Simone
'My Baby Just Cares For Me'
NOW 10

Eddie Cochran
'C'mon Everybody'
NOW 11

1961

Ben E. King
'Stand By Me'
NOW 9

Etta James
'I Just Want To Make Love To You'
NOW 33

1962

John Lee Hooker
'Boom Boom'
NOW 23

1965

Righteous Brothers
'Unchained Melody'
NOW 18

Righteous Brothers
'You've Lost That Lovin' Feelin''
NOW 19

Temptations
'My Girl'
NOW 21

1966

Dusty Springfield
'You Don't Have To Say You Love Me'
NOW 42

1967

Erma Franklin
'(Take A Little) Piece Of My Heart'
NOW 23

1968
Prince Buster
'Whine And Grine'
NOW 39

1969
The Hollies
'He Ain't Heavy He's My Brother'
NOW 13

Louis Armstrong
'We Have All The Time In The World'
NOW 29

1970
Free
'All Right Now'
NOW 19

1971
John Lennon
'Imagine'
NOW 45

Tony Christie
'(Is This The Way To) Amarillo'
NOW 60

1973
Michael Jackson
'Farewell My Summer Love'
NOW 4

Steve Miller Band
'The Joker'
NOW 18

Tony Christie
'Avenues And Alleyways'
NOW 61

1975
Queen
'Bohemian Rhapsody'
NOW 21

Hot Chocolate
'You Sexy Thing'
NOW 38

1976
Rose Royce
'Car Wash'
NOW 12

Abba
'Dancing Queen'
NOW 23

1977
Bob Marley & The Wailers
'One Love/ People Get Ready'
NOW 3

RELEASED 25 NOVEMBER 1985

ALSO HAPPENING IN NOVEMBER 1985

- The first version of Windows (Windows 1.0) was released by Microsoft
- This year's most-wanted toys were *Transformers* figures
- *Back to the Future* and *Rocky IV* were huge hits at the cinema
- **Fine Young Cannibals** released their self-titled debut album. **Shakin' Stevens** topped the charts at Christmas with 'Merry Christmas Everyone'
- In the world of literature, *The Handmaid's Tale* (Margaret Atwood) was published
- On television people were watching *Bergerac*, *Blankety Blank* and the first episodes of *Blind Date*

TRACKLISTING NOW 6

Record 1 Side 1

1 *One Vision* Queen
2 *When A Heart Beats* Nik Kershaw
3 *A Good Heart* Feargal Sharkey
4 *There Must Be An Angel (Playing With My Heart)* Eurythmics
5 *Alive And Kicking* Simple Minds
6 *It's Only Love (Live)* Tina Turner with Bryan Adams
7 *Empty Rooms* Gary Moore
8 *Lavender* Marillion

Record 1 Side 2

1 *Nikita* Elton John
2 *Running Up That Hill (A Deal With God)* Kate Bush
3 *Something About You* Level 42
4 *We Don't Need Another Hero (Thunderdome)* Tina Turner
5 *Don't Break My Heart* UB40
6 *Separate Lives* Phil Collins & Marilyn Martin
7 *She's So Beautiful* Cliff Richard

Record 2 Side 1

1 *Election Day* Arcadia
2 *I Got You Babe* UB40 Feat. Chrissie Hynde
3 *Blue* Fine Young Cannibals
4 *If I Was* Midge Ure
5 *Cities In Dust* Siouxsie & The Banshees
6 *Uncle Sam* Madness
7 *Lost Weekend* Lloyd Cole & The Commotions
8 *You Are My World* The Communards

Record 2 Side 2

1 *Just For Money* Paul Hardcastle
2 *Miami Vice Theme* Jan Hammer
3 *Body Rock* Maria Vidal
4 *Tarzan Boy* Baltimora
5 *Body And Soul* Mai Tai
6 *Single Life* Cameo
7 *Mated* David Grant & Jaki Graham

▶ For the first time since *NOW 3*, the sleeve did not feature the iconic pig. The porcine personality would not be seen again on subsequent volumes of the main *NOW* series.

▶ 'Alive And Kicking' by **Simple Minds** was included again on *NOW 23* after being featured in a trailer for the then brand-new Sky Premier League football coverage.

▶ This was the first appearance on a *NOW* by **Kate Bush**, who returned on *NOW 7* accompanied by **Peter Gabriel** and with 'The Sensual World' on *NOW 16*. 'Running Up That Hill' regained a top ten position in 2012 after featuring in the London Olympic closing ceremony.

32 TOP CHART HITS

RELEASED 11 AUGUST 1986

GABRIEL · WHAM! · DAVID BOWIE · GENESIS · THE HOUSEMARTINS · DOCTOR AND THE MEDICS · PET SHOP BOYS · LEVEL 42
MINDS · UB40 · A-HA · SLY FOX · OWEN PAUL · CHRIS DE BURGH · PATTI LA BELLE & MICHAEL McDONALD · SIMPLY RED · BILLY OCEAN
PLUS MANY MORE

ALSO HAPPENING IN AUGUST 1986

- Concern about the safety of nuclear power grew following the Chernobyl disaster
- The stars of *Grange Hill* did their part in the war on drugs with their song 'Just Say No', which reached the top ten in the charts
- The Panini football stickers and Garbage Pail Kids cards crazes swept playgrounds throughout the country
- Films *Top Gun*, *The Fly* and *Stand By Me* were released
- New albums included *Slippery When Wet* (**Bon Jovi**), *True Colors* (**Cyndi Lauper**) and *True Blue* (**Madonna**)

TRACKLISTING NOW 7

Record 1 Side 1

1 *Sledgehammer* Peter Gabriel
2 *Sing Our Own Song* UB40
3 *Let's Go All The Way* Sly Fox
4 *Lessons In Love* Level 42
5 *Opportunities (Let's Make Lots Of Money)* Pet Shop Boys
6 *Sinful!* Pete Wylie
7 *Camouflage* Stan Ridgway
8 *Paranoimia* Art of Noise with Max Headroom

Record 1 Side 2

1 *The Lady In Red* Chris De Burgh
2 *Absolute Beginners* David Bowie
3 *Invisible Touch* Genesis
4 *All The Things She Said* Simple Minds
5 *Happy Hour* The Housemartins
6 *Look Away* Big Country
7 *Brilliant Mind* Furniture
8 *Call Of The Wild* Midge Ure

Record 2 Side 1

1 *The Edge Of Heaven* Wham!
2 *My Favourite Waste Of Time* Owen Paul
3 *Too Good To Be Forgotten* Amazulu
4 *Spirit In The Sky* Doctor & The Medics
5 *Venus* Bananarama
6 *New Beginning (Mamba Seyra)* Bucks Fizz
7 *Hunting High And Low* A-ha
8 *Holding Back The Years* Simply Red
9 *A Kind Of Magic* Queen

Record 2 Side 2

1 *When The Going Gets Tough, The Tough Gets Going* Billy Ocean
2 *Set Me Free* Jaki Graham
3 *I Can't Wait* Nu Shooz
4 *Amityville (The House On The Hill)* Lovebug Starski
5 *Headlines* Midnight Star
6 *You And Me Tonight* Aurra
7 *On My Own* Patti Labelle and Michael McDonald
8 *Bang Zoom (Let's Go Go)* The Real Roxanne with Hitman Howie Tee

▶ 'Absolute Beginners' marked **David Bowie**'s third and final appearance to date on a NOW album. That's one less appearance than **Pato Banton.**

▶ **The Housemartins** commenced the longest consecutive run in the '80s (four editions), an accolade they share with **Bananarama** (*NOW 9–12*), **Inner City** (*NOW 13–16*), **T'Pau** (*NOW 10–13*) and **Jaki Graham** (*NOW 5–8*).

▶ The solitary appearance for **Chris De Burgh** in the *NOW* series. Fellow Chrises, **Isaak** ('Blue Hotel') and **Rea** ('Auberge') each also clocked up a single appearance, both on *NOW 19*.

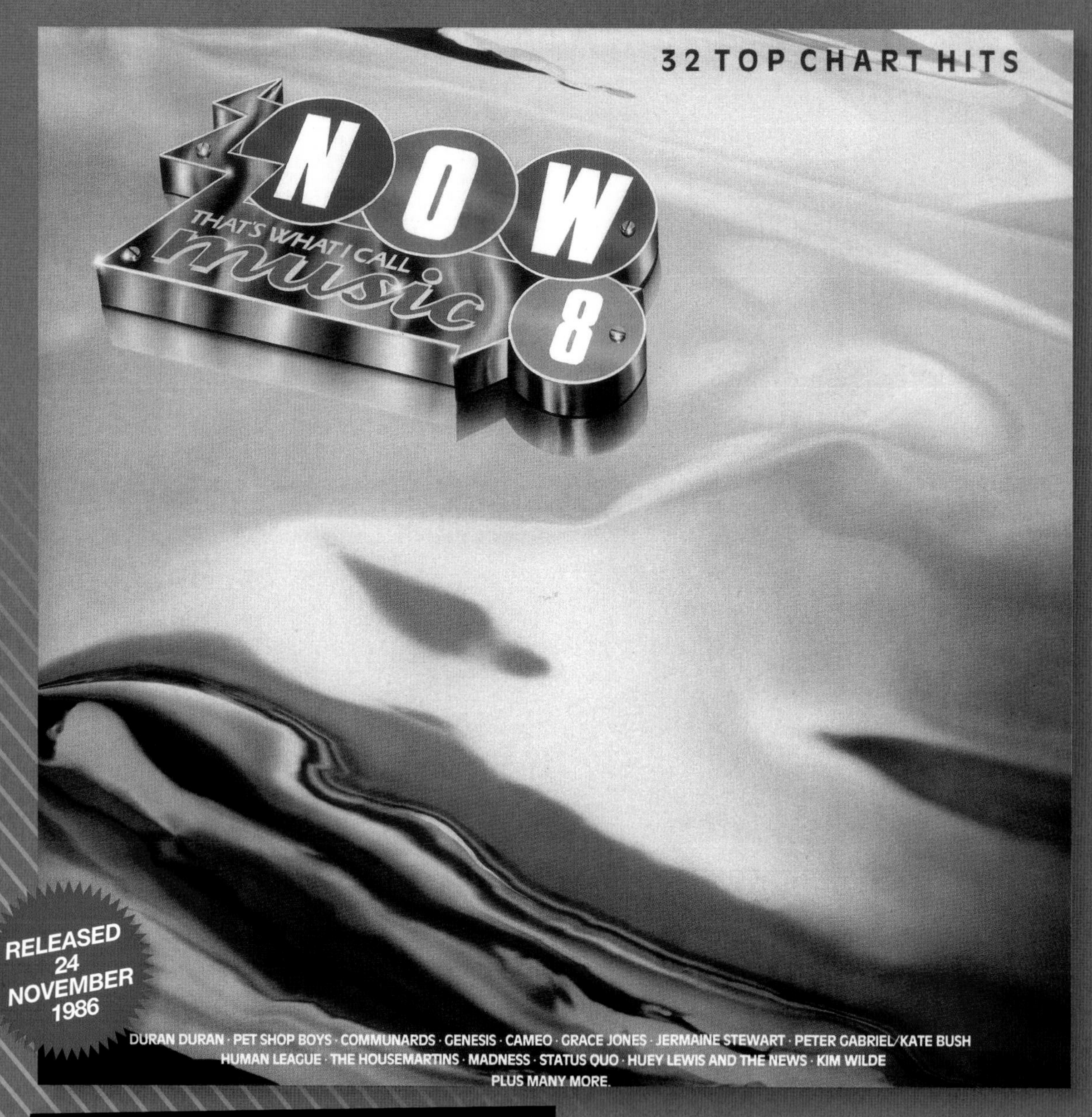

ALSO HAPPENING IN NOVEMBER 1986

- In the sporting world, 20-year-old Mike Tyson became the youngest-ever WBC World Heavyweight Champion, while in the UK Alex Ferguson took over as manager of Manchester United
- *Beadle's About* was first shown on television
- *Star Trek IV: The Voyage Home* was a hit in the cinema
- Album releases included *Licensed to Ill* (**Beastie Boys**), *Another Step* (**Kim Wilde**)
- Stephen King's *It* was published, showing just how terrifying clowns can be
- Christmas No.1 was 'Reet Petite' by **Jackie Wilson**

TRACKLISTING NOW 8

Record 1 Side 1

1 *Notorious* Duran Duran
2 *Suburbia* Pet Shop Boys
3 *Walk This Way* Run DMC
4 *Don't Leave Me This Way* The Communards
5 *Breakout* Swing Out Sister
6 *Higher Love* Steve Winwood
7 *(Forever) Live And Die* Orchestral Manoeuvres in the Dark
8 *In Too Deep* Genesis

Record 1 Side 2

1 *Word Up* Cameo
2 *I'm Not Perfect (But I'm Perfect For You)* Grace Jones
3 *Showing Out (Get Fresh At The Weekend)* Mel & Kim
4 *We Don't Have To Take Our Clothes Off* Jermaine Stewart
5 *Step Right Up* Jaki Graham
6 *What Have You Done For Me Lately* Janet Jackson
7 *Human* The Human League
8 *I Want to Wake Up With You* Boris Gardiner

Record 2 Side 1

1 *Don't Give Up* Peter Gabriel and Kate Bush
2 *Think For A Minute* The Housemartins
3 *(Waiting For) The Ghost-Train* Madness
4 *In The Army Now* Status Quo
5 *Stuck With You* Huey Lewis & The News
6 *One Great Thing* Big Country
7 *Greetings To The New Brunette* Billy Bragg
8 *(I Just) Died In Your Arms* Cutting Crew

Record 2 Side 2

1 *You Keep Me Hanging On* Kim Wilde
2 *Calling All The Heroes* It Bites
3 *Waterloo* Doctor & The Medics
4 *French Kissin' In The USA* Debbie Harry
5 *I Didn't Mean To Turn You On* Robert Palmer
6 *The Wizard* Paul Hardcastle
7 *(They Long To Be) Close To You* Gwen Guthrie
8 *Every Loser Wins* Nick Berry

▶ The only original *Top Of The Pops* theme song to appear on a *NOW* album was **Paul Hardcastle**'s 'The Wizard'. In the 1970s and again from 1998 to 2003, a version of **Led Zeppelin**'s 'Whole Lotta Love' was used; this was covered by **Goldbug** on *NOW 33.*

▶ **Janet Jackson**'s first UK hit, 'What Have You Done For Me Lately', brought her *NOW* tally level with brother **Michael**. She went on to feature nine times in total.

▶ **Cameo**'s 'Word Up' has been a hit four times by very different artists – **Cameo** themselves, Scottish rock band **Gun**, ex-Spice Girl **Melanie G** (as she was then named) and **Little Mix** in 2014. Only **Gun**'s version did not make it to a *NOW* tracklist.

30 TOP CHART HITS

RELEASED 23 MARCH 1987

BEN E. KING · BOY GEORGE · CURIOSITY KILLED THE CAT · SIMPLY RED · A-HA · FREDDIE MERCURY
5 STAR · MENTAL AS ANYTHING · GENESIS · UB40 · BON JOVI · WESTWORLD · JACKIE WILSON
PLUS MANY MORE

ALSO HAPPENING IN MARCH 1987

- **U2** released their chart-topping album *The Joshua Tree. Running in the Family* by **Level 42** is also released
- Van Gogh's *Sunflowers* was sold for a record £22.5 million
- Wrestling was at the height of its popularity, with Hulk Hogan as the WWF champion. *Wrestlemania III* was attended by over 90,000 people, setting an indoor attendance record which still stands today
- Cinema audiences were glued to *Lethal Weapon.* Later in the year *Robocop*, *Predator* and *Fatal Attraction* were also huge successes

TRACKLISTING NOW 9

Record 1 Side 1

1 *Reet Petite* **Jackie Wilson**
2 *Live It Up* **Mental As Anything**
3 *The Right Thing* **Simply Red**
4 *Sometimes* **Erasure**
5 *C'est La Vie* **Robbie Nevil**
6 *You Sexy Thing* **Hot Chocolate**
7 *It Doesn't Have To Be This Way* **The Blow Monkeys**
8 *Caravan Of Love* **The Housemartins**

Record 1 Side 2

1 *Everything I Own* **Boy George**
2 *Rat In Mi Kitchen* **UB40**
3 *Big Fun* **The Gap Band**
4 *Stay Out Of My Life* **Five Star**
5 *Heartache* **Pepsi & Shirlie**
6 *Trick Of The Night* **Bananarama**
7 *Take My Breath Away* **Berlin**

Record 2 Side 1

1 *The Great Pretender* **Freddie Mercury**
2 *Stand By Me* **Ben E. King**
3 *Down To Earth* **Curiosity Killed The Cat**
4 *So Cold The Night* **The Communards**
5 *Jack Your Body* **Steve 'Silk' Hurley**
6 *I Love My Radio (Midnight Radio)* **Taffy**
7 *Loving You Is Sweeter Than Ever* **Nick Kamen**
8 *Manhattan Skyline* **A-ha**

Record 2 Side 2

1 *Sonic Boom Boy* **Westworld**
2 *Livin' On A Prayer* **Bon Jovi**
3 *Land Of Confusion* **Genesis**
4 *The Final Countdown* **Europe**
5 *Over The Hills And Far Away* **Gary Moore**
6 *Cross That Bridge* **The Ward Brothers**
7 *Hymn To Her* **The Pretenders**

▶ *NOW* debuts for **Erasure** and **Bon Jovi. Erasure** featured twelve more times before **Bon Jovi** next materialised, ten years later on *NOW 34.* **Yazoo** – Vince Clarke of **Erasure**'s previous band – do not appear in the series. His former **Depeche Mode** pals made *their* debut after his departure ('Enjoy The Silence', *NOW 17*).

▶ **Ben E. King**'s 'Stand By Me' was the first Levi's Ad soundtrack song to be included on a *NOW*. Ten more followed spanning *NOW 11* (**Eddie Cochran**) to *NOW 42* (**Mr. Oizo**).

▶ **Jimmy Somerville** appeared ten times across the first twenty *NOW*s in three different guises (with **Bronski Beat, The Communards** and solo). 'So Cold The Night' is **The Communards**' third appearance.

ALSO HAPPENING IN NOVEMBER 1987

- Clearing up continued after the hurricane that swept the country in October caused an estimated £2 billion of damage
- The UK government unsuccessfully attempted to prevent publication of *Spycatcher*, the memoirs of former MI5 officer Peter Wright. Tom Clancy's *Patriot Games* was also a bestseller
- Sylvanian Families figures were the year's most-wanted toys
- At the cinema: *The Running Man*, *Three Men and a Baby* and *Planes, Trains and Automobiles*
- Christmas No.1 was 'Always on My Mind' (**Pet Shop Boys**)

TRACKLISTING NOW 10

CD1

1 *Barcelona* Freddie Mercury & Montserrat Caballé
2 *Rent* Pet Shop Boys
3 *Never Can Say Goodbye* The Communards
4 *Pump Up The Volume* M/A/R/R/S
5 *Labour Of Love* Hue And Cry
6 *The Real Thing* Jellybean feat. Steven Dante
7 *I Don't Want To Be A Hero* Johnny Hates Jazz
8 *Wanted* The Style Council
9 *China In Your Hand* T'Pau
10 *Alone* Heart
11 *Crazy Crazy Nights* Kiss
12 *Mony Mony* Billy Idol
13 *Here I Go Again* Whitesnake
14 *Rain In The Summertime* The Alarm
15 *Sugar Mice* Marillion

CD2

1 *Sweet Little Mystery* Wet Wet Wet
2 *Misfit* Curiosity Killed the Cat
3 *La Bamba* Los Lobos
4 *Wipe Out* The Beach Boys & The Fat Boys
5 *Love In The First Degree* Bananarama
6 *My Pretty One* Cliff Richard
7 *Hey Matthew* Karel Fialka
8 *Crockett's Theme* Jan Hammer
9 *My Baby Just Cares For Me* Nina Simone
10 *The Circus* Erasure
11 *Build* The Housemartins
12 *It's Over* Level 42
13 *When Smokey Sings* ABC
14 *Hourglass* Squeeze
15 *Fairytale Of New York* The Pogues feat. Kirsty MacColl

▶ This edition was the first to have an identical tracklist across vinyl, cassette and the increasingly popular CD format. Whilst CD variants of *NOW*s *4*, *8* and *9* were released, they featured fewer tracks than on vinyl.

▶ At the time this was the biggest selling *NOW* ever – a title it would hold until *NOW 29* seven years later.

▶ Christmas-referencing hits are usually nowhere to be seen on main *NOW* albums, having their own *NOW Christmas* series. 'Fairytale Of New York' by **The Pogues** featuring **Kirsty MacColl** is the unique and honourable exception.

30 TOP CHART HITS

NOW THAT'S WHAT I CALL music 11

RELEASED 21 MARCH 1988

PET SHOP BOYS · WET WET WET · T'PAU · MEL & KIM · MORRISSEY
BELINDA CARLISLE · KYLIE MINOGUE · BILLY OCEAN · BOMB THE BASS · JERMAINE STEWART
ANARAMA · EDDY GRANT · EDDIE COCHRAN · WHITESNAKE · JOHNNY HATES JAZZ · ELTON JOHN · THE MISSION
PLUS MANY MORE

ALSO HAPPENING IN MARCH 1988

- Eddie 'the Eagle' Edwards received a hero's welcome on his return from the Winter Olympics in Calgary, despite coming last in the 70m ski jump
- Plans were unveiled for Canary Wharf, set to be Europe's tallest skyscraper
- Students prepared to sit the first GCSE examinations that summer
- Films: *The Last Emperor*, *Beetlejuice*
- **Celine Dion** won the Eurovision Song Contest for Switzerland
- On television: *All Creatures Great and Small, Going Live!* and *Fireman Sam*

TRACKLISTING NOW 11

CD1

1 *Always On My Mind* **Pet Shop Boys**
2 *Heaven Is A Place On Earth* **Belinda Carlisle**
3 *Get Outta My Dreams, Get Into My Car* **Billy Ocean**
4 *Say It Again* **Jermaine Stewart**
5 *Gimme Hope Jo-anna* **Eddy Grant**
6 *C'mon Everybody* **Eddie Cochran**
7 *Suedehead* **Morrissey**
8 *Candle In The Wind* **Elton John**
9 *Angel Eyes (Home And Away)* **Wet Wet Wet**
10 *Turn Back The Clock* **Johnny Hates Jazz**
11 *Valentine* **T'Pau**
12 *Hot In The City* **Billy Idol**
13 *Mandinka* **Sinéad O'Connor**
14 *Tower Of Strength* **The Mission**
15 *Give Me All Your Love* **Whitesnake**

CD2

1 *I Should Be So Lucky* **Kylie Minogue**
2 *That's The Way It Is* **Mel & Kim**
3 *Come Into My Life* **Joyce Sims**
4 *Who Found Who* **Jellybean feat. Elisa Fiorillo**
5 *I Can't Help It* **Bananarama**
6 *Oh L'amour* **Dollar**
7 *Joe Le Taxi* **Vanessa Paradis**
8 *Stutter Rap (No Sleep Til Bedtime)* **Morris Minor and The Majors**
9 *Beat Dis* **Bomb The Bass**
10 *Doctorin' The House* **Coldcut feat. Yazz & The Plastic Population**
11 *House Arrest* **Krush**
12 *The Jack That House Built* **Jack N Chill**
13 *Rock Da House* **The Beatmasters feat. Cookie Crew**
14 *I'm Tired Of Getting Pushed Around* **Two Men A Drum Machine And A Trumpet**
15 *Rise To The Occasion* **Climie Fisher**

▶ 'I Should Be So Lucky' marked the first of twenty-three appearances for **Kylie Minogue**. As such she is ranked No.3 on the 'Most Featured Artist' leader board.

▶ 'Candle In The Wind', the UK's biggest selling song since records began, made its one and only appearance on a *NOW* release. This version was taken from Elton John's live album with the Melbourne Symphony Orchestra.

▶ Simon Climie made his first of three appearances with **Climie Fisher**. After a twelve year absence he returned as a songwriter for the **Honeyz** on *NOW 45* and **Stephen Gately** on *NOW 46*.

ALSO HAPPENING IN JULY 1988

- Thousands packed Wembley Stadium to see **Michael Jackson** perform
- The BBC Six O' Clock News temporarily went off the air when the studio was invaded by gay rights protesters. Newsreader Nicholas Witchell restrained one protester, leading to the memorable *Daily Mirror* headline 'Beeb Man Sits on Lesbian'
- Paul Gascoigne joined Tottenham Hotspur for the fee of £2 million
- At the cinema: *Short Circuit 2*, *Die Hard*, *A Fish Called Wanda*, *Cocktail*
- New album releases included *Kylie* (**Kylie Minogue**), *Straight Outta Compton* (**N.W.A**)

TRACKLISTING NOW 12

CD1

1 *With A Little Help From My Friends* Wet Wet Wet
2 *Circle In The Sand* Belinda Carlisle
3 *Wild World* Maxi Priest
4 *Give A Little Love* Aswad
5 *Love Changes (Everything)* Climie Fisher
6 *I Don't Wanna Go On With You Like That* Elton John
7 *Oh Patti (Don't Feel Sorry For Loverboy)* Scritti Politti
8 *In The Air Tonight* Phil Collins
9 *Don't Go* The Hothouse Flowers
10 *Everyday Is Like Sunday* Morrissey
11 *Mary's Prayer* Danny Wilson
12 *Heart Of Gold* Johnny Hates Jazz
13 *Don't Call Me Baby* Voice of the Beehive
14 *Can I Play With Madness* Iron Maiden
15 *These Dreams* Heart
16 *I Will Be With You* T'Pau

CD2

1 *Doctorin' The Tardis* The Timelords
2 *Boys (Summertime Love)* Sabrina
3 *I Want You Back* Bananarama
4 *I Think We're Alone Now* Tiffany
5 *Who's Leaving Who* Hazell Dean
6 *There's More To Love Than Boy Meets Girl* The Communards
7 *Get Lucky* Jermaine Stewart
8 *Nothing's Gonna Change My Love For You* Glenn Medeiros
9 *Theme From S-Express* S-Express
10 *Push It* Salt 'N' Pepa
11 *Bad Young Brother* Derek B
12 *The Payback Mix (Part One)* James Brown
13 *Car Wash* Rose Royce
14 *Pink Cadillac* Natalie Cole
15 *Just A Mirage* Jellybean feat. Adele Bertei
16 *A Love Supreme* Will Downing

▶ **Glenn Medeiros** was the first popstar from Hawaii to appear on a *NOW* album, but he wouldn't be the last – **Nicole Scherzinger** (first seen as a named artist on *NOW 68*) and **Bruno Mars** (*NOW 76*) also hail from the state.

▶ This was the only time metal legends **Iron Maiden** are featured, albeit not with their biggest hit. 'Bring Your Daughter To The Slaughter' was No.1 for two weeks at the start of 1991 but didn't appear on *NOW 19*.

▶ **The Timelords** were an early incarnation of the **KLF**. After 'Doctorin' The Tardis' was a hit the band published a book advising potential popstars how to get to No.1 without signing to a major record label. The next **KLF** single flopped.

ALSO HAPPENING IN NOVEMBER 1988

- George Bush Senior was elected as 41st US President
- *A Brief History of Time* by Stephen Hawking was published. It went on to sell over 10 million copies. Other bestsellers published in 1988 included *Matilda* (Roald Dahl) and *The Silence of the Lambs* by Thomas Harris
- At the cinema: *Child's Play*, *Buster*, *The Land Before Time*, *Who Framed Roger Rabbit?*
- **Dire Straits** released their greatest hits album *Money For Nothing*
- The Christmas No.1 was 'Mistletoe and Wine' (**Cliff Richard**)

TRACKLISTING NOW 13

CD1

1 *The Only Way Is Up* Yazz & The Plastic Population
2 *Teardrops* Womack & Womack
3 *A Little Respect* Erasure
4 *Harvest For The World* The Christians
5 *Ordinary Angel* Hue And Cry
6 *Breakfast In Bed* UB40 feat. Chrissie Hynde
7 *She Makes My Day* Robert Palmer
8 *Hands To Heaven* Breathe
9 *A Groovy Kind Of Love* Phil Collins
10 *Don't Worry, Be Happy* Bobby McFerrin
11 *Kiss* Art of Noise feat. Tom Jones
12 *Let's Stick Together* Bryan Ferry
13 *You Came* Kim Wilde
14 *Don't Make Me Wait* Bomb the Bass
15 *The Harder I Try* Brother Beyond
16 *He Ain't Heavy, He's My Brother* The Hollies

CD2

1 *The Twist (Yo Twist)* The Fat Boys & Chubby Checker
2 *Wee Rule* The Wee Papa Girl Rappers
3 *Twist And Shout* Salt 'N' Pepa
4 *The Race* Yello
5 *Big Fun* Inner City feat. Kevin Saunderson
6 *We Call It Acieed* D-Mob & Gary Haisman
7 *Burn It Up* The Beatmasters & P.P. Arnold
8 *Girl You Know It's True* Milli Vanilli
9 *Heaven In My Hands* Level 42
10 *Rush Hour* Jane Wiedlin
11 *I'm Gonna Be (500 Miles)* The Proclaimers
12 *Secret Garden* T'Pau
13 *I Want Your Love* Transvision Vamp
14 *I Don't Want Your Love* Duran Duran
15 *Love Is All That Matters* The Human League
16 *Martha's Harbour* All About Eve

▶ This was the last *NOW* to top a joint artist and compilation chart. A stand-alone compilation chart was launched in January 1989.

▶ *NOW 13* featured three No.1 singles. One was a cover version ('The Only Way Is Up' originally by **Otis Clay**), one featured in a movie ('A Groovy Kind Of Love' from *Buster*) and the third a re-release used in a TV ad for beer ('He Ain't Heavy, He's My Brother').

▶ Bassist Eg White left **Brother Beyond** before 'The Harder I Try' was a hit. His run of featured songs as a writer started with 'Leave Right Now' by **Will Young** on *NOW 57*.

32 TOP CHART HITS

MARC ALMOND featuring GENE PITNEY · PHIL COLLINS · ERASURE
BANANARAMA/LANANEENEENOONOO · YAZZ · SIMPLE MINDS · ROY ORBISON · PAULA ABDUL
BROTHER BEYOND · S'XPRESS · KIM WILDE · INXS
PLUS MANY MORE

RELEASED 20 MARCH 1989

ALSO HAPPENING IN MARCH 1989

- Iran broke off diplomatic relations with the UK over Salman Rushdie's highly controversial book *The Satanic Verses*. A fatwa was issued on the author by Iranian leader the Ayatollah Khomeini and Rushdie had to live under police protection for nine years
- Sky TV was launched in Europe
- *Rain Man* won four Oscars at the Academy Awards, including Best Film and Best Actor for Dustin Hoffman
- New albums included *Like a Prayer* (**Madonna**) and **Deacon Blue**'s *When the World Knows Your Name*

TRACKLISTING NOW 14

CD1

1 *Something's Gotten Hold Of My Heart* **Marc Almond feat. Gene Pitney**
2 *Two Hearts* **Phil Collins**
3 *Stop!* **Erasure**
4 *Help!* **Bananarama**
5 *Looking For Linda* **Hue And Cry**
6 *Fine Time* **Yazz**
7 *Four Letter Word* **Kim Wilde**
8 *Stop* **Sam Brown**
9 *You Got It* **Roy Orbison**
10 *She Drives Me Crazy* **Fine Young Cannibals**
11 *Need You Tonight* **INXS**
12 *Burning Bridges (On And Off And On Again)* **Status Quo**
13 *Big Area* **Then Jerico**
14 *The Last Of The Famous International Playboys* **Morrissey**
15 *Every Rose Has Its Thorn* **Poison**
16 *Belfast Child* **Simple Minds**

CD2

1 *Buffalo Stance* **Neneh Cherry**
2 *Good Life* **Inner City**
3 *Hey Music Lover* **S-Express**
4 *Blow The House Down* **Living in a Box**
5 *Promised Land* **The Style Council**
6 *Respect* **Adeva**
7 *Wild Thing* **Tone Lōc**
8 *I Live For Your Love* **Natalie Cole**
9 *First Time* **Robin Beck**
10 *Straight Up* **Paula Abdul**
11 *I Only Wanna Be With You* **Samantha Fox**
12 *Be My Twin* **Brother Beyond**
13 *Love Like A River* **Climie Fisher**
14 *All She Wants Is* **Duran Duran**
15 *Tracie* **Level 42**
16 *Love Changes Everything* **Michael Ball**

▶ For the first time two songs with the same title made the tracklisting – both **Erasure** and **Sam Brown** contributed singles called 'Stop'.

▶ **Bananarama**, assisted by French and Saunders, provided 1989's Comic Relief single here. At time of writing seventeen tracks raising money for that cause have featured in the series.

▶ Contrary to what **Poison** may have had you believe on their only *NOW* appearance, there are in fact some varieties of rose which do not have thorns. Perhaps unaware of this error **Miley Cyrus** later recorded her own version of the track.

RELEASED 14 AUGUST 1989

ALSO HAPPENING IN AUGUST 1989

- The *Marchioness* was sunk by the dredger *Bowbelle* on the River Thames, killing fifty-one people
- Electronic tagging of certain criminal offenders was introduced in the UK
- At the cinema: *Batman*, *Parenthood*, *Uncle Buck*, *Shirley Valentine*, *When Harry Met Sally*
- Albums released included *Sleeping with the Past* (**Elton John**)
- Television programmes making their debut in 1989 included *Fun House*, *Byker Grove* and *Birds of a Feather*. *Knightmare* and *The Krypton Factor* were both popular, as was *Challenge Anneka*

TRACKLISTING NOW 15

CD1

1 *I Want It All* Queen
2 *Kick It In* Simple Minds
3 *Good Thing* Fine Young Cannibals
4 *Americanos* Holly Johnson
5 *Baby I Don't Care* Transvision Vamp
6 *Mystify* INXS
7 *The Look* Roxette
8 *Rooms On Fire* Stevie Nicks
9 *My Brave Face* Paul McCartney
10 *Ferry Cross The Mersey* Gerry Marsden/Paul McCartney/ Holly Johnson and The Christians
11 *Song For Whoever* The Beautiful South
12 *Days* Kirsty MacColl
13 *The Second Summer Of Love* Danny Wilson
14 *Cry* Waterfront
15 *Violently* Hue and Cry
16 *The Best Of Me* Cliff Richard

CD2

1 *Back To Life (However Do You Want Me)* Soul II Soul feat. Caron Wheeler
2 *Manchild* Neneh Cherry
3 *Every Little Step* Bobby Brown
4 *Do You Love What You Feel* Inner City
5 *It is Time To Get Funky* D-Mob feat. LRS
6 *Joy And Pain* Donna Allen
7 *Licence To Kill* Gladys Knight
8 *Miss You Like Crazy* Natalie Cole
9 *It's Alright* Pet Shop Boys
10 *Swing The Mood* Jive Bunny & The Music Mixers
11 *You On My Mind* Swing Out Sister
12 *Cruel Summer* Bananarama
13 *Say No Go* De La Soul
14 *Blame It On The Bassline* Norman Cook & MC Wildski
15 *Just Keep Rockin'* Double Trouble & The Rebel MC
16 *Lullaby* The Cure

▶ Prior to a re-release of 'Everywhere' on *NOW 84*, this **Stevie Nicks** inclusion was the closest a Fleetwood or a Mac came to a *NOW*, although **Mark Morrison**'s misspelt *NOW 34* tribute forewarns the return of the AOR superstars.

▶ **Jive Bunny And The Mastermixers** would reach the No.1 spot with their first three singles. However, 'Swing The Mood' – their debut – is their sole entry to the *NOW* canon.

▶ Alongside fellow Scandinavians **Roxette** and **Swedish House Mafia, Ace Of Base** share the distinction of 'Swedish Band With Most Appearances' (six entries apiece). **Abba** have appeared only once.

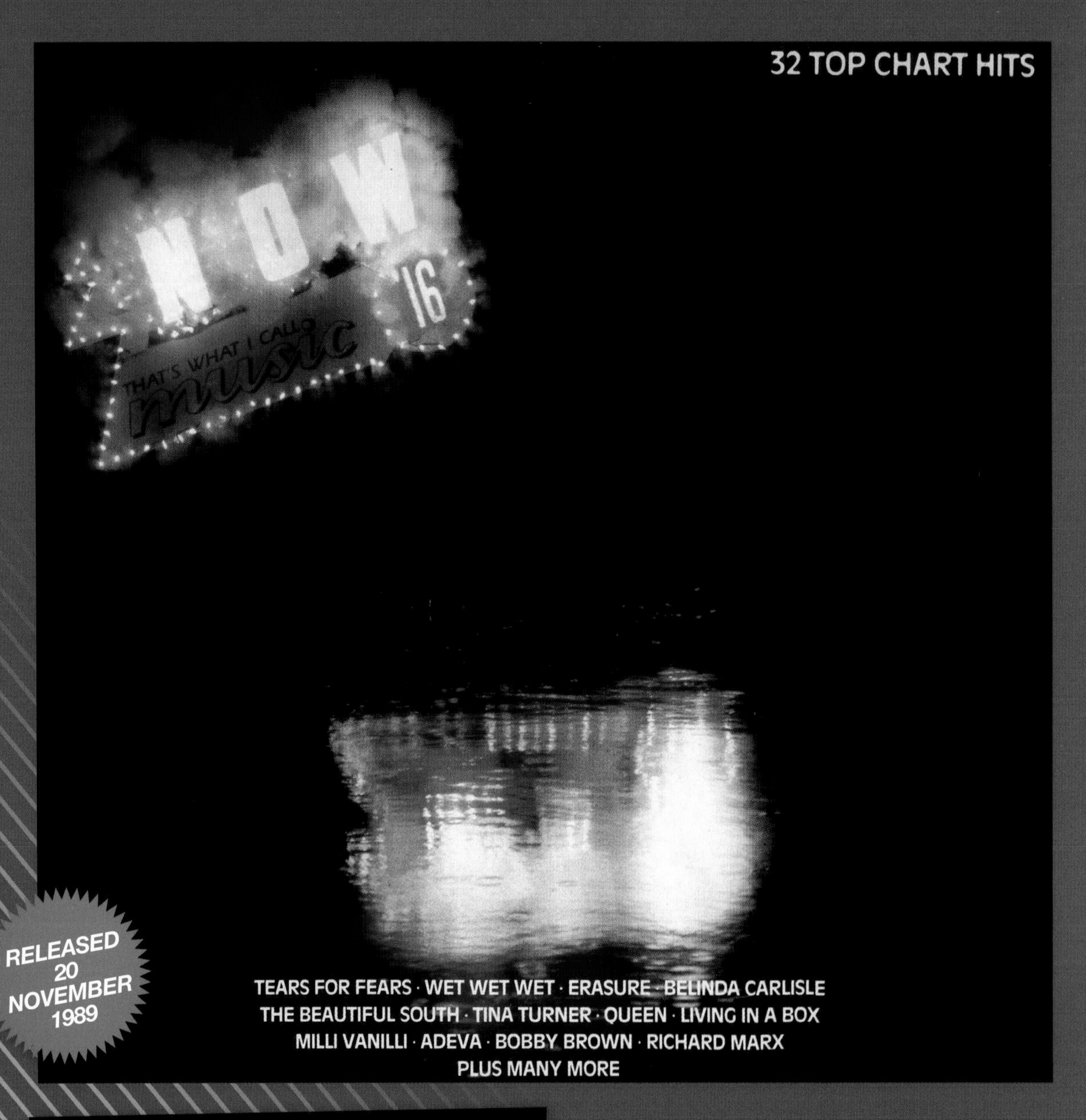

ALSO HAPPENING IN NOVEMBER 1989

- Television cameras were allowed to broadcast proceedings in the Houses of Parliament for the first time
- The final episode of *Blackadder* and Michael Palin's *Around the World in 80 Days* were both televised
- At the cinema: *Steel Magnolias*, *All Dogs Go to Heaven*, *The Little Mermaid*, *Back to the Future Part II*
- This year's albums included *Affection* (**Lisa Stansfield**) and *...But Seriously* (**Phil Collins**)
- Christmas No.1 was 'Do They Know it's Christmas?' (**Band Aid II**)

TRACKLISTING NOW 16

CD1

1 *Sowing The Seeds Of Love* Tears for Fears
2 *Leave A Light On* Belinda Carlisle
3 *Drama!* Erasure
4 *I Want That Man* Deborah Harry
5 *If Only I Could* Sydney Youngblood
6 *Name And Number* Curiosity Killed the Cat
7 *You Keep It All In* The Beautiful South
8 *Sweet Surrender* Wet Wet Wet
9 *Breakthru* Queen
10 *The Best* Tina Turner
11 *Born To Be Sold* Transvision Vamp
12 *Waterfall '89* Wendy & Lisa
13 *The Sensual World* Kate Bush
14 *I'm Not The Man I Used To Be* Fine Young Cannibals
15 *Sugarbox* Then Jerico
16 *Room In Your Heart* Living in a Box
17 *Right Here Waiting* Richard Marx
18 *Girl I'm Gonna Miss You* Milli Vanilli

CD2

1 *Street Tuff* Rebel MC & Double Trouble
2 *On Our Own* Bobby Brown
3 *Pump Up The Jam* Technotronic feat. Felly
4 *French Kiss* Lil Louis
5 *I Thank You* Adeva
6 *C'Mon And Get My Love* D-Mob feat. Cathy Dennis
7 *Eye Know* De La Soul
8 *Whatcha Gonna Do With My Lovin'* Inner City
9 *Can't Shake The Feeling* Big Fun
10 *I Just Don't Have The Heart* Cliff Richard
11 *Comment Te Dire Adieu?* Jimmy Somerville feat. June Miles Kingston
12 *Drive On* Brother Beyond
13 *You're History* Shakespears Sister
14 *Oh Well* Oh Well
15 *Kisses On The Wind* Neneh Cherry
16 *Do The Right Thing* Redhead Kingpin & The F.B.I.
17 *Wishing On A Star* Fresh 4 feat. Lizz E

▶ This was the last *NOW* released in the 1980s. As a bonus to CD purchasers, the silver discs contained three tracks not available on the vinyl or cassette – **Fine Young Cannibals, Lil' Louis** and **Brother Beyond.**

▶ Former Beatle **George Harrison** has no artist credit on any *NOW* album but did supply the searing guitar solo on **Belinda Carlisle**'s 'Leave A Light On'. Carlisle eventually appeared on nine *NOW*s over a period of eight years.

▶ 'Drama!' was **Erasure**'s fifth appearance of thirteen, and their second consecutive song title to end with an exclamation mark. Over the years eighteen track titles have ended this way, from **Thomas Dolby**'s 'Hyperactive!' on *NOW 2* to **Little Mix**'s 'Word Up!' on *NOW 87*.

32 TOP CHART HITS

NOW THAT'S WHAT I CALL MUSIC 17

FEATURING

ERASURE · PAULA ABDUL · PHIL COLLINS · UB40 · TINA TURNER
BEATS INTERNATIONAL · HAPPY MONDAYS · DEPECHE MODE
TECHNOTRONIC · BIZZ NIZZ · CANDY FLIP · REBEL MC
PLUS MANY MORE

RELEASED 23 APRIL 1990

ALSO HAPPENING IN APRIL 1990

- The Hubble Space Telescope was carried into space by the shuttle *Discovery*
- A riot took place at Strangeways Prison in Manchester
- A pop concert held in the recently freed Nelson Mandela's honour at Wembley Stadium was broadcast to more than sixty countries Performers included **Aswad**, **Neneh Cherry** and **Terence Trent D'Arby**
- Stephen Hendry became the youngest-ever world snooker champion, beating Jimmy White at the Crucible
- On television: *Blockbusters*, *Press Gang* and the first series of *You've Been Framed*

TRACKLISTING NOW 17

CD1

1 *Blue Savannah* **Erasure**
2 *Better World* **Rebel MC**
3 *Opposites Attract* **Paula Abdul**
4 *Dub Be Good To Me* **Beats International feat. Lindy Layton**
5 *Kingston Town* **UB40**
6 *Strawberry Fields Forever* **Candy Flip**
7 *I Don't Wanna Lose You* **Tina Turner**
8 *I Wish It Would Rain Down* **Phil Collins**
9 *Step On* **Happy Mondays**
10 *Loaded* **Primal Scream**
11 *Enjoy The Silence* **Depeche Mode**
12 *Real Real Real* **Jesus Jones**
13 *This Is How It Feels* **Inspiral Carpets**
14 *Shine On* **House Of Love**
15 *From Out Of Nowhere* **Faith No More**
16 *Hey You* **The Quireboys**

CD2

1 *This Beat Is Technotronic* **Technotronic feat. MC Eric**
2 *Happenin' All Over Again* **Lonnie Gordon**
3 *Don't You Love Me* **The 49ers**
4 *Read My Lips (Enough Is Enough)* **Jimmy Somerville**
5 *Stronger Than That* **Cliff Richard**
6 *Another Day In Paradise* **Jam Tronik**
7 *Moments In Soul* **J T & The Big Family**
8 *Got To Have Your Love* **Mantronix feat. Wondress**
9 *Don't Miss The Partyline* **Bizz Nizz**
10 *Everything Starts With An 'E'* **E-Zee Possee feat. MC Kinky**
11 *Put Your Hands Together* **D-Mob feat. Nuff Juice**
12 *Killer* **Adamski feat. Seal**
13 *Chime* **Orbital**
14 *Tomorrow* **Tongue N Cheek**
15 *Talking With Myself* **Electribe 101**
16 *I'd Rather Go Blind* **Sydney Youngblood**

▶ Only two volumes were released in 1990 (*NOW 17* and *NOW 18*). The same happened in 1991. However, every subsequent year has seen the now standardised release of three editions – timed to coincide with Easter, Summer and Christmas.

▶ Both the Creation and Factory record labels made their *NOW* debuts on this volume with **Primal Scream** and **Happy Mondays. New Order** did not appear until *NOW 25* with 'Regret'.

▶ One hit wonder **Bizz Nizz** landed their sole *NOW* entry here. However, Belgian producer Jean-Paul DeCoster returned as **2 Unlimited** on *NOW 20* and a further seven volumes.

MOST NUMBER ONE SINGLES BY *NOW* ALBUM

15
NOW 88

12
NOW 77 • 82 • 83

11
NOW 1 • 74 • 84

10
NOW 44 • 47 • 76 • 79 • 86 • 87

3484

TRACKS ON ALL 88 *NOWS*

12.5%

CREDITED AS 'FEATURING' AN ARTIST

437

TRACKS ON LAST TEN *NOWS*

30.9%

CREDITED AS 'FEATURING' AN ARTIST

LONGEST CONSECUTIVE *NOW* ALBUM RUNS

'Sound Of The Underground'
NOW 54

GIRLS ALOUD
13 HITS IN A ROW

'Walk This Way'
NOW 66

'Father And Son'
NOW 33

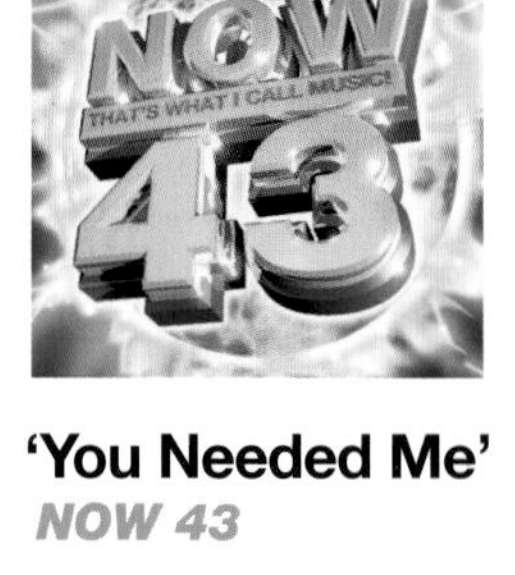

'You Needed Me'
NOW 43

'Five Colours In Her Hair'
NOW 58

McFLY
11 HITS IN A ROW

'The Heart Never Lies'
NOW 68

1836
DIFFERENT ARTISTS
716
APPEARED MORE THAN ONCE

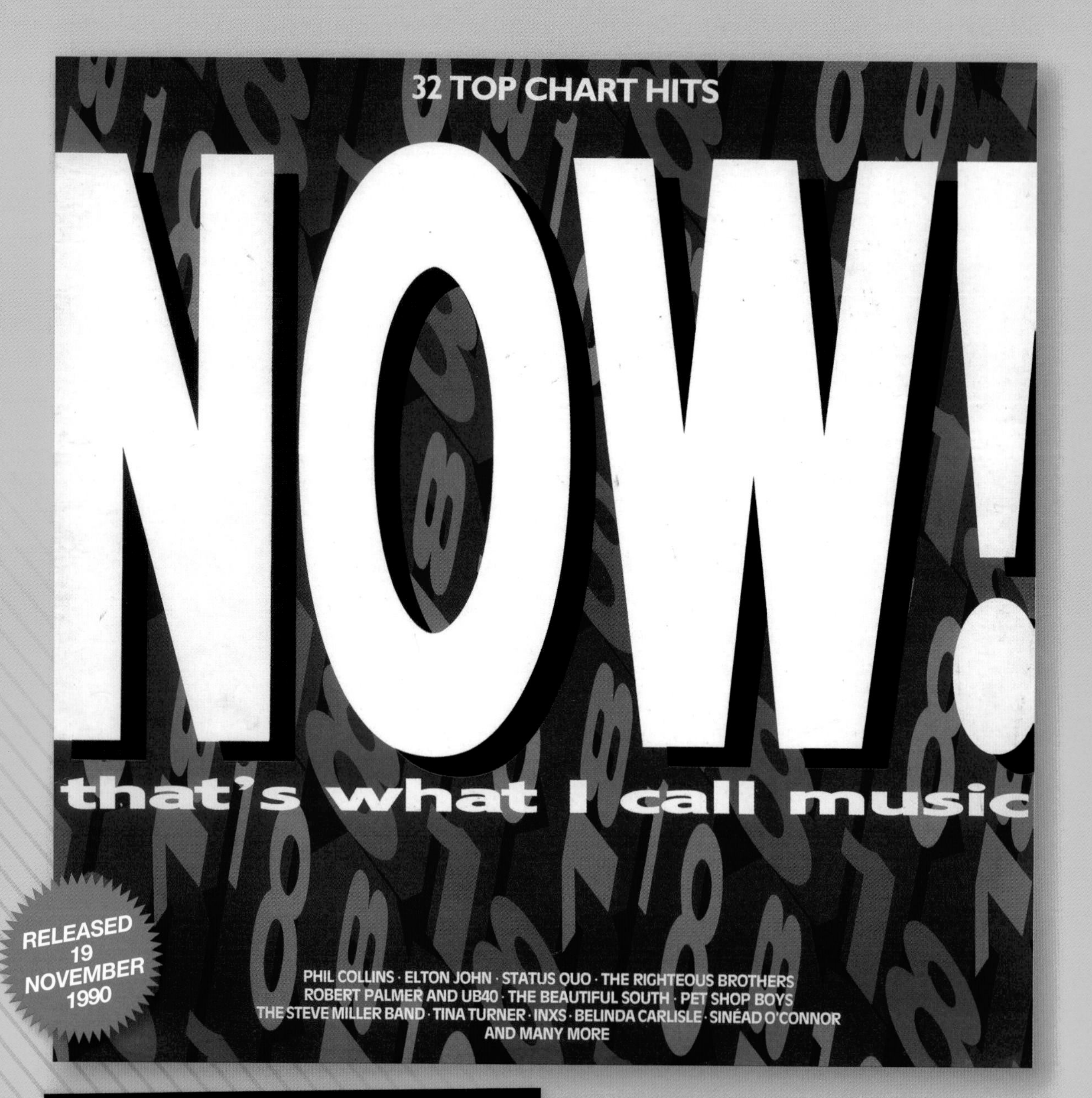

ALSO HAPPENING IN NOVEMBER 1990

- Margaret Thatcher resigned as Prime Minister and was replaced by John Major
- At the cinema: *Home Alone*, *The Krays*, *Dances With Wolves*
- The most-wanted toys were the Nintendo Game Boy, Sega Megadrive and Teenage Mutant Hero Turtles
- Albums released in 1990 included *I'm Your Baby Tonight* (**Whitney Houston**) and *Rhythm of Love* (**Kylie Minogue**)
- Bestsellers published in 1990: *Jurassic Park* (Michael Crichton), *The Stand* (Stephen King) and *The Buddha of Suburbia* (Hanif Kureishi)
- **Cliff Richard** scored another Christmas No.1 with 'Saviour's Day'

TRACKLISTING NOW 18

CD1

1 *A Little Time* The Beautiful South
2 *The Joker* Steve Miller Band
3 *Sacrifice* Elton John
4 *It Must Have Been Love* Roxette
5 *Something Happened On The Way To Heaven* Phil Collins
6 *Hold On* Wilson Phillips
7 *Nothing Compares 2 U* Sinéad O'Connor
8 *Unchained Melody* The Righteous Brothers
9 *(We Want) The Same Thing* Belinda Carlisle
10 *The Anniversary Waltz (Part One)* Status Quo
11 *Suicide Blonde* INXS
12 *Don't Ask Me* Public Image Ltd
13 *It's My Life* Talk Talk
14 *There She Goes* The La's
15 *Be Tender With Me Baby* Tina Turner
16 *I'll Be Your Baby Tonight* Robert Palmer feat. UB40

CD2

1 *So Hard* Pet Shop Boys
2 *Fascinating Rhythm* Bass-O-Matic
3 *Missing You* Soul II Soul feat. Kym Mazelle
4 *Tom's Diner* DNA feat. Suzanne Vega
5 *Englishman In New York* Sting
6 *Close To You Remix* The Cure
7 *I've Got You Under My Skin* Neneh Cherry
8 *Little Brother* Blue Pearl
9 *Step Back In Time* Kylie Minogue
10 *Don't Worry* Kim Appleby
11 *Megamix* Technotronic
12 *Itsy Bitsy Teenie Weenie Yellow Polka Dot Bikini* Bombalurina
13 *Where Are You Baby?* Betty Boo
14 *Dirty Cash (Money Talks)* The Adventures of Stevie V
15 *Have You Seen Her* MC Hammer
16 *To Love Somebody* Jimmy Somerville

▶ **Sinead O'Connor**'s 'Nothing Compares 2 U' was written by **Prince**, who also composed 'Kiss' by **Art Of Noise & Tom Jones** (*NOW 13*), 'I Would Die 4 U' by **Space Cowboy** (*NOW 52*), and 'Nasty Girl' by **Inaya Day** (*NOW 61*) as well as two hits of his own that appear on future editions.

▶ Former **Sex Pistol John Lydon**, aka **Johnny Rotten**, made his first appearance in the series as the leader of **Public Image Ltd**. He would later return as part of **Leftfield Lydon** on *NOW 26*.

▶ On its original 1984 release, **Talk Talk**'s 'It's My Life' missed the Top 40 altogether. Reissued in 1990 to promote a best-of album, it climbed to No.13. **No Doubt** promoted their greatest hits with a version of the song in 2003, reaching No.17 in the UK and the top ten in the States.

34 top chart hits

now!

that's what i call music

19

CHRIS REA · OLETA ADAMS · CHRIS ISAAK · THE CLASH
EMF · ROBERT PALMER · KIM APPLEBY · FREE
MC HAMMER · QUEEN · THE KLF · INXS · SEAL
AND MANY MORE

RELEASED 25 MARCH 1991

ALSO HAPPENING IN MARCH 1991

- The Government announced the abolition of the Poll Tax after widespread protests
- *Dances With Wolves* won six Oscars
- **Michael Jackson** signed a $1 billion contract with Sony
- There were new albums from **R.E.M.** (*Out of Time*) and **Roxette** (*Joyride*)
- **Bryan Adams** spent a record-breaking sixteen weeks at No.1 with '(Everything I Do) I Do It For You', featured on the soundtrack for *Robin Hood: Prince of Thieves*
- Television hits included *The Crystal Maze*, *Soldier Soldier*, *Mr Bean* and *Prime Suspect*

TRACKLISTING NOW 19

CD1

1 *Should I Stay Or Should I Go* The Clash
2 *She's A Woman* Scritti Politti feat. Shabba Ranks
3 *You Got The Love* The Source feat. Candi Staton
4 *3 A.M. Eternal (Live At The SSL)* The KLF feat. The Children of the Revolution
5 *Gonna Make You Sweat (Everybody Dance Now)* C & C Music Factory
6 *(I Wanna Give You) Devotion* Nomad feat. MC Mikee Freedom
7 *I Believe* EMF
8 *In Yer Face* 808 State
9 *Unfinished Sympathy* Massive
10 *Pray* M C Hammer
11 *G.L.A.D.* Kim Appleby
12 *What Do I Have To Do* Kylie Minogue
13 *The Stonk* Hale & Pace & The Stonkers
14 *Wiggle It* 2 In A Room
15 *Play That Funky Music* Vanilla Ice
16 *Bow Down Mister* Jesus Loves You
17 *Sadeness (Part 1)* Enigma
18 *Only You* Praise

CD2

1 *Get Here* Oleta Adams
2 *Cry For Help* Rick Astley
3 *Mercy Mercy Me/I Want You* Robert Palmer
4 *(I've Had) The Time Of My Life* Bill Medley & Jennifer Warnes
5 *You've Lost That Lovin' Feelin'* The Righteous Brothers
6 *Crazy* Seal
7 *This Is Your Life* Banderas
8 *Because I Love You (The Postman Song)* Stevie B
9 *Auberge* Chris Rea
10 *Blue Hotel* Chris Isaak
11 *All Right Now* Free
12 *Disappear* INXS
13 *Summer Rain* Belinda Carlisle
14 *Every Beat Of The Heart* The Railway Children
15 *Love Walked In* Thunder
16 *Innuendo* Queen

▶ *NOW 19* is the lowest-selling volume in the series. It was also the final *NOW* to have an accompanying video release.

▶ Due to sensitivities surrounding the Gulf War, **Massive Attack** were billed as 'Massive' for their *NOW* debut. They have a total of five *NOW* appearances to their name, three more than fellow Bristolians **Portishead.**

▶ Damon Rochefort from **Nomad** made his sole appearance here. He later found success as a scriptwriter for *Coronation Street*. The whereabouts, however, of **MC Mikee Freedom** are currently uncertain.

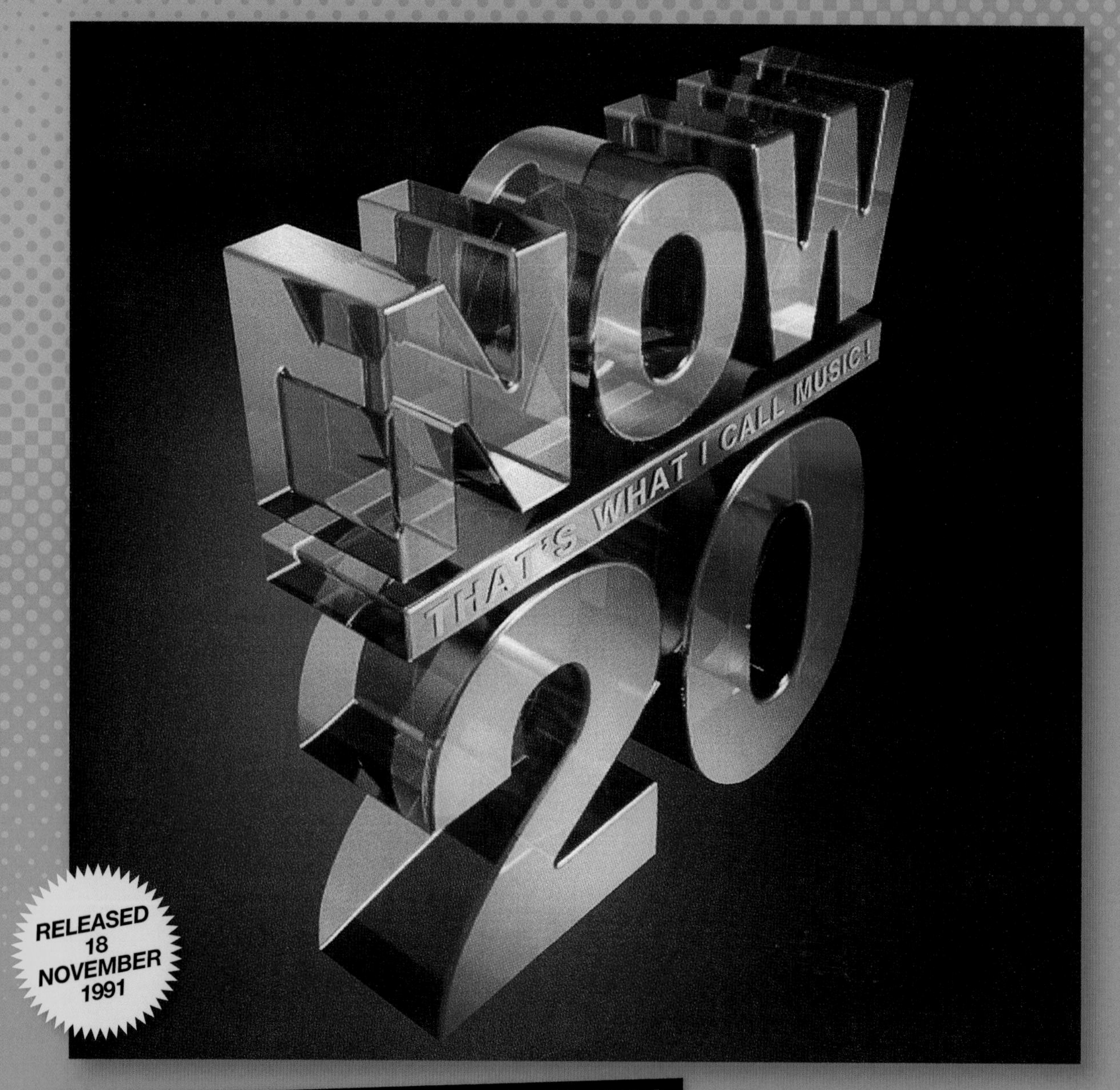

ALSO HAPPENING IN NOVEMBER 1991

- **Queen** front man Freddie Mercury died from pneumonia resulting from AIDS at the age of forty-five. **Queen** took the Christmas No.1 a month later with 'Bohemian Rhapsody / These Are the Days of Our Lives'
- At the cinema: *Cape Fear*, *The Addams Family*, *Beauty and the Beast*, *My Girl*
- The most-wanted toy was Thunderbirds' Tracy Island. Stocks ran out, prompting *Blue Peter* to show viewers how to make their own version
- Albums released in 1991 included *2Pacalypse Now* (**2Pac**) and *Achtung Baby* (**U2**)

TRACKLISTING NOW 20

CD1

1 *Dizzy* Vic Reeves & The Wonderstuff
2 *Live Your Life Be Free* Belinda Carlisle
3 *The Fly* U2
4 *Where The Streets Have No Name (I Can't Take My Eyes Off You)* Pet Shop Boys
5 *Love To Hate You* Erasure
6 *Sailing On The Seven Seas* Orchestral Manoeuvres in the Dark
7 *Something Got Me Started* Simply Red
8 *Change* Lisa Stansfield
9 *Sunshine On A Rainy Day* Zoë
10 *Let's Talk About Sex* Salt 'N' Pepa
11 *I Wanna Sex You Up* Color Me Badd
12 *Best Of You* Kenny Thomas
13 *Gett Off* Prince & The New Power Generation
14 *Faith (In The Power Of Love)* Rozalla
15 *Get Ready For This* 2 Unlimited
16 *Go* Moby
17 *It's Grim Up North* The Justified Ancients of Mu Mu
18 *Set Adrift On Memory Bliss* P.M. Dawn

CD2

1 *Don't Dream It's Over* Paul Young
2 *Caribbean Blue* Enya
3 *Saltwater* Julian Lennon
4 *Rush, Rush* Paula Abdul
5 *Any Dream Will Do* Jason Donovan
6 *Too Many Walls* Cathy Dennis
7 *This House* Alison Moyet
8 *Walking In Memphis* Marc Cohen
9 *My Town* Glass Tiger
10 *Wind Of Change* Scorpions
11 *Shining Star* INXS
12 *Joyride* Roxette
13 *Sit Down* James
14 *I Think I Love You* Voice of the Beehive
15 *Radio Wall Of Sound* Slade
16 *Always Look On The Bright Side Of Life* Monty Python
17 *American Pie* Don McLean

▶ Old and new comedic surrealists met for the only time in the series. **Monty Python** featured with their solitary *NOW* appearance whereas **Vic Reeves** would appear once more on *NOW 31*.

▶ **Pet Shop Boys'** cover of **U2**'s 'Where The Streets Have No Name' didn't go down too well. Appalled, in response **U2** issued a press release asking 'what have we done to deserve this?'

▶ 'American Pie' by **Don McLean** is the track with the longest-playing time on any *NOW*. It lasts eight minutes and thirty-four seconds in total.

ALSO HAPPENING IN APRIL 1992

- Euro Disney (now Disneyland Paris) opened in France. The park was not a success at first, but had an upswing in fortunes in 1995
- Four Los Angeles policemen were acquitted of beating motorist Rodney King, despite being caught on video. Subsequent riots caused over $800 million in damage
- The **Freddie Mercury** tribute concert was held at Wembley Stadium in front of a live audience of 72,000. All proceeds went to AIDS research
- At the cinema: *Beethoven*
- Albums released included *Diva* (**Annie Lennox**)

TRACKLISTING NOW 21

CD1

1 *Bohemian Rhapsody* **Queen**
2 *Goodnight Girl* **Wet Wet Wet**
3 *Stay* **Shakespears Sister**
4 *My Girl* **The Temptations**
5 *Stars* **Simply Red**
6 *Justified & Ancient* **The KLF feat. Tammy Wynette**
7 *It Must Be Love* **Madness**
8 *I Can't Dance* **Genesis**
9 *(Love Moves In) Mysterious Ways* **Julia Fordham**
10 *Weather With You* **Crowded House**
11 *Deeply Dippy* **Right Said Fred**
12 *To Be With You* **Mr. Big**
13 *Love Is Strange* **Everything but t he Girl**
14 *Church Of Your Heart* **Roxette**
15 *Driven By You* **Brian May**
16 *Welcome To The Cheap Seats* **The Wonder Stuff**
17 *Far Gone And Out* **The Jesus and Mary Chain**
18 *Born Of Frustration* **James**
19 *High* **The Cure**

CD2

1 *I Love Your Smile* **Shanice**
2 *I'm Doing Fine Now* **The Pasadenas**
3 *Give Me Just A Little More Time* **Kylie Minogue**
4 *Ride Like The Wind* **East Side Beat**
5 *Twilight Zone* **2 Unlimited**
6 *America: What Time Is Love?* **The KLF feat. The Children of the Revolution**
7 *A Deeper Love* **Clivilles & Cole**
8 *It's A Fine Day* **Opus III**
9 *Breath Of Life* **Erasure**
10 *Addams Groove* **Hammer**
11 *Expression* **Salt 'N' Pepa**
12 *We Got A Love Thang* **Ce Ce Peniston**
13 *Vibeology* **Paula Abdul**
14 *Make It On My Own* **Alison Limerick**
15 *Way Of The World* **Tina Turner**
16 *I Wonder Why* **Curtis Stigers**
17 *When You Tell Me That You Love Me* **Diana Ross**

▶ Following a series re-brand, Mark Goodier became the 'voice of *NOW*' on the TV Ads, a role he has repeated for every subsequent release.

▶ Kirsty Hawkshaw from **Opus III** is the daughter of composer Alan Hawkshaw. Amongst others, Alan composed the theme tunes to '*Grange Hill*' and '*Countdown*'. Sampled many times, elements of his 'Champ' track are used on 'Here Comes The Hotstepper' by **Ini Kamoze** (*NOW 31*).

▶ Stanley Kirk Burrell – aka **MC Hammer** – sold 50 million records and popularised voluminous trousers across his short career. He made his final appearance on *NOW 21*. Stop: Hammer time.

ALSO HAPPENING IN JULY 1992

- The Summer Olympics began in Barcelona. There were golds for Linford Christie (Men's 100m) and Sally Gunnell (Women's 400m Hurdles)
- New soap opera *Eldorado* launched on BBC 1. It was cancelled a year later
- At the cinema: *Boomerang, A League of Their Own, Honey, I Blew Up the Kid*
- *Diana: Her True Story* by Andrew Morton was published and created a storm of controversy in the media. After Princess Diana's death it was revealed that Diana herself was the main source for the book

TRACKLISTING NOW 22

CD1

1 *Take A Chance On Me* **Erasure**
2 *Finally* **Ce Ce Peniston**
3 *Please Don't Go* **KWS**
4 *It Only Takes A Minute* **Take That**
5 *Heartbeat* **Nick Berry**
6 *Rhythm Is A Dancer* **Snap!**
7 *Something Good* **Utah Saints**
8 *Friday I'm In Love* **The Cure**
9 *The Days Of Pearly Spencer* **Marc Almond**
10 *Bell Bottomed Tear* **The Beautiful South**
11 *Thunder* **Prince & The New Power Generation**
12 *Even Better Than The Real Thing* **U2**
13 *L.S.I.* **The Shamen**
14 *Disappointed* **Electronic**
15 *I Don't Care* **Shakespears Sister**
16 *Do Re Me So Far So Good* **Carter USM**
17 *Everything About You* **Ugly Kid Joe**
18 *On A Ragga Tip* **SL2**
19 *Blue Room* **The Orb**

CD2

1 *Hazard* **Richard Marx**
2 *The One* **Elton John**
3 *I Drove All Night* **Roy Orbison**
4 *Ain't No Doubt* **Jimmy Nail**
5 *Unchain My Heart* **Joe Cocker**
6 *You're All That Matters To Me* **Curtis Stigers**
7 *You Won't See Me Cry* **Wilson Phillips**
8 *Four Seasons In One Day* **Crowded House**
9 *Why* **Annie Lennox**
10 *Don't Let The Sun Go Down On Me* **George Michael and Elton John**
11 *One Shining Moment* **Diana Ross**
12 *Save The Best For Last* **Vanessa Williams**
13 *My Lovin' (You're Never Gonna Get It)* **En Vogue**
14 *Joy* **Soul II Soul**
15 *Don't You Worry 'Bout A Thing* **Incognito**

▶ 'Blue Room' by **The Orb** is recognised as the longest single track to become a UK top ten hit, at 39 minutes 57 seconds long – chart rules at the time classified recordings over forty minutes long to be albums. The version included here was somewhat edited down.

▶ **Elton John** and **George Michael**'s 'Don't Let The Sun Go Down On Me' had first been performed by the pair at Live Aid; when it went to No.1 in 1991 it was the first live recording to top the chart for ten years. George topped the chart with another live performance in 1993 – he's the only artist to appear on two No.1 singles recorded in concert.

▶ In 1992 there were twelve No.1 singles, and *NOW*s released that year also contained twelve chart toppers – but *NOW* doesn't boast a 1992 100% strike rate. 'Bohemian Rhapsody' and 'Don't Let The Sun Go Down On Me' climbed to No.1 in 1991. 'End Of The Road' by **Boyz II Men** and 'I Will Always Love You' by **Whitney Houston** were the 1992 UK No.1s that were missing.

ALSO HAPPENING IN NOVEMBER 1992

- Bill Clinton was elected as the 42nd US President
- *Ghostwatch* was broadcast on the BBC, terrifying a generation of children with such horrors as Michael Parkinson's possession by a demonic spirit
- The first episode of *Absolutely Fabulous* was broadcast
- **Madonna**'s controversial book *Sex* was published
- At the cinema: *Aladdin*, *Malcolm X*, *The Bodyguard*
- Whitney Houston's 'I Will Always Love You' was Christmas No.1. In total it spent ten weeks at the top of the charts

TRACKLISTING NOW 23

CD1

1 *Sleeping Satellite* Tasmin Archer
2 *Just Another Day* Jon Secada
3 *Would I Lie To You?* Charles & Eddie
4 *Shake Your Head* Was (Not Was)
5 *Iron Lion Zion* Bob Marley & The Wailers
6 *Faithful* Go West
7 *Too Funky* George Michael
8 *People Everyday* Arrested Development
9 *For Your Babies* Simply Red
10 *(Take A Little) Piece Of My Heart* Erma Franklin
11 *Too Much Love Will Kill You* Brian May
12 *Alive And Kicking* Simple Minds
13 *Boom Boom* John Lee Hooker
14 *Achy Breaky Heart* Billy Ray Cyrus
15 *Too Much Too Young* Little Angels
16 *Take This Heart* Richard Marx
17 *Jesus He Knows Me* Genesis
18 *Baby Don't Cry* INXS
19 *It's Only Natural* Crowded House

CD2

1 *Who Needs Love Like That* Erasure
2 *Ebeneezer Goode* The Shamen
3 *Run To You* Rage
4 *I'm Gonna Get You* Bizarre Inc feat. Angie Brown
5 *Temptation* Heaven 17
6 *House Of Love* East 17
7 *Don't You Want Me* The Farm
8 *Never Let Her Slip Away* Undercover
9 *Tetris* Dr Spin
10 *Supermarioland* Ambassadors of Funk feat. MC Mario
11 *How Do You Do!* Roxette
12 *Dancing Queen* Abba
13 *A Little Respect* Björn Again
14 *Be My Baby* Vanessa Paradis
15 *Let Me Take You There* Betty Boo
16 *Damn I Wish I Was Your Lover* Sophie B Hawkins
17 *Digging In The Dirt* Peter Gabriel
18 *Book Of Days* Enya
19 *Crying* Roy Orbison & k.d. lang
20 *Barcelona* Freddie Mercury & Montserrat Caballé

▶ The solitary *NOW* appearance for little-known pop combo **Abba** with a re-released 'Dancing Queen'. The single was released to promote their 'Gold' compilation, currently the second biggest-selling CD of all time in the UK.

▶ The **Rage** cover version of **Bryan Adams's** 'Run to You' featured a vocal performance from **Tony Jackson**. Tony also provided the vocal for *that* Um Bongo ad in the mid '80s.

▶ *NOW 23* marked penultimate appearances for both **Peter Gabriel** and **Genesis**. They would also both bow out on *NOW 24*.

ALSO HAPPENING IN APRIL 1993

- Plans were announced for Buckingham Palace to open to tourists to pay for the repairs to Windsor Castle, which had been damaged by fire the previous year
- The Grand National was declared void after a series of mishaps including a false start
- Actor Brandon Lee was accidently killed while filming *The Crow*
- At the cinema: *Indecent Proposal*, *The Madness of King George*
- Popular television programmes included *The Darling Buds of May*, *Lovejoy* and *Peak Practice*

TRACKLISTING NOW 24

CD1

1 *Young At Heart* The Bluebells
2 *Could It Be Magic* Take That
3 *Ain't No Love (Ain't No Use)* Sub Sub feat. Melanie Williams
4 *Exterminate!* Snap!
5 *We Are Family* Sister Sledge
6 *Informer* Snow
7 *Mr. Loverman* Shabba Ranks feat. Chevelle Franklin
8 *Oh Carolina* Shaggy
9 *Deep* East 17
10 *Step It Up* Stereo MCs
11 *Tennessee* Arrested Development
12 *Show Me Love* Robin S
13 *Independence* Lulu
14 *The Love I Lost* West End feat. Sybil
15 *No Limit* 2 Unlimited
16 *U Got 2 Know* Cappella
17 *Pressure Us* Sunscreem
18 *Born 2 B.R.E.E.D.* Monie Love
19 *Labour Of Love* Hue And Cry

CD2

1 *Ordinary World* Duran Duran
2 *Love Song For A Vampire* Annie Lennox
3 *Is It Like Today* World Party
4 *Constant Craving* k.d. lang
5 *In Your Care* Tasmin Archer
6 *Looking Through Patient Eyes* PM Dawn
7 *Sweet Harmony* The Beloved
8 *This Time* Dina Carroll
9 *Lady Godiva's Room* Simply Red
10 *Invisible Touch (Live)* Genesis
11 *Are You Gonna Go My Way* Lenny Kravitz
12 *I Feel You* Depeche Mode
13 *Steam* Peter Gabriel
14 *Cats In The Cradle* Ugly Kid Joe
15 *Easy* Faith No More
16 *I Put A Spell On You* Bryan Ferry
17 *Vienna* Ultravox
18 *Hope Of Deliverance* Paul McCartney

▶ **2 Unlimited's** 'No Limit' marked the start of five consecutive *NOW* appearances for the techno-touting denial enthusiasts. Lead singer **Anita Doth** was an Amsterdam traffic warden before joining the band, whilst rapper **Ray Slijngaard** used to be a chef.

▶ In 1981, 'Vienna' by **Ultravox** was famously denied the No.1 spot by 'Shaddup You Face' by **Joe Dolce.** Reissued in 1993, it was unlucky again, this time peaking at 13.

▶ 'Young At Heart', co-written by Siobhan Fahey of **Bananarama** and later **Shakespears Sister**, first appeared on *NOW 3*. **The Bluebells** saw the single finally top the chart ten years later after its use in a VW Golf TV advert.

ALSO HAPPENING IN AUGUST 1993

- Damon Hill celebrated his first Formula One victory in the Hungarian Grand Prix
- Buckingham Palace was opened to visitors for the first time
- At the cinema: *The Fugitive*, *Free Willy*, *Hocus Pocus*, *Coneheads* and *True Romance*
- This year's albums included *Siamese Dream* (**The Smashing Pumpkins**), *Emergency on Planet Earth* (**Jamiroquai**) and *Music Box* (**Mariah Carey**). **Billy Joel** released *River of Dreams*, which he said would be his final studio album

TRACKLISTING NOW 25

CD1

1 *Somebody To Love* George Michael & Queen
2 *What's Up?* 4 Non Blondes
3 *I Don't Wanna Fight* Tina Turner
4 *All That She Wants* Ace of Base
5 *Dreams* Gabrielle
6 *You Come From Earth* Lena Fiagbe
7 *Everybody Hurts* R.E.M.
8 *Regret* New Order
9 *Living On My Own* Freddie Mercury
10 *I Will Survive* Gloria Gaynor
11 *Sweat (A La La La La Long)* Inner Circle
12 *Tease Me* Chaka Demus & Pliers
13 *Shout (It Out)* Louchie Lou & Michie One
14 *Housecall* Shabba Ranks feat. Maxi Priest
15 *Come Undone* Duran Duran
16 *Sunflower* Paul Weller
17 *Ten Years Asleep* Kingmaker

CD2

1 *Tribal Dance* 2 Unlimited
2 *Luv 4 Luv* Robin S
3 *When I'm Good And Ready* Sybil
4 *This Is It* Dannii Minogue
5 *The Ultimate High* The Time Frequency
6 *Do You Really Want Me* Jon Secada
7 *If I Can't Have You* Kim Wilde
8 *West End Girls* East 17
9 *Nothin' My Love Can't Fix* Joey Lawrence
10 *Somewhere* Efua
11 *No Ordinary Love* Sade
12 *This I Swear* Richard Darbyshire
13 *Dream Of Me (Based On Love's Theme)* Orchestral Manoeuvres in the Dark
14 *U R The Best Thing* D:Ream
15 *Caught In The Middle* Juliet Roberts
16 *Break From The Old Routine* Oui 3
17 *I Want You* Utah Saints
18 *Zeroes And Ones* Jesus Jones

▶ 'Somewhere' by **Efua** is one of two singles on *NOW 25* to miss the Top 40 (**Lena Fiagbe** provides the other). Her husband **Jazzie B** was more successful, scoring thirteen Top 40 hits and six *NOW* entries with **Soul II Soul**.

▶ Making her *NOW* debut, **Gabrielle** holds the distinction of most entries from a British female artist – twelve as a solo performer and once with **East 17**.

▶ The first of five consecutive entries for **Chaka Demus**. Alongside **Pliers**, still the only Jamaican group to score three consecutive Top 5 Hits in the UK.

ALSO HAPPENING IN NOVEMBER 1993

- Graham Taylor resigned as manager after England failed to qualify for the World Cup
- At the cinema: *The Remains of the Day*, *Carlito's Way*, *The Piano*, *Robocop 3*, *Mrs Doubtfire*
- The year's most-wanted toys were the Power Rangers
- Popular television programmes included *Gladiators*, *Baywatch*, *Birds of a Feather* and *Eurotrash*. **Mr Blobby** from *Noel's House Party* scored the Christmas No.1
- Bestsellers published in 1993 included *Birdsong* (Sebastian Faulks), *Bravo Two Zero* (Andy McNab) and *Trainspotting* (Irvine Welsh)

TRACKLISTING NOW 26

CD1

1 *(I Can't Help) Falling In Love With You* UB40
2 *Go West* Pet Shop Boys
3 *Relax* Frankie Goes To Hollywood
4 *One Night In Heaven* M People
5 *Stay* Eternal
6 *Right Here* SWV
7 *Boom! Shake The Room* DJ Jazzy Jeff & The Fresh Prince
8 *Comin' On* The Shamen
9 *Here We Go* Stakka Bo
10 *She Don't Let Nobody* Chaka Demus & Pliers
11 *Disco Inferno* Tina Turner
12 *Big Scary Animal* Belinda Carlisle
13 *Two Princes* The Spin Doctors
14 *The Sidewinder Sleeps Tonite* R.E.M.
15 *This Garden* The Levellers
16 *Laid* James
17 *Distant Sun* Crowded House
18 *Creep* Radiohead
19 *I'd Do Anything For Love (But I Won't Do That)* Meat Loaf

CD2

1 *U Got 2 Let The Music* Cappella
2 *What Is Love* Haddaway
3 *Maximum Overdrive* 2 Unlimited
4 *Mr Vain* Culture Beat
5 *Give It Up* The Goodmen
6 *Open Up* Leftfield & Lydon
7 *Boom Shack-A-Lak* Apache Indian
8 *Feels Like Heaven* Urban Cookie Collective
9 *More And More* Captain Hollywood Project
10 *Free Love* Juliet Roberts
11 *Too Young To Die* Jamiroquai
12 *Don't Be A Stranger* Dina Carroll
13 *Pray* Take That
14 *Going Nowhere* Gabrielle
15 *Gotta Get It Right* Lena Fiagbe
16 *Wish* Soul II Soul
17 *So Natural* Lisa Stansfield
18 *Play Dead* Björk & David Arnold
19 *Heaven Help* Lenny Kravitz
20 *Tracks Of My Tears* Go West
21 *That's The Way Love Goes* Janet Jackson

▶ **Eternal** made their debut with 'Stay'. They would go on to appear eleven times over thirteen *NOW*s. **Louise Nurding** left the band after five of those appearances and went on to feature ten further times as a solo artist.

▶ The end of an era: **Culture Beat**'s 'Mr Vain' was the first No.1 single unavailable on seven-inch vinyl since the early 1950s. The German Eurodance extemporisers notched consecutive appearances on *NOW 26* and *27*.

▶ The prominent drum clatter on 'Give It Up' by **The Goodmen** would be heard again on **Simply Red**'s 'Fairground' a couple of years later. On *NOW 48* the Dutch dance duo returned under the **Chocolate Puma** alias.

ALSO HAPPENING IN MARCH 1994

- Nelson Mandela became President of South Africa
- Wonderbra's 'Hello Boys' ad campaign was blamed for distracting drivers, causing several car accidents
- *Schindler's List* won seven Oscars including Best Picture and Best Director for Steven Spielberg
- BBC Radio 5 Live went on air for the first time
- *Four Weddings and a Funeral* was a huge hit in cinemas. At the premiere Elizabeth Hurley (girlfriend of star Hugh Grant) wore *that* Versace dress held together with safety pins

TRACKLISTING NOW 27

CD1

1 *The Sign* **Ace Of Base**
2 *Twist And Shout* **Chaka Demus & Pliers**
3 *Things Can Only Get Better* **D:Ream**
4 *It's Alright* **East 17**
5 *Moving On Up* **M People**
6 *Save Our Love* **Eternal**
7 *Return To Innocence* **Enigma**
8 *For Whom The Bell Tolls* **The Bee Gees**
9 *Come In Out Of The Rain* **Wendy Moten**
10 *The Perfect Year* **Dina Carroll**
11 *Everyday* **Phil Collins**
12 *Now And Forever* **Richard Marx**
13 *Linger* **The Cranberries**
14 *Cornflake Girl* **Tori Amos**
15 *Good As Gold (Stupid As Mud)* **The Beautiful South**
16 *Rock And Roll Dreams Come Through* **Meat Loaf**
17 *Rocks* **Primal Scream**
18 *Hey Jealousy* **Gin Blossoms**
19 *Disarm* **The Smashing Pumpkins**

CD2

1 *Doop* **Doop**
2 *Wonderman* **Right Said Fred**
3 *Move On Baby* **Cappella**
4 *Anything* **Culture Beat**
5 *Let The Beat Control Your Body* **2 Unlimited**
6 *I Like To Move It* **Reel 2 Real feat. The Mad Stuntman**
7 *Come Baby Come* **K7**
8 *Teenage Sensation* **Credit To The Nation**
9 *The Way You Work It* **E.Y.C.**
10 *Here I Stand* **Bitty McLean**
11 *Sweet Lullaby* **Deep Forest**
12 *Violently Happy* **Björk**
13 *Uptight* **Shara Nelson**
14 *Because Of You* **Gabrielle**
15 *Nervous Breakdown* **Carleen Anderson**
16 *I Want You* **Juliet Roberts**
17 *Sail Away* **Urban Cookie Collective**
18 *Shine On* **Degrees of Motion feat. Biti**
19 *Lover* **Joe Roberts**

▶ The first of two taut appearances for the **Bee Gees**, however cover versions of their songs span back to *NOW 18* (**Jimmy Somerville**) and include two entries credited to **Steps** alone ('Tragedy' *NOW 44*, 'Chain Reaction' *NOW 50*).

▶ No.1 hit 'Doop' by **Doop** is one of five NOW entries where artist and song name are identical. **Oh Well** (*NOW 16*), **Absolutely Fabulous** (*NOW 28*), **Love City Groove** (*NOW 31*), and **Deepest Blue** (*NOW 55*) complete the illustrious quintet.

▶ Richard Marx's appearance as a songwriter (**Cliff Richard**'s 'Best Of Me', *NOW 15*) pre-dates his own debut as a performer on *NOW 16* ('Right Here Waiting'). *NOW 27* was his last appearance as either.

ALSO HAPPENING IN AUGUST 1994

- Shops in England and Wales were able to open legally on a Sunday for the first time
- **Lisa Marie Presley** and **Michael Jackson** were married
- At the cinema: *Forrest Gump*, *True Lies*, *The Mask*, *The Client* and the highly controversial *Natural Born Killers*
- Albums released included the debut from **Marilyn Manson**, *Portrait of an American Family*, *Dummy* **(Portishead)**, *The Holy Bible* **(Manic Street Preachers)** and *Definitely Maybe* **(Oasis)**
- Bestsellers published in 1994 included *Captain Corelli's Mandolin* (Louis de Bernières) and *Disclosure* (Michael Crichton)

TRACKLISTING NOW 28

CD1

1 *Love Is All Around* Wet Wet Wet
2 *I Swear* All-4-One
3 *Don't Turn Around* Ace of Base
4 *Shine* Aswad
5 *(Meet) The Flintstones* B52s
6 *Crazy For You* Let Loose
7 *U R The Best Thing* D:Ream
8 *Everybody's Talkin'* The Beautiful South
9 *I Believe* Marcella Detroit
10 *I'll Stand By You* The Pretenders
11 *Inside* Stiltskin
12 *Girls And Boys* Blur
13 *Renaissance* M People
14 *Just A Step From Heaven* Eternal
15 *Another Sad Love Song* Toni Braxton
16 *Searching* China Black
17 *You Don't Love Me (No No No)* Dawn Penn
18 *I Wanna Be Your Man* Chaka Demus & Pliers
19 *Always* Erasure
20 *Prayer For The Dying* Seal

CD2

1 *Swamp Thing* The Grid
2 *Everybody Gonfi Gon* Two Cowboys
3 *Get-A-Way* Maxx
4 *Go On Move* Reel 2 Real feat. The Mad Stuntman
5 *No Good (Start The Dance)* The Prodigy
6 *U & Me* Cappella
7 *Rock My Heart* Haddaway
8 *The Real Thing* 2 Unlimited
9 *Don't Give It Up* Sonic Surfers
10 *What's Up* DJ Miko
11 *Light My Fire* Club House feat. Carl
12 *The Real Thing* Toni Di Bart
13 *Sweets For My Sweet* C J Lewis
14 *Dedicated To The One I Love* Bitty McLean
15 *Whatta Man* Salt 'N' Pepa with En Vogue
16 *Your Body's Callin'* R. Kelly
17 *Dream On Dreamer* Brand New Heavies
18 *Caught In The Middle* Juliet Roberts
19 *Carry Me Home* Gloworm
20 *Absolutely Fabulous* Absolutely Fabulous

▶ Richard Curtis's first three movies all featured a soundtrack which delivered a No.1 single: **Wet Wet Wet**'s 'Love Is All Around' (*Four Weddings And A Funeral*), **Ronan Keating**'s 'When You Say Nothing At All' (*Notting Hill, NOW 44*), and **Geri Halliwell**'s 'It's Raining Men' (*Bridget Jones's Diary, NOW 49*).

▶ '**Aswad**'s 'Shine' was the first of four different songs with that title to appear in *NOW* history – a joint record. *NOW 67* boasts 'Shines' from both **Take That** and **Booty Luv**. **The Lovefreekz** took a fourth 'Shine' onto *NOW 60* – using his other alias **Lucid**, producer Mark Hadfield had also featured on *NOW 40.*

▶ 'Sticking with the subject, 'Shine' was remixed here by **The Beatmasters**, who had already featured with their own hits on *NOW 11* and *NOW 13.* They had previously remixed **The Shamen**'s paean to salmon farming with **Vera Lynn**, 'Ebeneezer Goode' (*NOW 23*).

ALSO HAPPENING IN NOVEMBER 1994

- The first UK National Lottery draw was held. Seven winners shared the jackpot of just under £5.9 million
- George Foreman regained the World Heavyweight Boxing Championship at the age of forty-five
- The first Eurostar train carried passengers through the Channel Tunnel
- The year's craze was Magic Eye pictures
- At the cinema: *Interview with the Vampire*, *Junior*, *Star Trek: Generations*
- Albums: *Bizarre Fruit* (**M People**) *CrazySexyCool* (**TLC**) *My Life* (**Mary J. Blige**)
- Christmas No.1 was **East 17**'s 'Stay Another Day'

TRACKLISTING NOW 29

CD1

1 *Baby Come Back* Pato Banton with Ali & Robin Campbell
2 *Hey Now (Girls Just Wanna Have Fun)* Cyndi Lauper
3 *Baby, I Love Your Way* Big Mountain
4 *Sure* Take That
5 *Sweetness* Michelle Gayle
6 *Saturday Night* Whigfield
7 *Another Night* MC Sar & The Real McCoy
8 *The Rhythm Of The Night* Corona
9 *True Faith* New Order
10 *Right Beside You* Sophie B. Hawkins
11 *7 Seconds* Youssou N'Dour/Neneh Cherry
12 *Stay (I Missed You)* Lisa Loeb And Nine Stories
13 *Mmm Mmm Mmm Mmm* Crash Test Dummies
14 *We Have All The Time In The World* Louis Armstrong
15 *Know By Now* Robert Palmer
16 *What's The Frequency, Kenneth?* R.E.M.
17 *Cigarettes & Alcohol* Oasis
18 *Love Is Strong* The Rolling Stones
19 *Zombie* The Cranberries

CD2

1 *Around The World* East 17
2 *Compliments On Your Kiss* Red Dragon feat. Brian and Tony Gold
3 *Gal Wine* Chaka Demus & Pliers
4 *She's Got That Vibe* R. Kelly
5 *Midnight At The Oasis* Brand New Heavies
6 *Stars* China Black
7 *What's Going On* Music Relief
8 *The Power Of Love* Celine Dion
9 *Confide In Me* Kylie Minogue
10 *Sly* Massive Attack
11 *So Good* Eternal
12 *Some Girls* Ultimate Kaos
13 *Can You Feel It?* Reel 2 Real feat. The Mad Stuntman
14 *Incredible* M Beat feat. General Levy
15 *Trouble* Shampoo
16 *Parklife* Blur feat. Phil Daniels
17 *I Love Saturday* Erasure
18 *When Do I Get To Sing 'My Way'* Sparks
19 *I Want The World* 2wo Third3

▶ On release, *NOW 29* was the biggest volume seller in the series, a record it held for another fifteen editions.

▶ **Big Mountain** spent three weeks at No.2 with their cover version of **Peter Frampton**'s 'Baby, I Love Your Way'. It was held at bay by **Wet Wet Wet** who started their fifteen-week run at No.1 with 'Love Is All Around' at the same time.

▶ **Ultimate KAOS** – originally **Sinitta**'s backing dancers – marked the first time a Simon Cowell guided act has appeared on a *NOW* release.

A *NOW* TIMES TABLE

Appearence counts by selected artists.

8

Geri Halliwell
Cast
Wiley

Geri Halliwell

7

Cheryl Cole
James
Chipmunk

Cheryl Cole

6

Christina Milian
Supergrass
N-Dubz

5

Adele
The Verve
Darius

4

Paula Abdul
Ocean Colour Scene
Pato Banton

3

Kate Bush
Depeche Mode
Dappy

David Gahan of Depeche Mode

2

Prince
The Rolling Stones
Sting

Keith Richards of The Rolling Stones

1

Whitney Houston
Sam Fox
Lionel Richie

Lionel Richie

THIS IS...

...How It Feels
Inspiral Carpets
NOW 17

...Hardcore
Pulp
NOW 39

...How We Do It
Montell Jordan
NOW 31

...Your Life
Banderas
NOW 19

...Not America
David Bowie
& Pat Metheny Group
NOW 5

David Bowie

QUESTIONS QUESTIONS

Where Is The Love? Black Eyed Peas *NOW 56*

What Difference Does It Make? The Smiths *NOW 2*

What is Love? Haddaway *NOW 26*

Why? Bronski Beat *NOW 4*

Whatcha Gonna Do With My Lovin'? Inner City *NOW 16*

What Do I Have To Do? Kylie Minogue *NOW 19*

What Have You Done For Me Lately? Janet Jackson *NOW 8*

Is It Any Wonder? Keane *NOW 64*

Who's That Chick? David Guetta *NOW 78*

Do I Wanna Know? Arctic Monkeys *NOW 86*

What Am I Fighting For? Unklejam *NOW 67*

SHOULD I STAY OR SHOULD I GO?

Stay
Eternal
NOW 26

Stay (I Missed You)
Lisa Loeb & Nine Stories
NOW 26

STAY

Stay
Shakespears Sister
NOW 20

Should I Stay Or Should I Go
The Clash
NOW 26

GO

Go
Moby
NOW 20

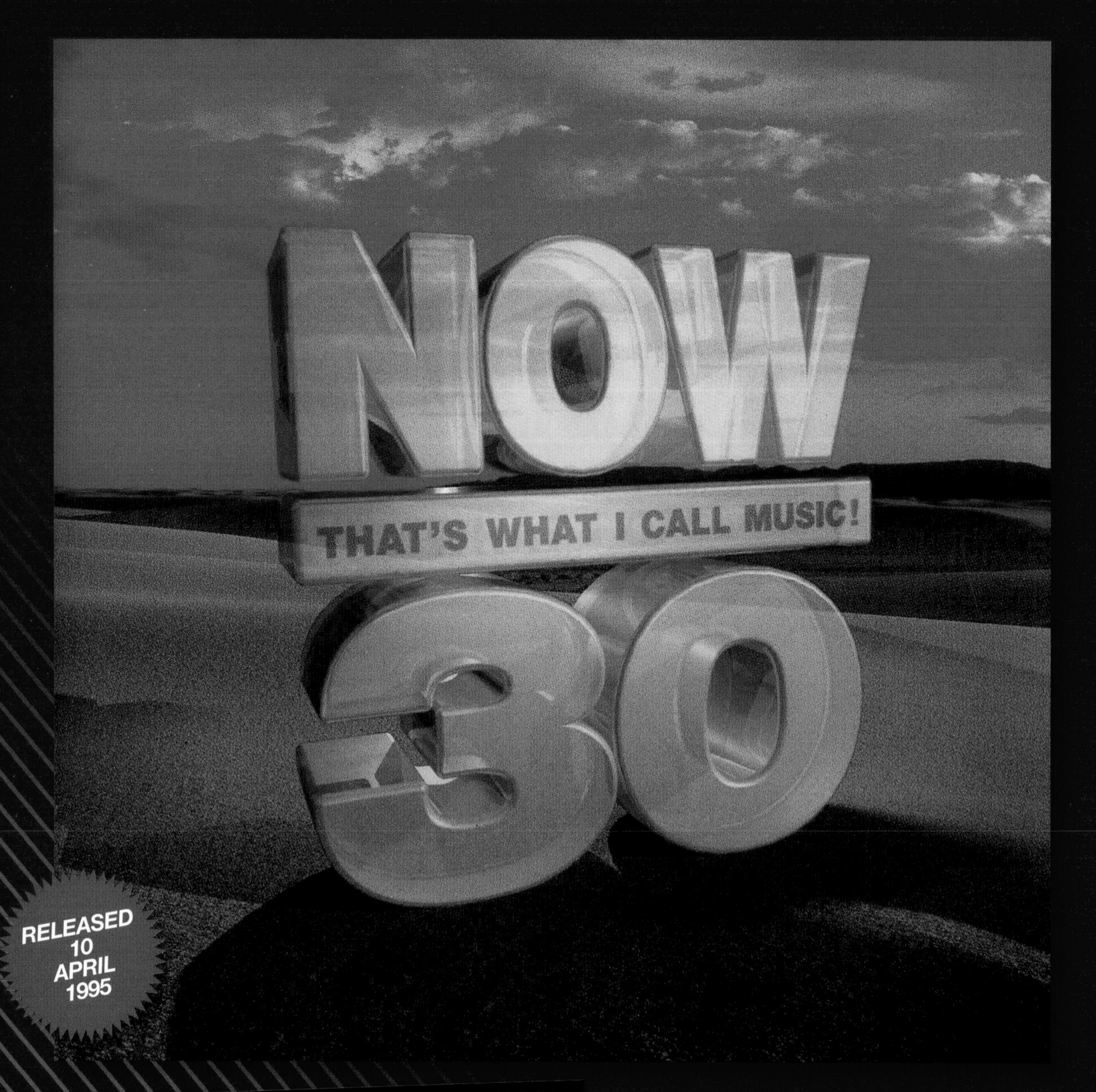

RELEASED 10 APRIL 1995

ALSO HAPPENING IN APRIL 1995

- Footballer Eric Cantona was given community service and banned from the game for eight months for kicking a spectator during a match
- *Four Weddings and a Funeral* won five Baftas, consolation for going home empty-handed at the Oscars
- The first episodes of *Father Ted* and *Hollyoaks* were broadcast
- Chris Evans took over The Radio 1 Breakfast Show
- At the cinema: *Bad Boys*, *The Basketball Diaries*
- Albums released included *Picture This* (**Wet Wet Wet**) and *Nobody Else* (**Take That**)

TRACKLISTING NOW 30

CD1

1 *Turn On, Tune In, Cop Out* Freak Power
2 *Whoops Now* Janet Jackson
3 *Love Me For A Reason* Boyzone
4 *Love Can Build A Bridge* Cher/Chrissie Hynde/Neneh Cherry with Eric Clapton
5 *Stay Another Day* East 17
6 *Over My Shoulder* Mike & The Mechanics
7 *Crocodile Shoes* Jimmy Nail
8 *Independent Love Song* Scarlet
9 *She's A River* Simple Minds
10 *Wake Up Boo!* The Boo Radleys
11 *Tell Me When* The Human League
12 *Sight For Sore Eyes* M People
13 *This Cowboy Song* Sting feat. Pato Banton
14 *Save It 'Til The Mourning After* Shut Up & Dance
15 *Bump 'N' Grind* R. Kelly
16 *Oh Baby I...* Eternal
17 *Protection* Massive Attack feat. Tracey Thorn
18 *Glory Box* Portishead
19 *Whatever* Oasis

CD2

1 *Don't Stop (Wiggle Wiggle)* The Outhere Brothers
2 *Don't Give Me Your Life* Alex Party
3 *U Sure Do* Strike
4 *The Bomb (These Sounds Fall Into My Mind)* Kenny Dope presents The Bucketheads
5 *Push The Feeling On* Nightcrawlers
6 *Always (Something There To Remind Me)* Tin Tin Out feat. Espiritu
7 *Baby Baby* Corona
8 *Axel F* Clock
9 *Set You Free* N-Trance
10 *You Belong To Me* JX
11 *Reach Up (Papa's Got A Brand New Pig Bag)* Perfecto Allstarz
12 *Cotton Eye Joe* Rednex
13 *Call It Love* Deuce
14 *Here I Go* 2 Unlimited
15 *Run Away* MC Sar & The Real McCoy
16 *Total Eclipse Of The Heart* Nicki French
17 *Suddenly* Sean Maguire
18 *Two Can Play That Game* Bobby Brown
19 *Hoochie Booty* Ultimate Kaos
20 *Bubbling Hot* Pato Banton with Ranking Roger
21 *One* Mica Paris

▶ **Eric Clapton**'s only credited appearance on a *NOW* was here – he played guitar on the Comic Relief single 'Love Can Build A Bridge'. He also featured prominently on 'I Wish It Would Rain Down' by **Phil Collins** on *NOW 17*.

▶ **Sean Maguire** (who played Aidan) joined a surprisingly long list of *EastEnders* cast members to have featured on *NOW* albums: **Sean Maguire, Nick Berry, Michelle Gayle** and **Martine McCutcheon** all made the leap from Albert Square to Top 40 success, with Martin Kemp of **Spandau Ballet** and Claire Grogan of **Altered Images** moving in the opposite direction.

▶ Simon Cowell's fellow X Factor judge and svengali Louis Walsh conceived **Boyzone** as 'an Irish answer to **Take That**', and following their first *NOW* inclusion here they would go on to appear another fourteen times, four more than Gary and the gang.

ALSO HAPPENING IN JULY 1995

- The OJ Simpson murder trial continued in Los Angeles
- Windows 95 launched with a huge worldwide marketing campaign
- eBay was founded
- At the cinema: *Apollo 13*, *Batman Forever*, *Pocahontas*, *Clueless*, *Waterworld*
- *Riverdance* enjoyed massive success both with its live shows and with the video release which became the UK's best-selling music video
- **Robbie Williams** quit **Take That**
- **Foo Fighters** released their self-titled debut album. Other albums included *Boombastic* (**Shaggy**) and *Garbage* (**Garbage**)

TRACKLISTING NOW 31

CD1

1 *Don't Want To Forgive Me Now* Wet Wet Wet
2 *A Girl Like You* Edwyn Collins
3 *Common People* Pulp
4 *Alright* Supergrass
5 *In The Summertime* Shaggy feat. Rayvon
6 *Here Comes The Hotstepper* Ini Kamoze
7 *3 Is Family* Dana Dawson
8 *Right In The Night (Fall In Love With Music)* Jam & Spoon feat. Plavka
9 *Hold My Body Tight* East 17
10 *Key To My Life* Boyzone
11 *Kiss From A Rose* Seal
12 *Days* Kirsty MacColl
13 *One Man In My Heart* The Human League
14 *Sour Times* Portishead
15 *Some Might Say* Oasis
16 *Buddy Holly* Weezer
17 *Roll To Me* Del Amitri
18 *I'm A Believer* EMF with Reeves & Mortimer
19 *White Lines (Don't Do It)* Duran Duran feat. Melle Mel & Grandmaster Flash & The Furious Five
20 *Hurts So Good* Jimmy Somerville

CD2

1 *Boom Boom Boom* The Outhere Brothers
2 *I've Got A Little Something For You* MN8
3 *This Is How We Do It* Montell Jordan
4 *Shoot Me With Your Love* D:Ream
5 *I Need Your Loving (Everybody's Gotta Learn Sometime)* Baby D
6 *Keep Warm* Jinny
7 *Dreamer* Livin' Joy
8 *Think Of You* Whigfield
9 *Whoomph! (There It Is)* Clock
10 *Humpin' Around* Bobby Brown
11 *Stuck On U* P J & Duncan
12 *Love City Groove* Love City Groove
13 *Swing Low Sweet Chariot* Ladysmith Black Mambazo feat. China Black
14 *Love Enuff* Soul II Soul
15 *Get Your Hands Off My Man* Junior Vasquez
16 *Freedom* Shiva
17 *Your Loving Arms* Billie Ray Martin
18 *I Need You* Deuce
19 *Son Of A Gun* JX
20 *Only Me* Hyperlogic

▶ This is the first time a *NOW* release had featured a minimum of forty tracks, a benchmark that exists to this day.

▶ With ten entries stretching back to the very first volume, 'White Lines' marked the final appearance to date for **Duran Duran**. Their 80s rivals **Spandau Ballet** have only ever appeared on the spin-off album *NOW Smash Hits of the 80s* in 1987.

▶ **Kirsty MacColl** is the only female solo artist to appear twice across the series with the same recording – 'Days' also appeared on *NOW 15*. **Juliet Roberts** appeared twice with 'Caught in the Middle', however it was in a remixed form the second time around (*NOW 28*).

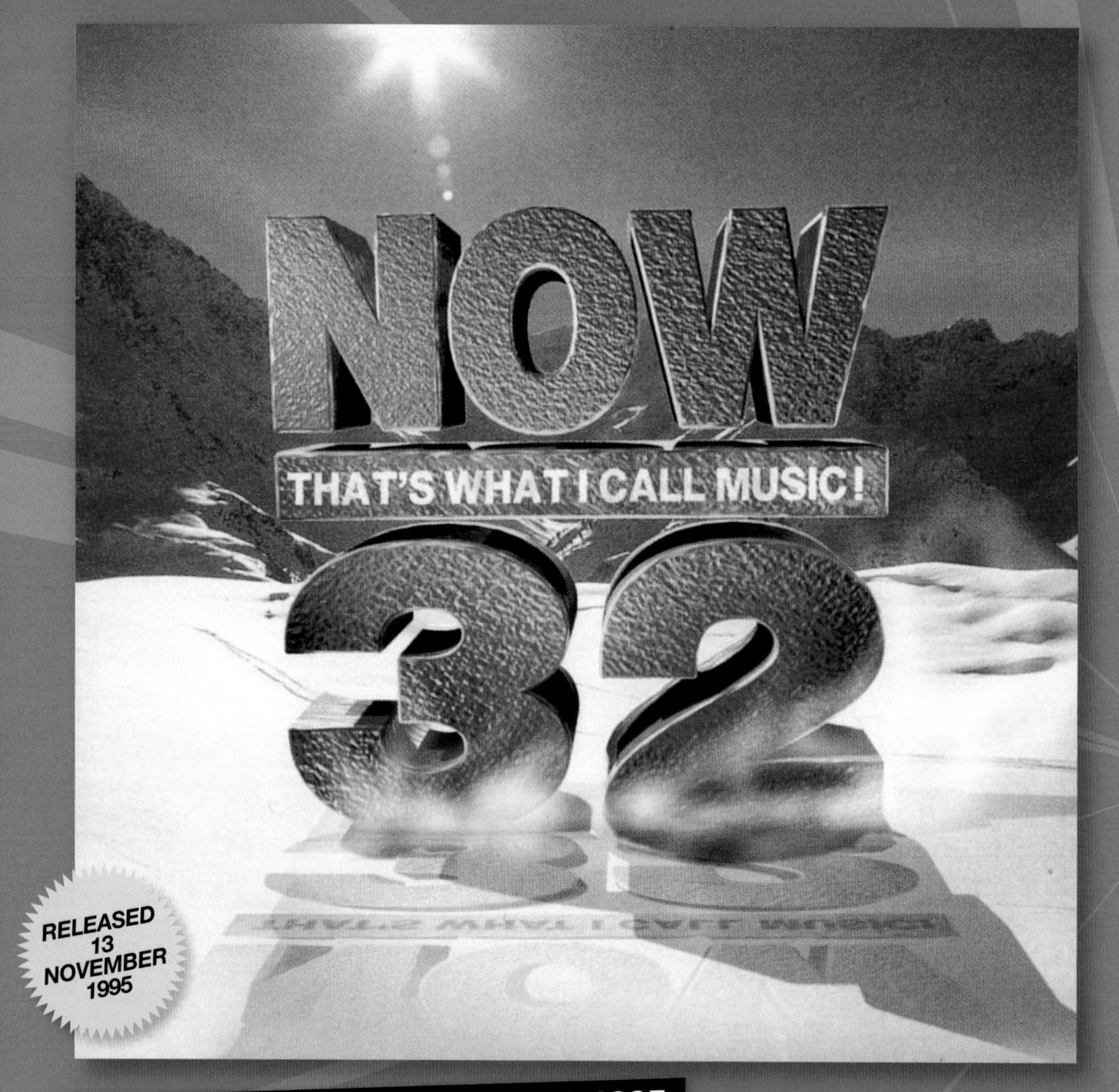

ALSO HAPPENING IN NOVEMBER 1995

- Princess Diana's *Panorama* interview with Martin Bashir was watched by 22 million people and causes a tabloid sensation
- Amazon.com sold its first book
- Sony's Playstation console was released in Europe
- At the cinema: *Casino*, *Toy Story*, *Ace Ventura: When Nature Calls.* Pierce Brosnan made his James Bond debut in *GoldenEye*
- Bestsellers published in 1995 included *The Horse Whisperer* (Nicholas Evans), *Angela's Ashes* (Frank McCourt) and *Long Walk to Freedom* (Nelson Mandela)

TRACKLISTING NOW 32

CD1

1 *Heaven For Everyone* Queen
2 *I'd Lie For You (And That's The Truth)* Meat Loaf
3 *Fairground* Simply Red
4 *Hold Me, Thrill Me, Kiss Me, Kill Me* U2
5 *GoldenEye* Tina Turner
6 *Walking In Memphis* Cher
7 *Pretenders To The Throne* The Beautiful South
8 *Light Of My Life* Louise
9 *Big River* Jimmy Nail
10 *Yeha-Noha* Sacred Spirit
11 *Lucky* Radiohead
12 *Sorted For E's & Wizz* Pulp
13 *Country House* Blur
14 *Alright* Cast
15 *Roll With It* Oasis
16 *Yes* McAlmont & Butler
17 *Broken Stones* Paul Weller
18 *I'm Only Sleeping* Suggs
19 *Come Together* The Smokin' Mojo Filters

CD2

1 *Gangsta's Paradise* Coolio feat. LV
2 *Boombastic* Shaggy
3 *Stayin' Alive* N-Trance feat. Ricardo Da Force
4 *I Feel Love* Donna Summer
5 *The Sunshine After The Rain* Berri
6 *Try Me Out* Corona
7 *I Luv U Baby* The Original
8 *Missing* Everything but the Girl
9 *Power Of A Woman* Eternal
10 *I Care* Soul II Soul
11 *La La La Hey Hey* The Outhere Brothers
12 *Big Time* Whigfield
13 *Wrap Me Up* Alex Party
14 *Higher State Of Consciousness* Josh Wink
15 *Renegade Master* Wildchild
16 *Inner City Life* Goldie Presents Metalheads
17 *Don't You Want Me* The Human League
18 *Fee Fi Fo Fum* Candy Girls feat. Sweet Pussy Pauline
19 *I Believe* Happy Clappers
20 *Dreams* Wild Colour
21 *Runaway* E'voke

Billed as a battle of Britpop heavyweights, **Blur** and **Oasis** released singles on the same day in August 1995, with the former's 'Country House' beating **Oasis**'s 'Roll With It' to the top spot. Had the Britpop spat never happened, 'I Luv U Baby' by **The Original** would have been No.1; all three are on this album.

The Smokin' Mojo Filters were a one-off 'supergroup' featuring, amongst others, **Paul McCartney, Paul Weller,** and **Noel Gallagher**. They got together to record a track in less than 24 hours for the *The Help Album* in aid of War Child. **Radiohead**'s 'Lucky' is taken from the same album.

Bernard Butler left **Suede** in late 1994. Less than a year later, with his only appearance in tandem with **David McAlmont**, he beat his old band onto a *NOW* by two editions. **Suede** would eventually notch up two inclusions, on *NOW*s *34* and *35*.

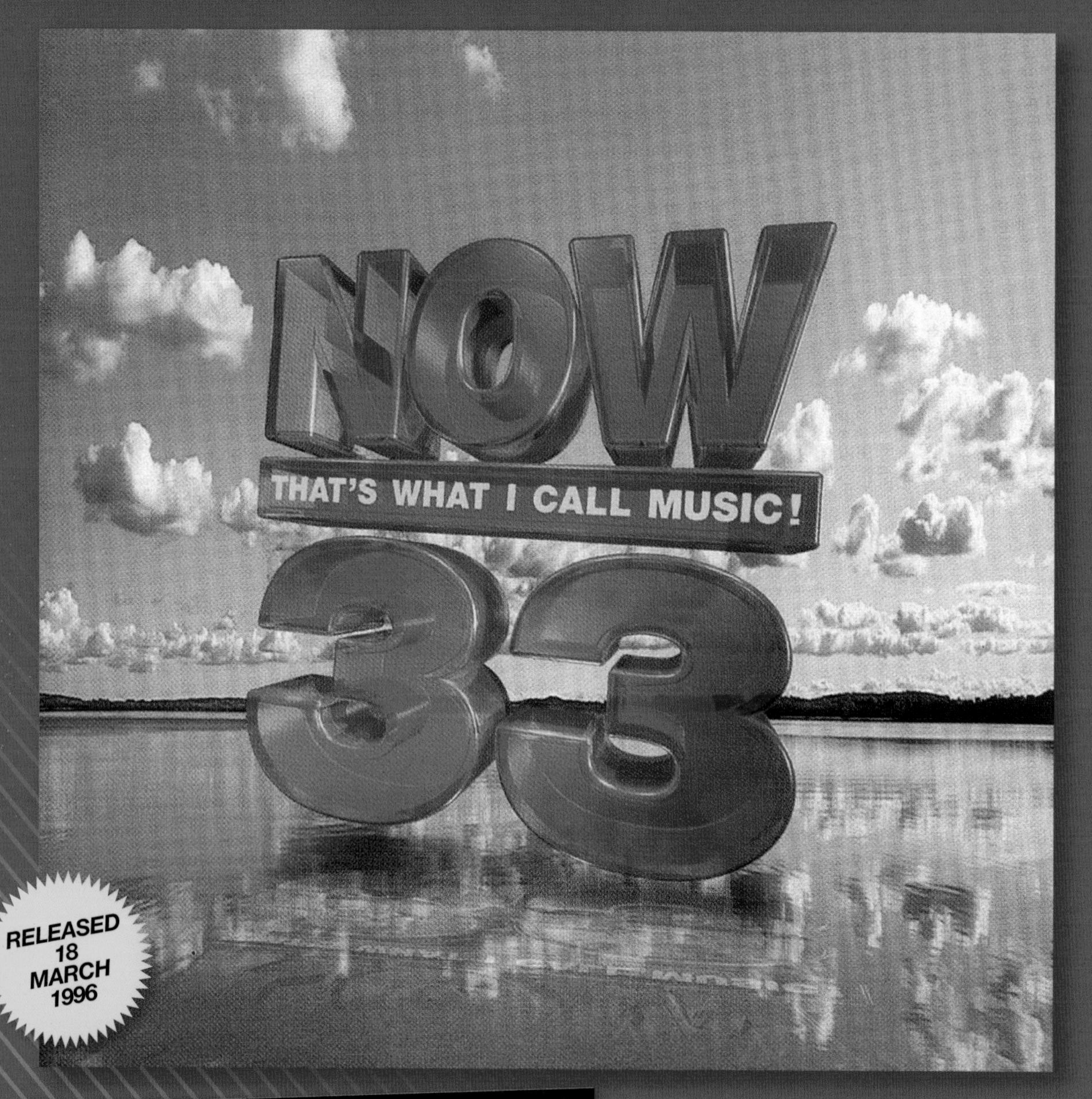

ALSO HAPPENING IN MARCH 1996

- British beef exports to Europe were banned over fears of Mad Cow Disease
- **Take That** split up in February. Hotlines were set up to counsel devastated fans
- *Braveheart* won five Academy Awards
- Tiger Woods became the youngest-ever winner of the US Masters
- At the cinema: *Fargo*, *The Juror*, *Broken Arrow*
- At the BRIT Awards, **Pulp**'s Jarvis Cocker invaded the stage during **Michael Jackson**'s performance of 'Earth Song'

TRACKLISTING NOW 33

CD1

1 *Too Much Love Will Kill You* Queen
2 *Don't Look Back In Anger* Oasis
3 *Spaceman* Babylon Zoo
4 *Going Out* Supergrass
5 *Disco 2000* Pulp
6 *One By One* Cher
7 *Not A Dry Eye In The House* Meat Loaf
8 *Anywhere Is* Enya
9 *'74–'75* The Connells
10 *Father And Son* Boyzone
11 *The Universal* Blur
12 *Out Of The Sinking* Paul Weller
13 *Sandstorm* Cast
14 *All I Need Is A Miracle* Mike + The Mechanics
15 *Fun Fun Fun* Status Quo with The Beach Boys
16 *Perseverance* Terrorvision
17 *Ladykillers* Lush
18 *Just The One* The Levellers
19 *Street Spirit (Fade Out)* Radiohead
20 *Live Forever* Oasis

CD2

1 *Lifted* Lighthouse Family
2 *Good Thing* Eternal
3 *I Just Want To Make Love To You* Etta James
4 *Never Never Love* Simply Red
5 *Give Me A Little More Time* Gabrielle
6 *Thunder* East 17
7 *I Got 5 On It* Luniz
8 *Walk Like A Champion* Kaliphz feat. Prince Naseem
9 *Why You Treat Me So Bad* Shaggy feat. Grand Puba
10 *So Pure* Baby D
11 *Passion* Gat Decor
12 *Disco's Revenge* Gusto
13 *I Need A Lover Tonight* Ken Doh
14 *Beautiful Life* Ace Of Base
15 *In Walked Love* Louise
16 *Not So Manic Now* Dubstar
17 *He's On The Phone* Saint Etienne
18 *Little Britain* Dreadzone
19 *Whole Lotta Love* Goldbug
20 *I Wanna Be A Hippy* Technohead

▶ 'Spaceman' by **Babylon Zoo** – the nom de plume of songwriter and musician Jas Mann – sold a million copies and spent five weeks at the top of the chart in 1996. It was the first time a male solo artist had made his debut at No.1.

▶ **Oasis** – who feature twice on *NOW 33* – chalked up a cumulative 134 weeks on the singles chart in 1996, a record previously held since 1981 by **Adam and the Ants.**

▶ A second showing for 'Too Much Love Will Kill You' (**Brian May**'s solo version appeared on *NOW 23*). Erroneously perceived as a tribute to Freddie Mercury, the song was originally recorded by **Queen** in the late 80s.

ALSO HAPPENING IN AUGUST 1996

- Prince Charles and Princess Diana divorce. Diana would henceforth be known as Diana, Princess of Wales
- The Summer Olympic Games in Atlanta were disappointing for Great Britain, with only one gold medal (for Matthew Pinsett and Steve Redgrave in Rowing)
- A replica of Shakespeare's Globe Theatre opened on the South Bank in London
- Rapper **Tupac Shakur** died after being shot in a drive-by attack
- At the cinema: *Independence Day*, *Matilda*, *The Crow: City of Angels*, *The Nutty Professor*

TRACKLISTING NOW 34

CD1

1 *Wannabe* Spice Girls
2 *Freedom* Robbie Williams
3 *Mysterious Girl* Peter Andre feat. Bubbler Ranx
4 *Good Enough* Dodgy
5 *The Day We Caught The Train* Ocean Colour Scene
6 *Theme From Mission: Impossible* Larry Mullen and Adam Clayton
7 *Born Slippy* Underworld
8 *There's Nothing I Won't Do* JX
9 *Ooh Aah... Just A Little Bit* Gina G
10 *Blurred* Pianoman
11 *Don't Stop Movin'* Livin' Joy
12 *Naked* Louise
13 *Return Of The Mack* Mark Morrison
14 *California Love* 2Pac feat. Dr Dre
15 *Groovin'* Pato Banton
16 *Jazz It Up* Reel 2 Real
17 *That Girl* Maxi Priest feat. Shaggy
18 *Macarena* Los Del Mar
19 *Sunshine* Umboza
20 *Higher State Of Consciousness* Wink
21 *Keep On Jumpin'* Todd Terry feat. Martha Wash and Jocelyn Brown
22 *Children* Robert Miles

CD2

1 *Jesus To A Child* George Michael
2 *Wonderwall* Oasis
3 *Slight Return* The Bluetones
4 *Peacock Suit* Paul Weller
5 *Hey God* Bon Jovi
6 *The Only Thing That Looks Good On Me Is You* Bryan Adams
7 *In Too Deep* Belinda Carlisle
8 *Cecilia* Suggs feat. Louchie Lou and Michie One
9 *Charmless Man* Blur
10 *Trash* Suede
11 *One Of Us* Joan Osborne
12 *Instinct* Crowded House
13 *Ocean Drive* Lighthouse Family
14 *On Silent Wings* Tina Turner
15 *Wrong* Everything But The Girl
16 *How Bizarre* OMC
17 *Walking On The Milky Way* Orchestral Manoeuvres In The Dark
18 *Female Of The Species* Space
19 *Walkaway* Cast
20 *Coming Home Now* Boyzone

▶ The **Spice Girls** made their first appearance here. 'Wannabe' was recorded in less than an hour and is the biggest-selling single by an all-female group in UK history. Of ten tracks released as singles from the first two **Spice Girls** albums, only '2 Become 1' isn't on a *NOW*.

▶ It was an auspicious edition for debuts: the man with the most credits of all (29), **Robbie Williams**, arrived here – his first effort a version of *NOW 3* and *7* stalwarts **Wham!**'s 'Freedom'. Chief **Wham!** man **George Michael**'s comeback solo single 'Jesus To A Child' also featured on this *NOW*.

▶ **U2** bassist **Adam Clayton** and drummer **Larry Mullen** have more credited appearances on *NOW* albums than their more fêted band mates Bono and The Edge as a consequence of 'Theme From Mission: Impossible' making its mark on *NOW 34*.

ALSO HAPPENING IN NOVEMBER 1996

- Bill Clinton was re-elected for a second term as US President
- The *Toy Story* Buzz Lightyear figure was this year's most wanted toy
- At the cinema: Baz Luhrmann's *Romeo + Juliet*, *The English Patient*, *Star Trek: First Contact*
- **The Spice Girls** released their debut album, *Spice*. They reached Christmas No.1 with '2 Become 1'
- Published in 1996 : *The Beach* (Alex Garland), *A Game of Thrones* (George RR Martin), *Fight Club* (Chuck Palahniuk)
- Popular TV: *Shooting Stars*, *The Fast Show*, *Never Mind the Buzzcocks*

TRACKLISTING NOW 35

CD1

1 *Say You'll Be There* **Spice Girls**
2 *Fastlove* **George Michael**
3 *Flava* **Peter Andre**
4 *If You Ever* **East 17 feat. Gabrielle**
5 *Breakfast At Tiffany's* **Deep Blue Something**
6 *Se A Vida E (That's The Way Life Is)* **Pet Shop Boys**
7 *You're Gorgeous* **Babybird**
8 *Rotterdam* **The Beautiful South**
9 *If You're Thinking Of Me* **Dodgy**
10 *Don't Dream It's Over* **Crowded House**
11 *Marblehead Johnson* **The Bluetones**
12 *The Riverboat Song* **Ocean Colour Scene**
13 *If It Makes You Happy* **Sheryl Crow**
14 *Milk* **Garbage feat. Tricky**
15 *Woman* **Neneh Cherry**
16 *Goodbye Heartbreak* **Lighthouse Family**
17 *Something Changed* **Pulp**
18 *Flying* **Cast**
19 *Beautiful Ones* **Suede**
20 *Always Breaking My Heart* **Belinda Carlisle**

CD2

1 *Escaping* **Dina Carroll**
2 *Words* **Boyzone**
3 *Someday* **Eternal**
4 *I'll Never Break Your Heart* **Backstreet Boys**
5 *Love II Love* **Damage**
6 *Oh What A Night* **Clock**
7 *Undivided Love* **Louise**
8 *When I Fall In Love* **Ant & Dec**
9 *Don't Make Me Wait* **911**
10 *My Love Is For Real* **Strike**
11 *Insomnia* **Faithless**
12 *Seven Days And One Week* **BBE**
13 *I'm Alive* **Stretch 'N' Vern**
14 *Stamp!* **Healy And Amos**
15 *Follow The Rules* **Livin' Joy**
16 *Jump To My Beat* **Wildchild**
17 *Pearl's Girl* **Underworld**
18 *Neighbourhood* **Space**
19 *Possibly Maybe* **Bjork**
20 *Chasing Rainbows* **Shed Seven**

▶ *NOW 35* was the last in the series to be manufactured on vinyl.

▶ The second appearance for 'Don't Dream its Over', **Paul Young**'s cover version beat **Crowded House**'s re-released original by fifteen volumes (it first appeared on *NOW 20* in 1991).

▶ Jeremy Healy from **Healy & Amos** made his *NOW* debut with the **E-Zee Posse** on *NOW 17* and had a hand in **Gwen Stefani**'s 'Wind It Up' on *NOW 66*. To date, his old band **Haysi Fantayzee** remain unchronicled by *NOW*.

ALSO HAPPENING IN MARCH 1997

- Channel 5 began broadcasting in the UK
- *The English Patient* won nine Oscars
- The first cloned mammal was announced by scientists – Dolly the sheep
- Nintendo's N64 console was released in Europe
- Rapper The Notorious B.I.G. was killed in a drive-by shooting
- At the cinema: *Liar Liar*, *The Devil's Own*, *Austin Powers*
- Albums released in 1997 included *Pop* **(U2)**, *Life After Death* **(The Notorious B.I.G.)** and *Aquarium* **(Aqua)**

TRACKLISTING NOW 36

CD1

1 *Mama* **Spice Girls**
2 *Say What You Want* **Texas**
3 *Alone* **The Bee Gees**
4 *Don't Marry Her* **The Beautiful South**
5 *Don't Speak* **No Doubt**
6 *Your Woman* **White Town**
7 *Remember Me* **The Blueboy**
8 *Virtual Insanity* **Jamiroquai**
9 *One And One* **Robert Miles feat. Maria Nayler**
10 *Spinning The Wheel* **George Michael**
11 *Horny* **Mark Morrison**
12 *Natural* **Peter Andre**
13 *Love Guaranteed* **Damage**
14 *Don't You Love Me* **Eternal**
15 *Walk On By* **Gabrielle**
16 *I Can Make You Feel Good* **Kavana**
17 *Hey Child* **East 17**
18 *A Different Beat* **Boyzone**
19 *Anywhere For You* **Backstreet Boys**
20 *The Day We Find Love* **911**

CD2

1 *Discothèque* **U2**
2 *Breathe* **The Prodigy**
3 *Block Rockin' Beats* **The Chemical Brothers**
4 *Nancy Boy* **Placebo**
5 *What Do You Want From Me?* **Monaco**
6 *Everyday Is A Winding Road* **Sheryl Crow**
7 *Beetlebum* **Blur**
8 *She's A Star* **James**
9 *Wide Open Space* **Mansun**
10 *Free Me* **Cast**
11 *Dark Clouds* **Space**
12 *Waterloo Sunset* **Cathy Dennis**
13 *Everybody Knows (Except You)* **The Divine Comedy**
14 *Indestructible* **Alisha's Attic**
15 *Shout* **Ant & Dec**
16 *You Got The Love* **The Source feat. Candi Staton**
17 *Encore Une Fois* **Sash!**
18 *Bellissima* **DJ Quicksilver**
19 *Flash* **BBE**
20 *Passion* **Amen! UK**

▶ 'The second of three appearances for 'You Got The Love' by **The Source** featuring **Candi Staton** (see also *NOW 19* and *NOW 63*). Two cover versions by **Florence + the Machine** (one with **Dizzee Rascal**) also followed on *NOW 74* and *NOW 76*. It is the most chronicled song in *NOW* history.

▶ German production outfit **Sash!** can count themselves extremely unlucky having reached No.2 in the singles chart on five separate occasions without ever getting to No.1 Their first four hits were sung in four different languages – they can be found on *NOW*s *36* to *39*.

▶ Glasgow band **Texas**'s twelve appearances was until recently a record for a Scottish act – however **Calvin Harris** has now overtaken them on seventeen, assisted by a dazzling array of guest vocalists.

ALSO HAPPENING IN JULY 1997

- Mike Tyson's licence to box was revoked after he bit off part of Evander Holyfield's ear
- *Harry Potter and the Philosopher's Stone* was published. It went on to sell over 107 million copies worldwide, becoming one of the top five bestselling books of all time
- At the cinema: *Men in Black*, *Air Force One*, *Contact*
- *Be Here Now* (**Oasis**) became the fastest selling album in UK history. *The Fat of the Land* (**The Prodigy**) was also hugely successful

TRACKLISTING NOW 37

CD1

1 *MMMBop* Hanson
2 *I Wanna Be The Only One* Eternal feat. Bebe Winans
3 *Lovefool* The Cardigans
4 *Just A Girl* No Doubt
5 *Ecuador* Sash! feat. Rodriguez
6 *Where Do You Go* No Mercy
7 *Who Do You Think You Are* Spice Girls
8 *Free* Ultra Naté
9 *Closer Than Close* Rosie Gaines
10 *Star People* George Michael
11 *Don't Let Go (Love)* En Vogue
12 *You Might Need Somebody* Shola Ama
13 *C U When U Get There* Coolio feat. 40 Thevz
14 *Smokin' Me Out* Warren G feat. Ron Isley
15 *I Believe I Can Fly* R. Kelly
16 *Wonderful Tonight* Damage
17 *The Journey* 911
18 *Isn't It A Wonder* Boyzone
19 *Quit Playing Games (With My Heart)* Backstreet Boys
20 *Hey DJ! (Play That Song)* N-Tyce
21 *I'll Be* Foxy Brown feat. Jay-Z

CD2

1 *If I Never See You Again* Wet Wet Wet
2 *Staring At The Sun* U2
3 *Bitter Sweet Symphony* The Verve
4 *Love Is The Law* Seahorses
5 *100 Mile High City* Ocean Colour Scene
6 *Old Before I Die* Robbie Williams
7 *Guiding Star* Cast
8 *Young Boy* Paul McCartney
9 *A Change Would Do You Good* Sheryl Crow
10 *Paranoid Android* Radiohead
11 *Halo* Texas
12 *Sun Hits The Sky* Supergrass
13 *Waltzing Along* James
14 *On Your Own* Blur
15 *Scooby Snacks* Fun Lovin' Criminals
16 *The Saint* Orbital
17 *Nightmare* Brainbug
18 *Ain't Nobody* The Course
19 *Something Goin' On* Todd Terry feat. Martha Wash and Jocelyn Brown
20 *Give Me Love* Diddy

▶ Summer 1997 was a high-water mark for Britpop on *NOW* albums – CD2 here features tracks from **The Verve, Ocean Colour Scene, Cast, Radiohead, Supergrass** and **Blur** with **Seahorses** making their only appearance. Guitarist John Squire's former band **Stone Roses** are not be found on any *NOW*.

▶ **Coolio**'s 'C U When You Get There' based its melody on Pachelbel's 'Canon In D Major'. However, he wasn't the first to do so in the *NOW* series – **Pet Shop Boys**' 'Go West' on volume 26 utilised the same piece of classical music.

▶ **No Mercy** were masterminded by Frank Farian who had already scored two of the biggest singles of all time with **Boney M.** Previously, **Milli Vanilli** – another Farian project – appeared on *NOW 13* and *NOW 16*.

ALSO HAPPENING IN NOVEMBER 1997

- Construction began on the Millennium Dome
- Top-selling toys this year included Teletubbies, Beanie Babies and the Tamagotchi
- At the cinema: *Bean*, *Alien: Resurrection*, *Spice World: the Movie*
- Albums: *Come On Over* (**Shania Twain**), *Spice World* (**Spice Girls**) *All Saints* (**All Saints**), *Left of the Middle* (**Natalie Imbruglia**). The Spice Girls scored another Christmas No.1 with 'Too Much'
- Bestsellers published in 1997: *Sex and the City* (Candace Bushnell), *The God of Small Things* (Arundhati Roy), *The Bible Code* (Michael Drosnin)

TRACKLISTING NOW 38

CD1

1 *Tubthumping* Chumbawamba
2 *Spice Up Your Life* Spice Girls
3 *Where's The Love* Hanson
4 *Picture Of You* Boyzone
5 *As Long As You Love Me* Backstreet Boys
6 *Angel Of Mine* Eternal
7 *Raincloud* Lighthouse Family
8 *Got 'Til Its Gone* Janet Jackson
9 *You've Got A Friend* The Brand New Heavies
10 *I Know Where It's At* All Saints
11 *Arms Around The World* Louise
12 *Freed From Desire* Gala
13 *Stay* Sash! feat. La Trec
14 *Sunchyme* Dario G
15 *Never Gonna Let You Go* Tina Moore
16 *You Sexy Thing* Hot Chocolate
17 *Da Ya Think I'm Sexy* N-Trance feat. Rod Stewart
18 *Phenomenon* LL Cool J
19 *Party People…Friday Night* 911
20 *Maria* Ricky Martin
21 *Samba De Janeiro* Bellini
22 *Free* DJ Quicksilver

CD2

1 *Yesterday* Wet Wet Wet
2 *You Have Been Loved* George Michael
3 *The Drugs Don't Work* The Verve
4 *Stand By Me* Oasis
5 *All You Good Good People* Embrace
6 *Don't Leave* Faithless
7 *Karma Police* Radiohead
8 *James Bond Theme* Moby
9 *Choose Life* PF Project feat. Ewan McGregor
10 *Lazy Days* Robbie Williams
11 *A Life Less Ordinary* Ash
12 *Black Eyed Boy* Texas
13 *Bitch* Meredith Brooks
14 *Janie, Don't Take Your Love To Town* Jon Bon Jovi
15 *Better Day* Ocean Colour Scene
16 *I'm So Lonely* Cast
17 *Earthbound* Conner Reeves
18 *Lonely* Peter Andre
19 *4 Seasons Of Loneliness* Boyz II Men

As Spicemania continued to grip the nation, combat-trousered rival girlband **All Saints** entered the fray and went on to chalk up eight appearances. Half the band, the Appleton sisters, then placed three consecutive singles on *NOW 53* to *55*.

We bid a fond farewell to **Rod Stewart** with this dance remix of 'Da Ya Think I'm Sexy'. Despite only two credits to his name, Rod's *NOW* career stretches back to the very first volume, whose featured song 'Baby Jane' remains his last UK No.1 single to date.

The third Top 10 appearance and second *NOW* check-in for **Hot Chocolate**'s 'You Sexy Thing'. A hit in 1975 (denied the top spot by **Queen**'s 'Bohemian Rhapsody' – *NOW 21*), 1987 (*NOW 9*) and here from 1997, this re-release coincided with its inclusion in *The Full Monty* film.

ALSO HAPPENING IN APRIL 1998

- *Titanic* won eleven Oscars at the Academy Awards, including Best Song for 'My Heart Will Go On'
- At the cinema: *Sliding Doors*, *City of Angels*, *Twilight*, *The Big Lebowski*
- George Michael was arrested for lewd behaviour in a Beverly Hills public toilet. This incident was later used as the basis for his video 'Outside'
- The Apple iMac computer was launched
- *Coronation Street*'s Deirdre Rachid was released from prison after the 'Free the Weatherfield One' campaign
- TV show *South Park* gained in popularity

TRACKLISTING NOW 39

CD1

1 *Never Ever* All Saints
2 *High* Lighthouse Family
3 *Together Again* Janet Jackson
4 *Stop* Spice Girls
5 *Torn* Natalie Imbruglia
6 *Kiss The Rain* Billie Myers
7 *Angels* Robbie Williams
8 *Perfect Day* Various Artists
9 *Baby Can I Hold You* Boyzone
10 *Here's Where The Story Ends* Tin Tin Out feat. Shelley Nelson
11 *The Ballad Of Tom Jones* Space with Cerys of Catatonia
12 *Insane* Texas
13 *Weird* Hanson
14 *How Do I Live* LeAnn Rimes
15 *You're Still The One* Shania Twain
16 *Tomorrow Never Dies* Sheryl Crow
17 *No Surprises* Radiohead
18 *Lucky Man* The Verve
19 *This Is Hardcore* Pulp

CD2

1 *Let Me Entertain You* Robbie Williams
2 *Mulder And Scully* Catatonia
3 *Brimful Of Asha (Norman Cook Remix)* Cornershop
4 *It's Like That* Run D.M.C. vs Jason Nevins
5 *Renegade Master '98* Wildchild
6 *Bamboogie* Bamboo
7 *Found A Cure* Ultra Naté
8 *La Primavera* Sash!
9 *Barbie Girl* Aqua
10 *5,6,7,8* Steps
11 *Let's Go Round Again* Louise
12 *Amnesia* Chumbawamba
13 *Let Me Show You* Camisra
14 *Planet Love* DJ Quicksilver
15 *Treat Infamy* Rest Assured
16 *Prince Igor* Warren G feat. Sissel
17 *Ain't That Just The Way* Lutricia McNeal
18 *Whine And Grine* Prince Buster
19 *The Beat Goes On* The All Seeing I
20 *Believe* Goldie
21 *II I Have To Give* Backstreet Boys
22 *No Way No Way* Vanilla

▶ 'Together Again' by **Janet Jackson** was also the opening track on the first edition of the U.S. version of the *NOW That's What I Call Music* series. The album was a seventeen-song single disc.

▶ **Natalie Imbruglia** spent four weeks at No.2 with 'Torn' which is one of the best-selling songs never to reach No.1. It was kept off the top spot by **Aqua**'s million-selling 'Barbie Girl', also included here.

▶ We bid a fond farewell to **Pulp** on *NOW 39* (five entries) but a hearty Hello to **Steps** who started a Gold standard fourteen-song run here (including two credits on *NOW 42*).

ALSO HAPPENING IN AUGUST 1998

- Bill Clinton admitted 'improper physical contact' with intern Monica Lewinsky after previously denying any wrongdoing
- Internet company Google was founded
- At the cinema: *Blade*, *There's Something About Mary*, *Saving Private Ryan*, *Armageddon*, *Lethal Weapon 4*
- Albums released included *Follow the Leader* (**Korn**), *Postcards from Heaven* (**Lighthouse Family**), *The Miseducation of Lauryn Hill* (**Lauryn Hill**) and *This is My Truth Tell Me Yours* (**Manic Street Preachers**)
- *The Royle Family*, *Cold Feet* and *Who Wants to be a Millionaire* all made their debuts on television

TRACKLISTING NOW 40

CD1

1 *The Grease Megamix* John Travolta And Olivia Newton-John
2 *Viva Forever* Spice Girls
3 *Looking For Love* Karen Ramirez
4 *Because We Want To* Billie
5 *Lady Marmalade* All Saints
6 *Horny* Mousse T. vs Hot 'n' Juicy
7 *Feel It* The Tamperer feat. Maya
8 *Doctor Jones* Aqua
9 *Last Thing On My Mind* Steps
10 *You Make Me Feel Like Dancing* Leo Sayer
11 *Kung Fu Fighting* Bus Stop feat. Carl Douglas
12 *New Kind Of Medicine* Ultra Naté
13 *Stranded* Lutricia McNeal
14 *Lost In Space* Lighthouse Family
15 *All That I Need* Boyzone
16 *Under The Bridge* All Saints
17 *All My Life* K-Ci & JoJo
18 *I Get Lonely* Janet Jackson
19 *Be Careful* Sparkle feat. R. Kelly
20 *Kiss The Girl* Peter Andre

CD2

1 *The Boys Of Summer* Don Henley
2 *Dance The Night Away* The Mavericks
3 *Save Tonight* Eagle Eye Cherry
4 *Road Rage* Catatonia
5 *Big Mistake* Natalie Imbruglia
6 *Come Back To What You Know* Embrace
7 *Sonnet* The Verve
8 *Teardrop* Massive Attack
9 *Legacy* Mansun
10 *Three Lions '98* Baddiel, Skinner and the Lightning Seeds
11 *Vindaloo* Fat Les
12 *The Rockafeller Skank* Fatboy Slim
13 *Needin' U* David Morales presents The Face
14 *I Can't Help Myself* Lucid
15 *Keep On Dancin' (Let's Go)* Perpetual Motion
16 *Everybody Dance (The Horn Song)* Barbara Tucker
17 *Where Are You* Imaani
18 *Night Fever* Adam Garcia
19 *Do You Love Me Boy?* Kerri-Ann
20 *No Tengo Dinero* Los Umbrellos

▶ Drummer and vocalist with **The Eagles** throughout the 1970s, **Don Henley** released his solo single 'Boys Of Summer' in 1985 and reached No.12. Hoping for better in 1998, the re-release again stalled two places outside the Top 10. Four years later **DJ Sammy** finally took the song into the Top 3 and was rewarded with a spot on *NOW 54.*

▶ As the World Cup in France was taking place there were football-related singles occupying the top two of the chart: **Baddiel, Skinner and the Lightning Seeds** with 'Three Lions '98' and **Fat Les**'s 'Vindaloo'. Comedian Keith Allen provided vocals on the latter and his daughter **Lily,** later a popstar in her own right with nine *NOW* credits, appeared in the video.

▶ **Red Hot Chili Peppers** have never appeared on a *NOW*. The closest they have come is via **All Saints'** cover of 'Under The Bridge', which omitted the final verse's more overt references to drug addiction.

ALSO HAPPENING IN NOVEMBER 1998

- Impeachment hearings began against President Clinton
- Europe prepared for the launch of the single currency on 1 January 1999
- Digital television launched in the UK
- This year's most wanted toys were ProYo Yo-Yos and the interactive Furby
- At the cinema: *Elizabeth*, *Meet Joe Black*, *A Bug's Life*
- Albums: *Supposed Former Infatuation Junkie* (**Alanis Morissette**), *Without You I'm Nothing* (**Placebo**), Believe (**Cher**), *My Love is Your Love* (**Whitney Houston**)
- The **Spice Girls** were Christmas No.1 again with 'Goodbye'

TRACKLISTING NOW 41

CD1

1 *No Matter What* Boyzone
2 *Millennium* Robbie Williams
3 *Perfect 10* The Beautiful South
4 *Sweetest Thing* U2
5 *I Just Wanna Be Loved* Culture Club
6 *Life Is A Flower* Ace Of Base
7 *Crush* Jennifer Paige
8 *Heartbeat* Steps
9 *Finally Found* Honeyz
10 *Each Time* E17
11 *Little Bit Of Lovin'* Kele Le Roc
12 *Everything's Gonna Be Alright* Sweetbox
13 *Come Back Darling* UB40
14 *I Want You Back* Melanie B feat. Missy 'Misdemeanor' Elliott
15 *Bootie Call* All Saints
16 *Turn Back Time* Aqua
17 *Too Much* Spice Girls
18 *Someone Loves You Honey* Lutricia McNeal
19 *Question Of Faith* Lighthouse Family
20 *True Colors* Phil Collins
21 *Every Time* Janet Jackson

CD1

1 *Girlfriend* Billie
2 *More Than A Woman* 911
3 *Sex On The Beach* T-Spoon
4 *If You Buy This Record Your Life Will Be Better* The Tamperer feat. Maya
5 *Music Sounds Better With You* Stardust
6 *Up And Down* Vengaboys
7 *Move Mania* Sash! feat. Shannon
8 *Would You..?* Touch and Go
9 *Dreams* The Corrs
10 *My Favourite Game* The Cardigans
11 *Sit Down '98* James
12 *Gangster Trippin'* Fatboy Slim
13 *Falling In Love Again* Eagle Eye Cherry
14 *My Favourite Mistake* Sheryl Crow
15 *No Regrets* Robbie Williams
16 *We Gotta Get Out Of This Place* Space
17 *My Weakness Is None Of Your Business* Embrace
18 *The Incidentals* Alisha's Attic
19 *Relax* Deetah
20 *Home Alone* R. Kelly feat. Keith Murray
21 *Tell Me Ma* Sham Rock

▶ Released as a single in three different versions across nine years, 'Sit Down' by **James** made its second *NOW* appearance here (originally *NOW 20*). This version was the band's highest charting hit since the original.

▶ Eurodance behemoths **Vengaboys** scored seven consecutive Top 10 hits, six consecutive *NOW* entries and sold 25 million records around the globe. Boom, boom, boom, boom indeed.

▶ British band **Touch and Go**'s massive European hit has enjoyed a TV ad afterlife. The follow up single was called 'Straight… To Number One'. It failed to chart.

APPLE
KAJAGOOGOO
NOW 1

FUN
GAP BAND
NOW 9

AREA
THEN JERICHO
NOW 14

GIRL
PRECOCIOUS BRATS
NOW 45

MISTAKE
NATALIE IMBRUGLIA
NOW 40

RIVER
JIMMY NAIL
NOW 32

SUR
THE THRILLS
NOW 32

SCARY ANIMAL
BELINDA CARLISLE
NOW 26

NOW BODY LANGUAGE

NO...

...Good (Start The Dance)
Prodigy
NOW 28

...Limit
2 Unlimited
NOW 24

...Matter What
Boyzone
NOW 41

...Regrets
Robbie Williams
NOW 41

...Ordinary Love
Sade
NOW 25

...Surprises
Radiohead
NOW 39

Thom Yorke of Radiohead

I'M NOT ALONE

will.i.am and **Calvin Harris** are two of *NOW*s most promiscuous, serial collaborators. However, one man unites them both

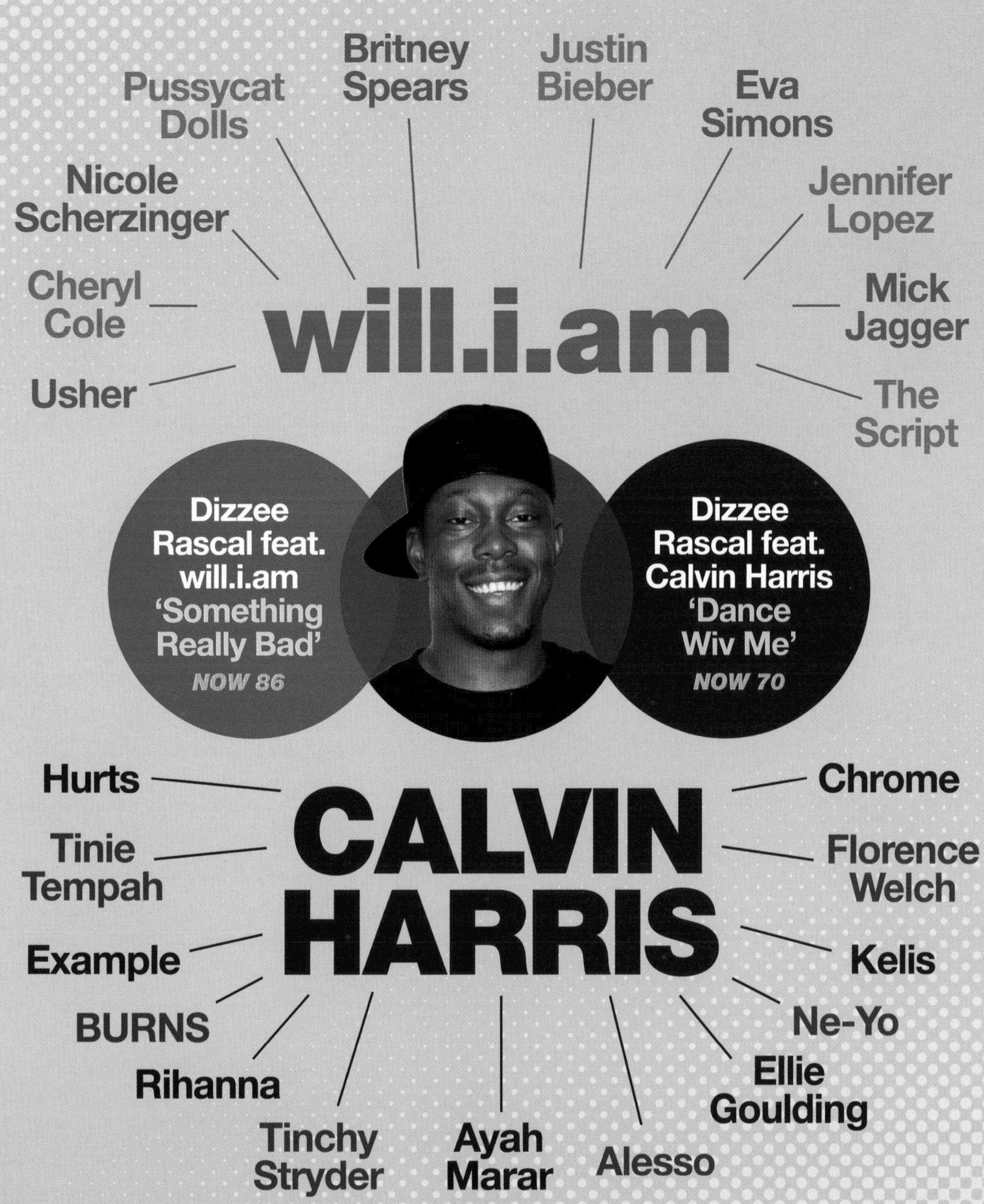

ALSO HAPPENING IN MARCH 1999

- Glenn Hoddle was sacked as England manager following the controversy over comments he made that were offensive to people with disabilities
- *Shakespeare in Love* won seven Oscars, including Best Picture and Best Director. Gwyneth Paltrow gave a very weepy acceptance speech when collecting her Best Actress award
- At the cinema: *Lock, Stock and Two Smoking Barrels*, *Cruel Intentions*, *The Matrix*
- Albums released included *Performance and Cocktails* **(Stereophonics)**, *13* **(Blur)**, *Central Reservation* **(Beth Orton)**, and *FanMail* **(TLC)**

TRACKLISTING NOW 42

CD1

1 *When The Going Gets Tough* Boyzone
2 *Better Best Forgotten* Steps
3 *Believe* Cher
4 *Thank Abba For The Music* Steps, Tina Cousins, Cleopatra, B*witched & Billie
5 *Goodbye* Spice Girls
6 *End Of The Line* Honeyz
7 *Honey To The Bee* Billie
8 *What Can I Do* The Corrs
9 *Big Big World* Emilia
10 *Killin' Time '99* Tina Cousins
11 *We Like To Party (The Vengabus)* Vengaboys
12 *Witch Doctor* Cartoons
13 *Always Have Always Will* Ace of Base
14 *You Should Be* Blockster
15 *Enjoy Yourself* A+
16 *El Paraiso Rico* Deetah
17 *More Than This* Emmie
18 *Protect Your Mind (For The Love Of A Princess)* DJ Sakin & Friends
19 *Popped* Fool Boona
20 *Colour The World* Sash!
21 *Over You* Justin

CD2

1 *Strong* Robbie Williams
2 *Fly Away* Lenny Kravitz
3 *Praise You* Fatboy Slim
4 *You Don't Know Me* Armand Van Helden/ Duane Harden
5 *Flat Beat* Mr. Oizo
6 *Erase/Rewind* The Cardigans
7 *Just Looking* Stereophonics
8 *Walk Like A Panther* The All Seeing I feat. Tony Christie
9 *National Express* The Divine Comedy
10 *Tequila* Terrorvision
11 *How Long's A Tear Take To Dry* The Beautiful South
12 *Wish I Could Fly* Roxette
13 *A Little Bit More* 911
14 *These Are The Times* Dru Hill
15 *My Love* Kele Le Roc
16 *War Of Nerves* All Saints
17 *Inkanyezi Nezazi (The Star and The Wiseman)* Ladysmith Black Mambazo
18 *Tender* Blur
19 *You Don't Have To Say You Love Me* Dusty Springfield

▶ **Cher** went out with a bang on *NOW 42* – 'Believe' may be her last *NOW* credit to date but it remains the highest-selling single by a solo female artist in the UK. It's the first *NOW* sighting of future **Girls Aloud** songwriter and producer Brian Higgins.

▶ **Dusty Springfield**'s 'You Don't Have To Say You Love Me' was recorded in 1966, making this the longest gap between original release and appearing on a *NOW*. The song was included on *NOW 42* as a tribute – Dusty died on 2 March 1999. This is the only time the death of an artist has been marked in this way without a contemporary hit single.

▶ Released by popular demand after a performance on the 1999 Brit Awards, the medley 'Thank Abba For The Music' was the only time sibling-heavy Irish girl band **B*Witched** and sibling-heavier Mancunian girl band **Cleopatra** featured on a *NOW*.

ALSO HAPPENING IN JULY 1999

- David and Victoria Beckham were married. Details of the lavish ceremony are widely reported, including the golden thrones they sat on
- A total solar eclipse occured over the UK on 11 August
- Microsoft released the first version of MSN Messenger
- The Napster music file-sharing website was launched
- At the cinema: *American Pie*, *Eyes Wide Shut*, *The Blair Witch Project*
- Albums released included *On How Life Is* **(Macy Gray)**, *The Writing's on the Wall* **(Destiny's Child)**

TRACKLISTING NOW 43

CD1

1 *Perfect Moment* Martine McCutcheon
2 *You Needed Me* Boyzone
3 *I Want It That Way* Backstreet Boys
4 *Sweet Like Chocolate* Shanks & Bigfoot
5 *Bring It All Back* S Club 7
6 *Boom, Boom, Boom, Boom!!* Vengaboys
7 *9pm (Till I Come)* ATB
8 *Turn Around* Phats & Small
9 *Red Alert* Basement Jaxx
10 *Without Love* Dina Carroll
11 *Look At Me* Geri Halliwell
12 *I Breathe Again* Adam Rickitt
13 *Viva La Radio* Lolly
14 *Doodah* Cartoons
15 *Say It Again* Precious
16 *Love Of A Lifetime* Honeyz
17 *Private Number* 911
18 *Your Kisses Are Charity* Culture Club
19 *Greatest Day* Beverley Knight
20 *Word Up* Melanie G
21 *Dayz Like That* Fierce
22 *Forever* Tina Cousins

CD2

1 *Everybody's Free (To Wear Sunscreen)* Baz Luhrmann
2 *In Our Lifetime* Texas
3 *You Get What You Give* New Radicals
4 *Pumping On Your Stereo* Supergrass
5 *Lovestruck* Madness
6 *Ooh La La* The Wiseguys
7 *Hey Boy Hey Girl* The Chemical Brothers
8 *Right Here Right Now* Fatboy Slim
9 *Saltwater* Chicane feat. Maire Brennan
10 *Cloud Number Nine* Bryan Adams
11 *Coffee & TV* Blur
12 *Beat Mama* Cast
13 *Pick A Part That's New* Stereophonics
14 *Bring It On* Gomez
15 *Secret Smile* Semisonic
16 *I Know What I'm Here For* James
17 *Synth & Strings* Yomanda
18 *Better Off Alone* DJ Jurgen presents Alice DeeJay
19 *To Be In Love* Masters at Work feat. India

▶ *NOW 43* was the first edition to appear on minidisc. The format only ran for six volumes before it was noted that minidisc was not the format of the future.

▶ **Phats and Small**'s sole entry to the *NOW* canon trailed their punningly titled 1999 album *Now Phats What I Small Music*. Expect a call from our lawyers.

▶ **Semisonic**'s solitary entry shouldn't elicit too much sympathy for front man Dan Wilson. He went on to co-write three songs on **Adele**'s 27-million-selling *21* album including the blockbuster 'Someone Like You' (*NOW 79*).

ALSO HAPPENING IN NOVEMBER 1999

- As the world prepared for the dawn of the new millennium, fears grew that the Y2K bug would cause computers to fail
- At the cinema: *The Bone Collector*, *The World is Not Enough*, *Sleepy Hollow*, *Toy Story 2*
- Albums released: *Westlife* (**Westlife**), *Rainbow* (**Mariah Carey**), *Affirmation* (**Savage Garden**), *Willennium* (**Will Smith**)
- Christmas No.1 was 'I Have a Dream / Seasons in the Sun' (**Westlife**)
- Bestsellers published in 1999: *Girl With a Pearl Earring* (Tracy Chevalier), *Bridget Jones: the Edge of Reason* (Helen Fielding), *Chocolat* (Joanne Harris)

TRACKLISTING NOW 44

CD1

1 *...Baby One More Time* Britney Spears
2 *That Don't Impress Me Much* Shania Twain
3 *Mambo No 5 (A Little Bit Of...)* Lou Bega
4 *Blue (Da Ba Dee)* Eiffel 65
5 *Tragedy* Steps
6 *Mi Chico Latino* Geri Halliwell
7 *She's The One* Robbie Williams
8 *When You Say Nothing At All* Ronan Keating
9 *Northern Star* Melanie C
10 *Kiss Me* Sixpence None the Richer
11 *Summer Son* Texas
12 *Sing It Back* Moloko
13 *Sun Is Shining* Bob Marley vs Funkstar De Luxe
14 *Not Over You Yet* Diana Ross
15 *When The Heartache Is Over* Tina Turner
16 *Canned Heat* Jamiroquai
17 *Burning Down The House* Tom Jones and The Cardigans
18 *Drinking In L.A.* Bran Van 3000
19 *Moving* Supergrass
20 *You'll Be In My Heart* Phil Collins

CD2

1 *If I Could Turn Back The Hands Of Time* R. Kelly
2 *Lift Me Up* Geri Halliwell
3 *What I Am* Tin Tin Out feat. Emma Bunton
4 *I've Got You* Martine McCutcheon
5 *Larger Than Life* Backstreet Boys
6 *Give It To You* Jordan Knight
7 *Sunshine* Gabrielle
8 *Never Let You Down* Honeyz
9 *S Club Party* S Club 7
10 *Mickey* Lolly
11 *2 Times* Ann Lee
12 *We're Going To Ibiza* Vengaboys
13 *Bailamos* Enrique Iglesias
14 *(Mucho Mambo) Sway* Shaft
15 *Don't Stop!* ATB
16 *The Launch* DJ Jean
17 *I See You Baby* Groove Armada feat. Gram'ma Funk
18 *King Of My Castle* Wamdue Project
19 *Back In My Life* Alice DeeJay
20 *Turn It Around* Alena

▶ The last *NOW* to be released in the 1990s, *NOW 44* is in the record books as the best-selling compilation album of all time in the UK, having sold 2.3 million copies since release.

▶ American teenager **Britney Spears** opened her account with 'Baby One More Time', which reached No.1 in every country it charted in. It's one of the thirty best selling UK singles since records began.

▶ Four consecutive summer No.1 singles featured: **Geri Halliwell**'s 'Mi Chico Latino', **Lou Bega**'s 'Mambo No.5', **Vengaboys**' 'We're Going To Ibiza', and **Eiffel 65**'s 'Blue (Da Ba Dee)'.

ALSO HAPPENING IN APRIL 2000

- The London Eye (also known as the Millennium Wheel) opened on the bank of the River Thames
- At the cinema: *Girl Interrupted*, *Boys Don't Cry*, *Erin Brockovich*, *American Psycho*, *Kevin and Perry Go Large*, *Being John Malkovich*
- Albums released included *Aquarius* (**Aqua**), *No Strings Attached* (**'N Sync**), *Not That Kind* (**Anastacia**) and *Can't Take Me Home* (**Pink**), *Invincible* (**Five**) and *Oops!... I Did it Again* (**Britney Spears**)
- Popular television programmes included *Da Ali G Show*, *Castaway 2000* and *The Big Breakfast*

TRACKLISTING NOW 45

CD1

1 *Rise* Gabrielle
2 *Never Be The Same Again* Melanie C feat. Lisa 'Left Eye' Lopes
3 *Fill Me In* Craig David
4 *Born To Make You Happy* Britney Spears
5 *Show Me The Meaning Of Being Lonely* Backstreet Boys
6 *Sitting Down Here* Lene Martin
7 *Mama Told Me Not To Come* Tom Jones & The Stereophonics
8 *Man I Feel Like A Woman* Shania Twain
9 *Bag It Up* Geri Halliwell
10 *You're My Number One* S Club 7
11 *Cartoon Heroes* Aqua
12 *Shalala Lala* Vengaboys
13 *Ooh Stick You* Daphne & Celeste
14 *See Ya* Atomic Kitten
15 *Don't Call Me Baby* Madison Avenue
16 *Love Me* Martine McCutcheon
17 *Say You'll Be Mine* Steps
18 *Won't Take It Lying Down* Honeyz
19 *Rewind* Precious
20 *Get It On Tonite* Montell Jordan
21 *Sweet Love 2k* Fierce
22 *Every Day I Love You More* Boyzone

CD2

1 *Don't Give Up* Chicane feat. Bryan Adams
2 *Toca's Miracle* Fragma
3 *The Time Is Now* Moloko
4 *Re Rewind (The Crowd Say Bo Selecta)* Artful Dodger feat. Craig David
5 *A Little Bit Of Luck* DJ Luck & MC Neat
6 *Thong Song* Sisqo
7 *Money* Jamelia feat. Beenie Man
8 *Caught Out There* Kelis
9 *Movin' Too Fast* Artful Dodger feat. Romina Johnson
10 *In Your Arms (Rescue Me)* Nu Generation
11 *Bingo Bango* Basement Jaxx
12 *Killer 2000* ATB
13 *Adelante* Sash!
14 *Merry Christmas Mr Lawrence (Heart Of Asia)* Watergate
15 *Everybody* Progress presents The Boy Wunda
16 *Blow Ya Mind* Lock 'N' Load
17 *Big Girl* Precocious Brats feat. Kevin & Perry
18 *Hammer To The Heart* The Tamperer Featuring Maya
19 *Cognoscenti vs Intelligentsia* Cuban Boys
20 *It's Only Us* Robbie Williams
21 *All The Small Things* Blink-182
22 *Natural Blues* Moby
23 *Imagine* John Lennon

▶ On the opening *NOW* of a new millennium, two artists took the distinction of being the first acts to appear across three separate decades: congratulations to renowned lungsmiths **Tom Jones** and **Bryan Adams**.

▶ 'It's Only Us' by **Robbie Williams** was actually a double A-sided single with 'She's The One'. Although 'It's Only Us' was the official lead track, 'She's the One' proved the more popular and as such turned up on the preceding *NOW*.

▶ Twenty-nine years after its original release, **John Lennon** made his sole *NOW* appearance with 'Imagine' – the joint second-longest gap between original release and *NOW* inclusion (alongside 'Reet Petite' by **Jackie Wilson**, *NOW 9*).

ALSO HAPPENING IN JULY 2000

- The Office for National Statistics revealed one in four UK homes now used the Internet
- The first series of UK *Big Brother* was broadcast and immediately became a huge ratings hit. Housemate 'Nasty Nick' Bateman received lots of media attention for his game-playing strategy
- At the cinema: *High Fidelity*, *Stuart Little*, *28 Days*, *Big Momma's House*, *Mission: Impossible II*, *Chicken Run*
- Albums released included *Parachutes* (**Coldplay**), *Fragments of Freedom* (**Morcheeba**), *7* (**S Club 7**) and **Ronan Keating**'s self-titled debut album

TRACKLISTING NOW 46

CD1

1 *Oops... I Did It Again* Britney Spears
2 *Reach* S Club 7
3 *It Feels So Good* Sonique
4 *Shackles (Praise You)* Mary Mary
5 *Gotta Tell You* Samantha Mumba
6 *When A Woman* Gabrielle
7 *Spinning Around* Kylie Minogue
8 *Sex Bomb* Tom Jones & Mousse T.
9 *The Bad Touch* Bloodhound Gang
10 *Don't Be Stupid (You Know I Love You)* Shania Twain
11 *Day And Night* Billie Piper
12 *2 Faced* Louise
13 *Try Again* Aaliyah
14 *Bye Bye Bye* *NSYNC
15 *Ghetto Romance* Damage
16 *When I Said Goodbye* Steps
17 *New Beginning* Stephen Gately
18 *The One* Backstreet Boys
19 *Porcelain* Moby
20 *Yellow* Coldplay
21 *A Song For The Lovers* Richard Ashcroft

CD2

1 *You See The Trouble With Me* Black Legend
2 *Groovejet (If This Ain't Love)* Spiller feat. Sophie Ellis-Bextor
3 *Sandstorm* Darude
4 *O.T.B. (On The Beach)* York
5 *I Need Your Lovin' (Like The Sunshine)* Marc Et Claude
6 *The Power Of Love* Frankie Goes To Hollywood
7 *When The World Is Running Down (You Can't Go Wrong)* Different Gear vs The Police
8 *Luvstruck* Southside Spinners
9 *Will I Ever* Alice DeeJay
10 *It's My Turn* Angelic
11 *Airwave* Rank 1
12 *Girls Like Us* B15 Project feat. Crissy D & Lady G
13 *Summer Of Love* Lonyo Comme Ci Comme Ca
14 *Crazy Love* M.J. Cole
15 *Masterblaster 2000* DJ Luck & MC Neat feat. JJ
16 *Freak Like Me* Tru Faith & Dub Conspiracy
17 *Call Me* Jamelia
18 *Uncle John From Jamaica* Vengaboys
19 *Flee Fly Flo* Fe-M@il
20 *For Sure* Scooch
21 *I Want Your Love* Atomic Kitten
22 *Deeper Shade Of Blue* Steps

▶ Only one *Blue Peter* presenter's daughter has appeared nine times on a *NOW* album. **Sophie Ellis-Bextor**'s first hit credited as a solo artist, recorded with **Spiller**, ended up as the seventh biggest-selling single of the year.

▶ **Frankie Goes To Hollywood** had appeared all the way back on *NOW 2* with 'Relax' and *NOW 3* with 'Two Tribes'. Finally, 43 editions later, their third hit 'The Power Of Love' made it onto a *NOW* via a remixed, re-released version.

▶ **Tom Jones** has appeared seven times on a *NOW* release but never by himself. His No.3 hit 'Sex Bomb' with **Mousse T.** featured within a run of four consecutive appearances (*NOW 44* to *47*) and was his highest charting hit for thirteen years.

ALSO HAPPENING IN NOVEMBER 2000

- George W. Bush won the US Presidential election amid controversy over votes in Florida
- Judith Keppel became the first person to win £1,000,000 on the UK version of *Who Wants to Be a Millionaire?*
- Nokia released the 3310 mobile phone – 126 million units were eventually sold
- Films: *Charlie's Angels*, *Coyote Ugly*, *What Lies Beneath*
- Albums released included *Forever* (**Spice Girls**), *It's All About the Stragglers* (**Artful Dodger**) and *One Touch* (**Sugababes**). The Christmas No.1 was **Bob the Builder**'s 'Can We Fix It?'

TRACKLISTING NOW 47

CD1

1 *Rock DJ* Robbie Williams
2 *Lady (Hear Me Tonight)* Modjo
3 *Life Is A Rollercoaster* Ronan Keating
4 *In Demand* Texas
5 *It's My Life* Bon Jovi
6 *Beautiful Day* U2
7 *Babylon* David Gray
8 *Pure Shores* All Saints
9 *Holler* Spice Girls
10 *Body Groove* Architechs feat. Nana
11 *7 Days* Craig David
12 *Body II Body* Samantha Mumba
13 *Lucky* Britney Spears
14 *Can't Fight The Moonlight* LeAnn Rimes
15 *Natural* S Club 7
16 *It's Gonna Be Me* *NSYNC
17 *I'm Outta Love* Anastacia
18 *You Need Love Like I Do* Tom Jones & Heather Small
19 *Kids* Robbie Williams & Kylie Minogue
20 *Trouble* Coldplay

CD2

1 *I'm Over You* Martine McCutcheon
2 *On A Night Like This* Kylie Minogue
3 *Stomp* Steps
4 *Absolutely Everybody* Vanessa Amorosi
5 *Walk Of Life* Billie Piper
6 *Out Of Your Mind* True Steppers and Dane Bowers feat. Victoria Beckham
7 *I Turn To You* Melanie C
8 *Silence* Delerium feat. Sarah McLachlan
9 *Sky* Sonique
10 *Kernkraft 400* Zombie Nation
11 *Time To Burn* Storm
12 *Feel The Beat* Darude
13 *Ordinary World* Aurora
14 *You Take My Breath Away* SuReaL
15 *Who The Hell Are You* Madison Avenue
16 *Doom's Night* Azzido Da Bass
17 *Who Let The Dogs Out?* B-Boyz
18 *Country Grammar (Hot...)* Nelly
19 *Unleash The Dragon* SisQó
20 *Tell Me* Melanie B
21 *Beautiful Inside* Louise
22 *Should I Stay* Gabrielle

Four **Spice Girls** related acts appeared on *NOW 47*. The next four volumes all featured two solo **Spice Girls** tracks apiece.

An alternative version of 'Who Let The Dogs Out?' was performed here by **B-Boyz** and captured for posterity rather than the **Baha Men**'s No.2 hit. The **B-Boyz** version did not chart.

William Orbit appeared as a producer for **Blur** on *NOW 42* and *NOW 43* but delivered a co-write here on **All Saints**' 'Pure Shores'. It went on to become the second biggest-selling single of the year.

ALSO HAPPENING IN APRIL 2001

- Wikipedia was launched
- An outbreak of Foot-and-Mouth disease caused a crisis for the UK farming and tourist industries
- Albums released included *Just Enough Education to Perform* (**Stereophonics**), *Echo Park* (**Feeder**), *All for You* (**Janet Jackson**) and *All Rise* (**Blue**)
- *EastEnders* viewers found out who shot Phil. Elsewhere, *Celebrity Big Brother* was screened for the first time
- At the cinema: *Bridget Jones's Diary*, *Miss Congeniality*, *Save the Last Dance*, *The Wedding Planner*
- **Mariah Carey** signed a four-album, $80 million contract with Virgin Records

TRACKLISTING NOW 48

CD1

1 *Whole Again* **Atomic Kitten**
2 *Pure and Simple* **Hear'Say**
3 *Never Had A Dream Come True* **S Club 7**
4 *I'm Like A Bird* **Nelly Furtado**
5 *It Wasn't Me* **Shaggy feat. Ricardo 'Rikrok' Ducent**
6 *Clint Eastwood* **Gorillaz**
7 *Chillin* **Modjo**
8 *I Wanna Be U* **Chocolate Puma**
9 *Everytime You Need Me* **Fragma feat. Maria Rubia**
10 *Always Come Back To Your Love* **Samantha Mumba**
11 *Stronger* **Britney Spears**
12 *It's The Way You Make Me Feel* **Steps**
13 *What Took You So Long?* **Emma Bunton**
14 *The Way You Make Me Feel* **Ronan Keating**
15 *Shape Of My Heart* **Backstreet Boys**
16 *I Need You* **LeAnn Rimes**
17 *Still Be Lovin' You* **Damage**
18 *Paradise* **Kaci**
19 *On The Radio* **Martine McCutcheon**
20 *Please Stay* **Kylie Minogue**
21 *Can We Fix It* **Bob The Builder**

CD2

1 *Somewhere Over The Rainbow* **Eva Cassidy**
2 *Stuck In A Moment You Can't Get Out Of* **U2**
3 *Mr. Writer* **Stereophonics**
4 *Don't Panic* **Coldplay**
5 *Inner Smile* **Texas**
6 *Let Love Be Your Energy* **Robbie Williams**
7 *Buck Rogers* **Feeder**
8 *Last Resort* **Papa Roach**
9 *Chase The Sun* **Planet Funk**
10 *Played A Live (The Bongo Song)* **Safri Duo**
11 *Dream To Me* **Dario G**
12 *American Dream* **Jakatta**
13 *I Put A Spell On You* **Sonique**
14 *Feels So Good* **Melanie B**
15 *Case Of The Ex* **Mýa**
16 *Straight Up* **Chanté Moore**
17 *Stutter* **Joe**
18 *Show Me The Money* **Architechs**
19 *Piano Loco* **DJ Luck & MC Neat**
20 *Loco* **Fun Lovin' Criminals**

▶ Animated character **Bob The Builder** sold over a million copies of 'Can We Fix It', which was 2000's biggest-selling single. Other cartoon characters to be credited on *NOW* albums include **Crazy Frog** and **Gorillaz**, but definitely not **The Cartoons**, who aren't cartoons.

▶ Unremarked upon in her lifetime, **Eva Cassidy**'s music gained in popularity after repeated exposure on Terry Wogan's Radio 2 show and *Top Of The Pops 2*. Whilst 'Over The Rainbow' didn't quite make the top forty, the album *Songbird* would go on to sell close to 2 million copies in the UK.

▶ Before *X Factor*, *Pop Idol* and *Fame Academy* there was *PopStars*. Alongside **Hear'Say**, the UK series also gifted us **Liberty X** (seven *NOW* appearances) and **Darius Danesh** (a not too shabby five). Upon release, 'Pure and Simple' was the biggest-selling debut single of all time (550,000 copies in its first week).

ALSO HAPPENING IN JULY 2001

- R&B singer **Aaliyah** was killed in a plane crash in the Bahamas on 25 August, aged twenty-two
- Music file-sharing website Napster was shut down due to a US court order
- At the cinema: *Shrek, Jurassic Park III*, *Lara Croft: Tomb Raider*
- Albums released included *Songs in A Minor* (**Alicia Keys**), *Origin of Symmetry* (**Muse**) and *White Blood Cells* (**The White Stripes**)
- TV: *Brass Eye* controversy and the first episode of *The Office* was broadcast
- Richard and Judy left *This Morning*

TRACKLISTING NOW 49

CD1

1 *Eternity* Robbie Williams
2 *Out Of Reach* Gabrielle
3 *Eternal Flame* Atomic Kitten
4 *All Rise* Blue
5 *Don't Stop Movin'* S Club 7
6 *It's Raining Men* Geri Halliwell
7 *Lovin' Each Day* Ronan Keating
8 *Have A Nice Day* Stereophonics
9 *Teenage Dirtbag* Wheatus
10 *The Rock Show* Blink-182
11 *Elevation* U2
12 *Ms. Jackson* Outkast
13 *Survivor* Destiny's Child
14 *The Way To Your Love* Hear'Say
15 *More Than That* Backstreet Boys
16 *Don't Let Me Be The Last To Know* Britney Spears
17 *Close To You* Marti Pellow
18 *Thank You* Dido
19 *Destiny* Zero 7
20 *Pyramid Song* Radiohead

CD2

1 *Electric Avenue* Eddy Grant
2 *19-2000* Gorillaz
3 *Do You Really Like It?* DJ Pied Piper and the Masters Of Ceremonies
4 *All I Want* Mis-Teeq
5 *Another Chance* Roger Sanchez
6 *Romeo* Basement Jaxx
7 *Meet Her At The Love Parade 2001* Da Hool
8 *Castles In The Sky* Ian Van Dahl
9 *You Are Alive* Fragma
10 *Here And Now* Steps
11 *Upside Down* A*Teens
12 *Perfect Bliss* Bellefire
13 *I Don't Want A Lover (2001 Mix)* Texas
14 *Never Enough* Boris Dlugosch feat. Róisín Murphy
15 *All For You* Janet Jackson
16 *Who's That Girl?* Eve
17 *Ride Wit Me* Nelly feat. City Spud
18 *Dance For Me* SisQó
19 *Ring Ring Ring* Aaron Soul
20 *So What If I?* Damage
21 *Lullaby* Melanie B

▶ **Dido Florian Cloud de Bounevialle O'Malley Armstrong** made her one and only *NOW* appearance to date with 'Thank You'. Its parent album *No Angel* went on to sell 21 million copies worldwide.

▶ The **New Radicals** appeared only once (*NOW 43*) but Gregg Alexander made his second appearance here as a songwriter for hire penning 'Lovin' Each Day' for **Ronan Keating** ('Life Is A Rollercoaster' appeared on *NOW 47*).

▶ **Atomic Kitten**'s 'Eternal Flame' was the first single to feature new member Jenny Frost, whose own *NOW* career pre-dated that of her new band (as part of Eurovision hopefuls Precious on *NOW 43* and *NOW 45*).

ALSO HAPPENING IN NOVEMBER 2001

- At the cinema: *Harry Potter and the Philosopher's Stone*, *American Pie*, *Legally Blond*
- Albums released included *Britney* (**Britney Spears**), *Swing When You're Winning* (**Robbie Williams**), *They Don't Know* (**So Solid Crew**), *World of Our Own* (**Westlife**), *HIStory Volume I* (**Michael Jackson**) and *Laundry Service* (**Shakira**)
- Bestsellers published in 2001 included *Life of Pi* (Yann Martel) and *Atonement* (Ian McEwan)
- The Christmas No.1 was 'Somethin' Stupid' by **Robbie Williams** and **Nicole Kidman**, from the film *Moulin Rouge*

TRACKLISTING NOW 50

CD1

1 *Can't Get You Out Of My Head* Kylie Minogue
2 *Uptown Girl* Westlife
3 *Hey Baby* DJ Ötzi
4 *Mambo No 5* Bob The Builder
5 *Chain Reaction* Steps
6 *Let's Dance* Five
7 *Take Me Home* Sophie Ellis-Bextor
8 *Perfect Gentleman* Wyclef Jean
9 *What Would You Do?* City High
10 *If You Come Back* Blue
11 *Turn Off The Light* Nelly Furtado
12 *Heaven Is A Halfpipe* OPM
13 *Bohemian Like You* The Dandy Warhols
14 *Smooth Criminal* Alien Ant Farm
15 *Fat Lip* Sum 41
16 *A Little Respect* Wheatus
17 *Sing* Travis
18 *Ain't It Funny* Jennifer Lopez
19 *Take My Breath Away* Emma Bunton
20 *Don't Need The Sun (To Shine To Make Me Smile)* Gabrielle
21 *(I Wish I Knew How It Would Feel To Be) Free / One* Lighthouse Family
22 *What If* Kate Winslet

CD2

1 *Rapture* iiO
2 *Starlight* Supermen Lovers
3 *Little L* Jamiroquai
4 *Bootylicious* Destiny's Child
5 *Purple Hills* D12
6 *Let Me Blow Ya Mind* Eve feat. Gwen Stefani
7 *I'm A Slave 4 U* Britney Spears
8 *One Night Stand* Mis-Teeq
9 *Family Affair* Mary J. Blige
10 *Baby Come On Over* Samantha Mumba
11 *Thinking It Over* Liberty
12 *Not Such An Innocent Girl* Victoria Beckham
13 *Stuck In The Middle With You* Louise
14 *Scream If You Wanna Go Faster* Geri Halliwell
15 *Things That Go Bump In The Night* Allstars
16 *Set You Free* N-Trance
17 *Flawless* The Ones
18 *Digital Love* Daft Punk
19 *Superstylin* Groove Armada
20 *2 People* Jean Jacques Smoothie
21 *21 Seconds* So Solid Crew
22 *Because I Got High* Afroman

▶ **Kylie Minogue**'s biggest-selling single since 1988,'Can't Get You Out Of My Head', was co-written by Cathy Dennis (who appeared on *NOW*s *16, 20* and *36* as a performer) and Rob Davis of 70s glam rockers **Mud.** Davis had already contributed his writing skills to 'Groovejet' on *NOW 48.*

▶ **Billy Joel** is yet to make an appearance on a *NOW* album. Until then, we've got **Westlife.** 'Uptown Girl' was the sixth of fourteen No.1 singles for the Irish boyband, who finally split in 2012 after selling 11 million albums in the UK alone.

▶ **Destiny's Child** made their final appearance here, although members **Beyoncé** and **Kelly Rowland** would be back as solo artists. Also not to be seen again: behatted slider **Jamiroquai**, Lancashire liberators **N-Trance**, and the **Lighthouse Family.**

ALSO HAPPENING IN MARCH 2002

- The Queen Mother died at the age of 101
- DAB radio launched in the UK
- There were Oscar wins for *A Beautiful Mind* (four), *The Fellowship of the Ring* (four) and *Moulin Rouge* (two)
- At the cinema: *Ice Age*, *Ali G Indahouse*, *Ali*, *A Beautiful Mind*
- Albums released included *Original Pirate Material* (**The Streets**) and *A New Day Has Come* by **Celine Dion**
- On television, *24* made its debut on BBC2 and *Little Britain* continued to be viewed by millions

TRACKLISTING NOW 51

CD1

1 *Hero* Enrique Iglesias
2 *Fly By II* Blue
3 *Me Julie* Ali G feat. Shaggy
4 *Gotta Get Thru This* Daniel Bedingfield
5 *More Than A Woman* Aaliyah
6 *Somethin' Stupid* Robbie Williams and Nicole Kidman
7 *The World's Greatest* R. Kelly
8 *Have You Ever* S Club 7
9 *Overprotected* Britney Spears
10 *Murder On The Dancefloor* Sophie Ellis-Bextor
11 *In Your Eyes* Kylie Minogue
12 *Point Of View* DB Boulevard
13 *Something* Lasgo
14 *ResuRection* PPK
15 *The Whistle Song (Blow My Whistle Baby)* DJ Aligator Project
16 *True Love Never Dies* Flip & Fill feat. Kelly Llorenna
17 *Everybody* Hear'Say
18 *The Land Of Make Believe* Allstars
19 *A Mind Of Its Own* Victoria Beckham
20 *Words Are Not Enough* Steps
21 *Calling* Geri Halliwell
22 *I Will Always Love You* Rik Waller

CD2

1 *Handbags and Gladrags* Stereophonics
2 *How You Remind Me* Nickelback
3 *Movies* Alien Ant Farm
4 *In Too Deep* Sum 41
5 *Addicted To Bass* Puretone
6 *Am To PM* Christina Milian
7 *Always On Time* Ja Rule feat. Ashanti
8 *Caramel* City High feat. Eve
9 *Shoulda Woulda Coulda* Beverley Knight
10 *Lately* Samantha Mumba
11 *Drowning* Backstreet Boys
12 *Dance For Me* Mary J. Blige
13 *Crazy Rap* Afroman
14 *Bad Babysitter* Princess Superstar feat. High & Mighty
15 *Oi!* Platinum 45's feat. More Fire Crew
16 *It's Love (Trippin')* Goldtrix presents Andrea Brown
17 *Lazy* X-Press 2 feat. David Byrne
18 *So Lonely* Jakatta
19 *Star Guitar* The Chemical Brothers
20 *Drifting Away* Lange feat. Skye
21 *I Don't Wanna Lose My Way* Dreamcatcher

▶ Fourth and final appearance for a song titled 'In Too Deep', courtesy here of **Sum 41. Dead or Alive** (*NOW 5*), **Genesis** (*NOW 8*) and **Belinda Carlisle** (*NOW 34*) have all utilised the same name.

▶ Sixteen years after *NOW 7* **Allstars** provided the second Bucks Fizz related track to appear in the series. 'Land of Make Believe' was co-written by former **King Crimson** member Pete Sinfield. **King Crimson** have yet to appear on a *NOW*.

▶ **Sophie Ellis-Bextor**'s 'Murder On The Dancefloor' features a bass line by super-sessioneer Guy Pratt. His work with **Madonna** and **Michael Jackson** has not been chronicled on a *NOW*, however his co-write of Jimmy Nails 'Ain't No Doubt' can be found on *NOW 22*.

ALSO HAPPENING IN JULY 2002

- A man was arrested after beheading a statue of Margaret Thatcher, using a cricket bat and metal pole
- Rio Ferdinand transferred to Manchester United for a record £29.1 million
- At the Commonwealth Games in Manchester there were gold medals for Paula Radcliffe in the 5000 metres and Jonathan Edwards in the triple jump
- At the cinema: *Austin Powers in Goldmember*, *Resident Evil*, *Scooby Doo*, *Minority Report*
- Albums released included *Heathen Chemistry* (**Oasis**), *By the Way* (**Red Hot Chilli Peppers**) and **Linkin Park**'s *Reanimation*

TRACKLISTING NOW 52

CD1

1 *If Tomorrow Never Comes* Ronan Keating
2 *Just A Little* Liberty X
3 *Freeek!* George Michael
4 *Freak Like Me* Sugababes
5 *Love At First Sight* Kylie Minogue
6 *Escape* Enrique Iglesias
7 *Get Over You* Sophie Ellis-Bextor
8 *One Step Closer* S Club Juniors
9 *Follow Da Leader 2002* Nigel & Marvin
10 *The Logical Song* Scooter
11 *Forever* Dee Dee
12 *Shooting Star* Flip & Fill
13 *Be Cool* Paffendorf
14 *Tell It To My Heart* Kelly Llorenna
15 *Shake Ur Body* Shy FX & T-Power feat. Di
16 *It Just Won't Do* Tim Deluxe feat. Sam Obernik
17 *At Night* Shakedown
18 *Dove (I'll Be Loving You)* Moony
19 *Luv Da Sunshine* Intenso Project
20 *(Take Me Away) Into The Night* 4 Strings
21 *Like A Prayer* Mad'House
22 *You* S Club 7

CD2

1 *It's OK!* Atomic Kitten
2 *I'm Not A Girl, Not Yet A Woman* Britney Spears
3 *Foolish* Ashanti
4 *No More Drama* Mary J. Blige
5 *Girlfriend* *NSYNC
6 *When You Look At Me* Christina Milian
7 *Hot In Herre* Nelly feat. Dani Stevenson
8 *It Takes More* Ms. Dynamite
9 *Lil' Big Man* Omero Mumba
10 *Rock The Boat* Aaliyah
11 *Freak Mode* The Reelists
12 *My Culture* 1 Giant Leap
13 *Just A Little Girl* Amy Studt
14 *Soak Up The Sun* Sheryl Crow
15 *Pounding* Doves
16 *I Would Die 4 U* The Space Cowboy
17 *American English* Idlewild
18 *Blurry* Puddle of Mudd
19 *We Are All Made Of Stars* Moby
20 *Stop Crying Your Heart Out* Oasis

▶ The only **Madonna** cover version in the entire series, **Mad'House**'s take on 'Like A Prayer', appeared here. 'Material Girl' was sampled on **The Tamperer**'s 'If You Buy This Record Your Life Will Be Better' on *NOW 41*, 'La Isla Bonita' plundered for **Deetah**'s 'El Paradiso Rico' on *NOW 42*, while the strings from 'Papa Don't Preach' were used by **Progress presents The Boy Wunda** on 'Everybody' from *NOW 45.*

▶ First time around for **Sugababes**, whose 'Freak Like Me' heralded a remarkable run of nineteen appearances in twenty-four *NOW*s. That leaves them as the second most compiled girl band in the history of the series – we've yet to meet the winners.

▶ Some necessary S Club admin: **S Club 7** featured nine times, before changing their name to (just) **S Club** for two further involvements. **S Club Juniors**, who debuted here, showed up twice before changing *their* name to **S Club 8**. Hope that's clear.

ALSO HAPPENING IN NOVEMBER 2002

- Controversy erupted over Channel 4 broadcasting Gunther von Hagens performing the first public autopsy in Britain in more than 170 years
- **Michael Jackson** dangled his baby son over the edge of his hotel balcony
- **Girls Aloud** were formed on *Popstars: the Rivals.* Their track 'Sound of the Underground' was the Christmas No.1
- At the cinema: H*arry Potter and the Chamber of Secrets*, *8 Mile*, *Bowling for Columbine*
- Albums released included *One Love* (**Blue**), *Justified* (**Justin Timberlake**), *Escapology* (**Robbie Williams**) and *Slicker Than Your Average* (**Craig David**)

TRACKLISTING NOW 53

CD1

1 *Heaven* DJ Sammy & Yanou feat. Do
2 *Aserejé (The Ketchup Song)* Las Ketchup
3 *Love To See You Cry* Enrique Eglesias
4 *Round Round* Sugababes
5 *The Tide Is High (Get The Feeling)* Atomic Kitten
6 *One Love* Blue
7 *Colourblind* Darius
8 *What I Go To School For* Busted
9 *Got To Have Your Love* Liberty X
10 *It's All Gravy* Romeo feat. Christina Milian
11 *I'm Right Here* Samantha Mumba
12 *What You Got* Abs
13 *I Love Rock 'n' Roll* Britney Spears
14 *Automatic High* S Club Juniors
15 *Come Into My World* Kylie Minogue
16 *My Vision* Jakatta feat. Seal
17 *Music Gets The Best Of Me* Sophie Ellis-Bextor
18 *Heart Of Gold* Kelly Llorenna
19 *Walk On Water* Milk Inc.
20 *Because The Night* Jan Wayne
21 *Pray* Lasgo
22 *Posse* Scooter

CD2

1 *In My Place* Coldplay
2 *Little By Little* Oasis
3 *Electrical Storm* U2
4 *Hero* Chad Kroeger feat. Josey Scott
5 *Check The Meaning* Richard Ashcroft
6 *Imagine* Eva Cassidy
7 *A Thousand Miles* Vanessa Carlton
8 *You Were Right* Badly Drawn Boy
9 *I Love It When We Do* Ronan Keating
10 *Fantasy* Appleton
11 *Dy-Na-Mi-Tee* Ms. Dynamite
12 *Feel It Boy* Beenie Man feat. Janet Jackson
13 *James Dean (I Wanna Know)* Daniel Bedingfield
14 *Without Me* Eminem
15 *She Hates Me* Puddle Of Mudd
16 *Girl All The Bad Guys Want* Bowling for Soup
17 *Grace* Supergrass
18 *Jam Side Down* Status Quo
19 *Fascinated* Raven Maize
20 *Shiny Disco Balls* Who Da Funk feat. Jessica Eve
21 *Starry Eyed Surprise* Oakenfold feat. Shifty Shellshock

▶ The last of four consecutive appearances for Northern dance diva **Kelly Llorena.** Kelly has appeared twice with the same song, providing the vocals for **N-Trance**'s 'Set You free' on *NOW 30* and *NOW 50.*

▶ **Busted**'s *NOW* career burns as brightly – and as quickly – as their Top 40 run, with seven consecutive appearances from their eight Top 3 hits across two years. No.1 'Crashed The Wedding' was released too late to make it onto *NOW 56*.

▶ 'Aserejé (The Ketchup Song)' – **Las Ketchup**'s only *NOW* appearance – reached No.1 in twenty-seven countries. The chorus's lyrics are actually a 'spanglish' translation of 'Rappers Delight' by **Sugarhill Gang**.

NOW SPECIAL EDITIONS

By 1985 *NOW* was established as the premium compilation series in the shops, and highly regarded as a mark of quality. It was a logical move to widen the brief and, starting with *NOW That's What I Call Christmas*, genre-focused albums began to appear.

The following year the first *NOW Summer* was released, and in 1987 a tie-in with *Smash Hits* magazine resulted in an overview of the 1980s up to that point.

Since then there have been numerous iterations of the *NOW Dance* concept, alongside many eras and styles of music that have all been afforded the luxury of a *NOW* volume.

Our round up of the *NOW* special editions concludes with a look at the various DVDs and interactive games that have been released over the last thirteen years.

THE
CHRISTMAS
ALBUM
18 ORIGINAL CHRISTMAS HITS

THE
CHRISTMAS
COMPACT
DISC
16 ORIGINAL CHRISTMAS HITS

NOW!
THE CHRISTMAS ALBUM

CHRISTMAS

NOW
MASSIVE CHRISTMAS HITS
XMAS

NOW
THAT'S WHAT I CALL
XMAS

NOW
THAT'S WHAT I CALL
XMAS

NOW
THAT'S WHAT I CALL
CHRISTMAS

NOW
THAT'S WHAT I CALL
CHRISTMAS

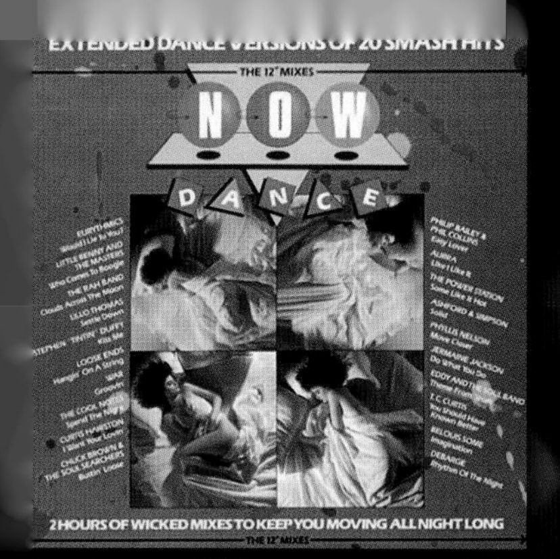
EXTENDED DANCE VERSIONS OF 20 SMASH HITS
THE 12" MIXES
NOW
DANCE
2 HOURS OF WICKED MIXES TO KEEP YOU MOVING ALL NIGHT LONG

20 SMASH DANCE HITS OF THE YEAR
THE 12" MIXES
NOW
DANCE 86
DIANA ROSS CHAIN REACTION
JERMAINE STEWART WE DON'T HAVE TO
COMMUNARDS DON'T LEAVE ME THIS WAY
FIVE STAR CAN'T WAIT ANOTHER MINUTE
MIDNIGHT STAR MIDAS TOUCH
GWEN GUTHRIE AIN'T NOTHIN' GOIN' ON BUT THE RENT
TIMEX SOCIAL CLUB RUMORS
JOYCE SIMS ALL AND ALL
CASHFLOW MINE ALL MINE
ARETHA FRANKLIN WHO'S ZOOMIN' WHO?
TAVARES HEAVEN MUST BE MISSING AN ANGEL
PAUL HARDCASTLE DON'T WASTE MY TIME
JAKI GRAHAM BREAKING AWAY
GRACE JONES PULL UP TO THE BUMPER
SINITTA SO MACHO
BRONSKI BEAT HIT THAT PERFECT BEAT
PHIL FEARON I CAN PROVE IT
BORIS GARDINER I WANNA WAKE UP WITH YOU

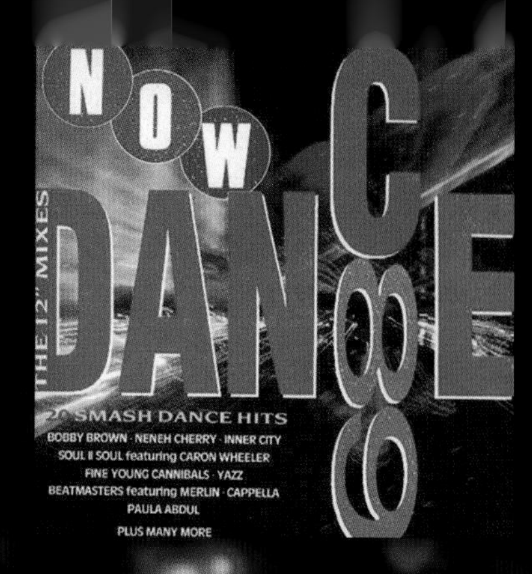
NOW
DANCE
THE 12" MIXES
20 SMASH DANCE HITS
BOBBY BROWN · NENEH CHERRY · INNER CITY
SOUL II SOUL featuring CARON WHEELER
FINE YOUNG CANNIBALS · YAZZ
BEATMASTERS featuring MERLIN · CAPPELLA
PAULA ABDUL
PLUS MANY MORE

DANCE

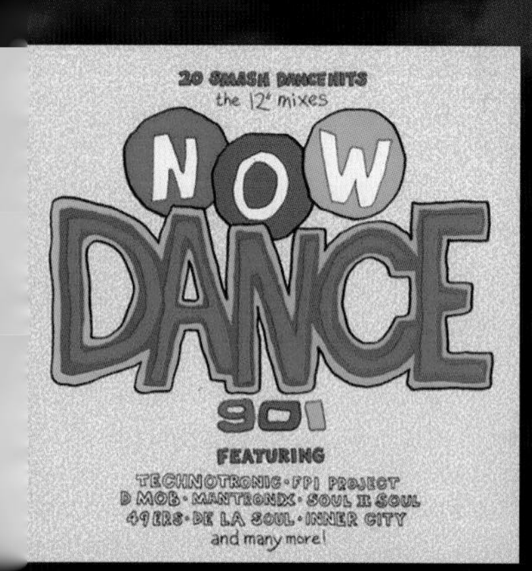
20 SMASH DANCE HITS
the 12" mixes
NOW
DANCE
901
FEATURING
TECHNOTRONIC · FPI PROJECT
D MOB · MANTRONIX · SOUL II SOUL
49 ERS · DE LA SOUL · INNER CITY
and many more!

NOW
DANCE
902
FEATURING
ADVENTURES OF STEVIE V · ADAMSKI · SOUL II SOUL
MAXI PRIEST · YAZZ · BETTY BOO · BOBBY BROWN · CHAD JACKSON
AND MANY MORE

THE 12" MIXES
DANCE
903
FEATURING:
TECHNOTRONIC BETTY BOO BASS-O-MATIC MONIE LOVE
NENEH CHERRY BLUE PEARL LOOSE ENDS INNOCENCE
Plus Many More

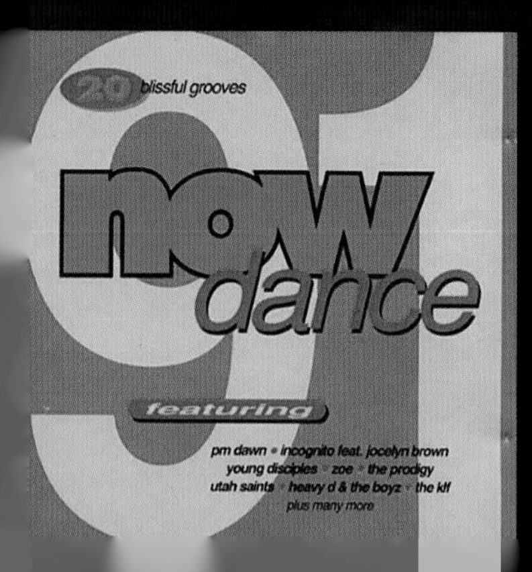
20 blissful grooves
now
dance
featuring
pm dawn · incognito feat. jocelyn brown
young disciples · zoe · the prodigy
utah saints · heavy d & the boyz · the klf
plus many more

NOW
dance
bizarre inc · was (not was) · east 17 · the shamen
utah saints · soul II soul · ce ce peniston
u2 · rage

20 buzzin' beats
NOW
dance
FEATURING: ace of base · louchie lou & michie one
inner circle · 2 unlimited · gabrielle · dina carroll
and many more!

Originating as early as 1985, the *NOW Dance* offshoot really got into its stride in the 1990s and early 2000s, averaging more than one volume per year in that period.

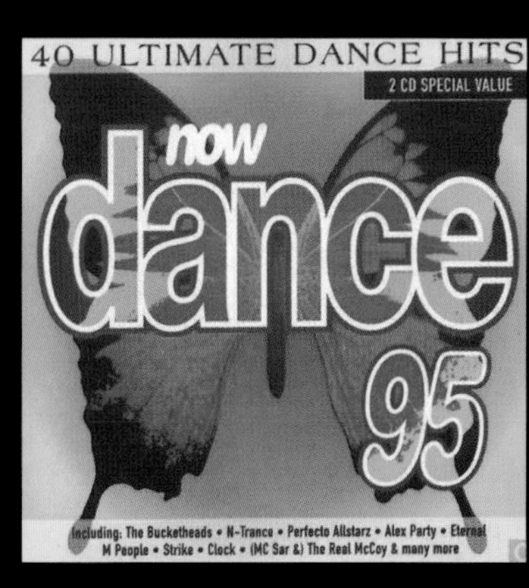

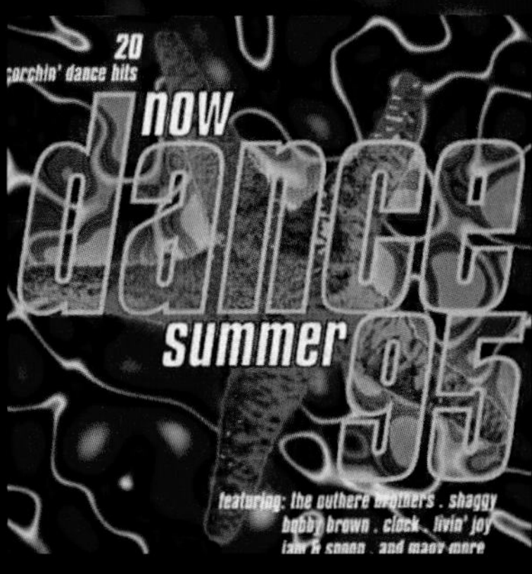

NOW
DANCE
2000
Virgin

NOW
DANCE
2001
Virgin

NOW
DANCE
2001
PART 2
Virgin

NOW
DANCE
2002

NOW
DANCE
2002
PART TWO

NOW
DANCE
2003

NOW
DANCE
2003
PART TWO

NOW
DANCE
2004

NOW
41 BRAND NEW DANCE HITS
DANCE

Whilst these two titles are not part of the *NOW Dance* series, they show that dance-based albums continue to be released.

SPECIAL EDITIONS

Decades, genres, seasons, countries, weddings: the *NOW* team have turned their attention to all of these over the years.

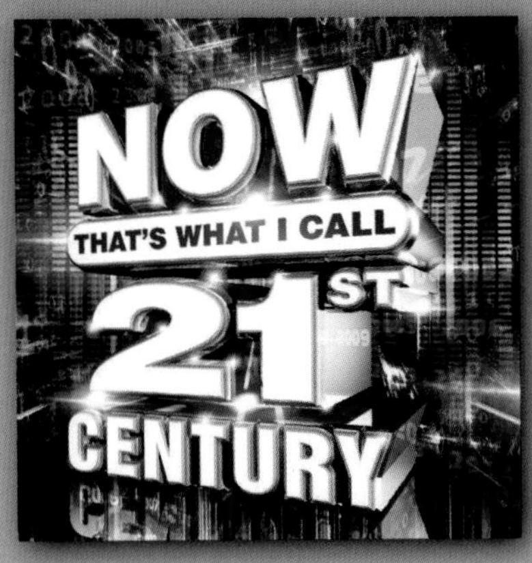

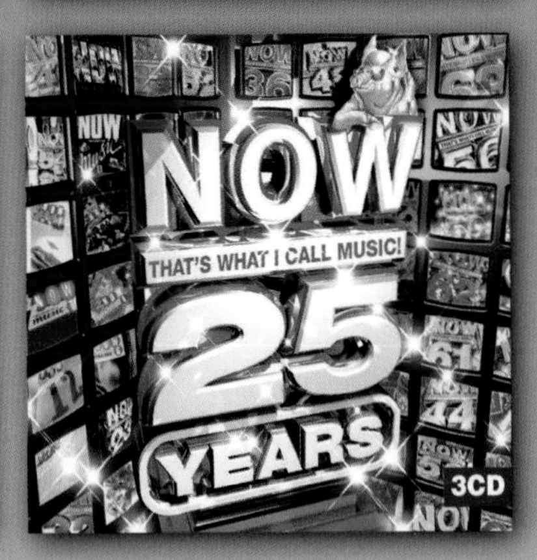

THE
SUMMER
ALBUM
30 ORIGINAL SUMMER HITS

NOW
THAT'S WHAT I CALL
CHILL

NOW
THAT'S WHAT I CALL
SUMMER

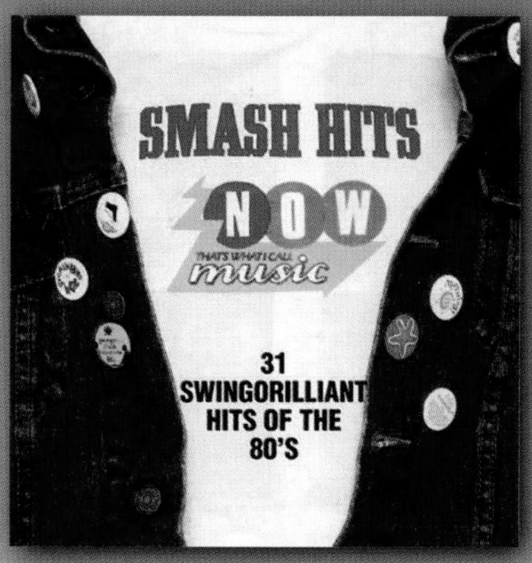
SMASH HITS
NOW
THAT'S WHAT I CALL
music
31
SWINGORILLIANT
HITS OF THE
80'S

NOW
THAT'S WHAT I CALL
REGGAE

NOW
THAT'S WHAT I CALL
FEEL
GOOD

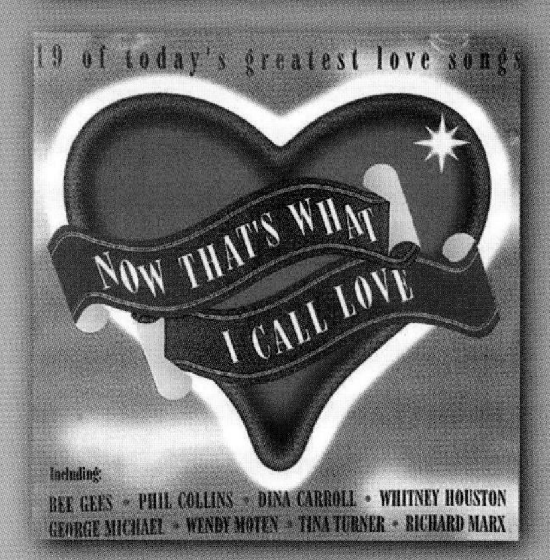
19 of today's greatest love songs
NOW THAT'S WHAT
I CALL LOVE
Including:
BEE GEES • PHIL COLLINS • DINA CARROLL • WHITNEY HOUSTON
GEORGE MICHAEL • WENDY MOTEN • TINA TURNER • RICHARD MARX

NOW
THAT'S WHAT I CALL
LOVE

NOW
THAT'S WHAT I CALL
LOVE

NOW
THAT'S WHAT I CALL
NO.1'S

Official
NOW
THAT'S WHAT I CALL A
No.1
Classic Number 1's to celebrate 60 years of the Official Singles Chart

NOW
THAT'S WHAT I CALL
R&B

NOW
THAT'S WHAT I CALL
RUNNING

NOW
THAT'S WHAT I CALL
RUNNING
2014

NOW
THAT'S WHAT I CALL
CLUB HITS

NOW
THAT'S WHAT I CALL
Disney

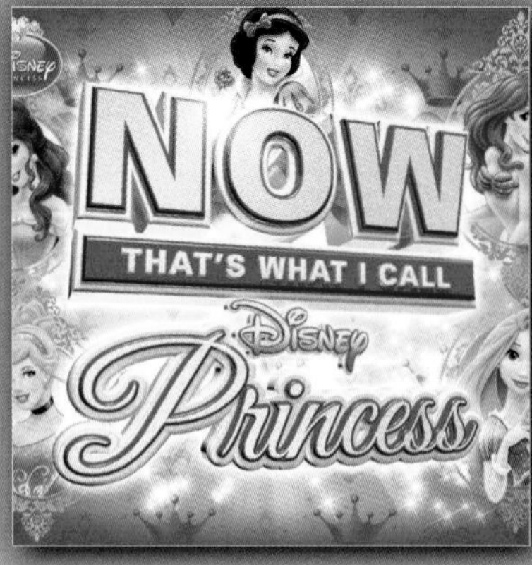
NOW
THAT'S WHAT I CALL
Disney
Princess

NOW
THAT'S WHAT I CALL
DISCO

NOW
THAT'S WHAT I CALL
music
'86

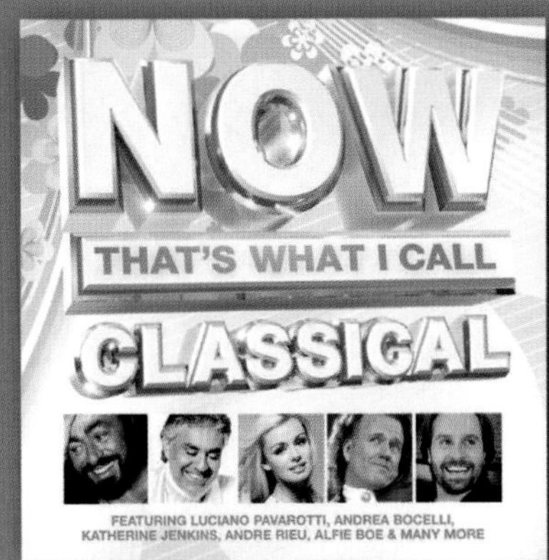
NOW
THAT'S WHAT I CALL
CLASSICAL
FEATURING LUCIANO PAVAROTTI, ANDREA BOCELLI,
KATHERINE JENKINS, ANDRE RIEU, ALFIE BOE & MANY MORE

NOW
THAT'S WHAT I CALL
RELAXING
CLASSICAL

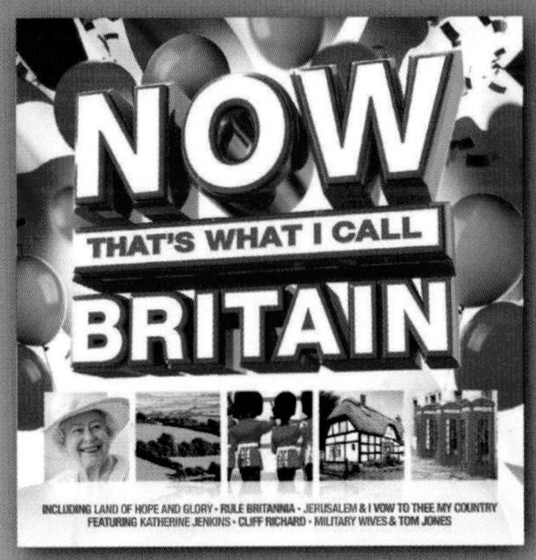
NOW
THAT'S WHAT I CALL
BRITAIN
INCLUDING LAND OF HOPE AND GLORY • RULE BRITANNIA • JERUSALEM & I VOW TO THEE MY COUNTRY
FEATURING KATHERINE JENKINS • CLIFF RICHARD • MILITARY WIVES & TOM JONES

NOW
THAT'S WHAT I CALL
MOVIES

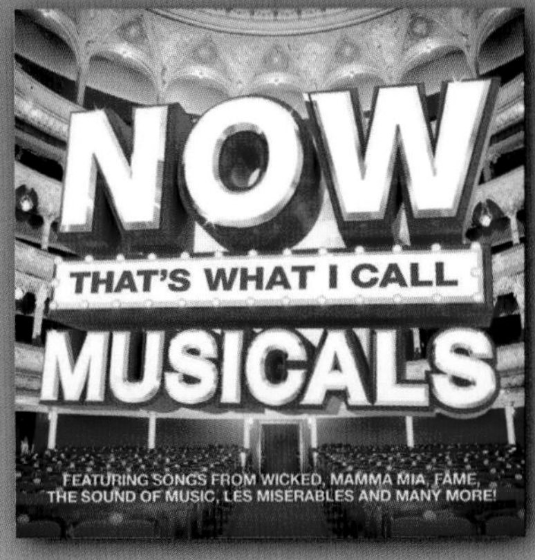
NOW
THAT'S WHAT I CALL
MUSICALS
FEATURING SONGS FROM WICKED, MAMMA MIA, FAME,
THE SOUND OF MUSIC, LES MISERABLES AND MANY MORE!

NOW
THAT'S WHAT I CALL MUSIC!
USA

NOW
THAT'S WHAT I CALL
ROCK

NOW
THAT'S WHAT I CALL A
WEDDING!

SPECIAL EDITION DVDS

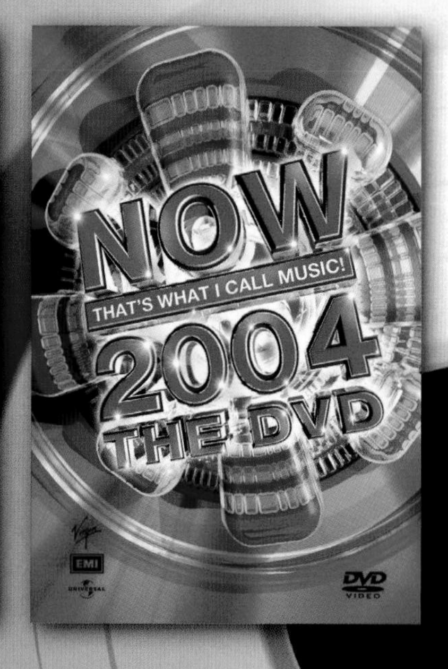

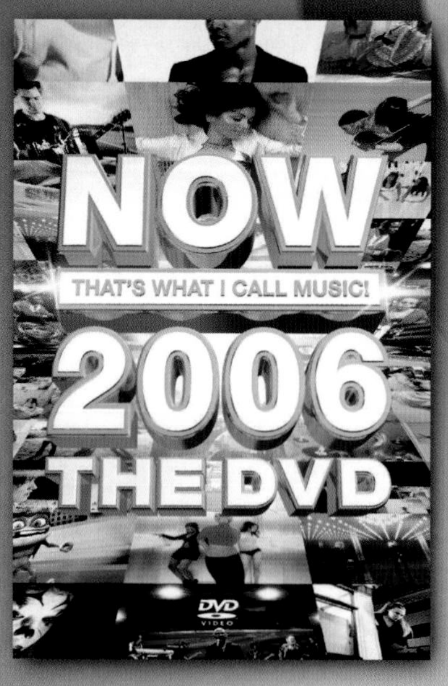

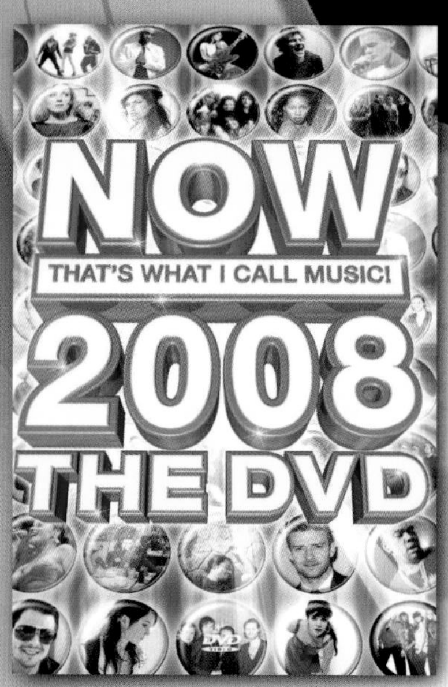

Since the rise of the DVD format at the turn of the century, *NOW* has explored annual video compilations as well as interactive quizzes and a charity disc of comedy.

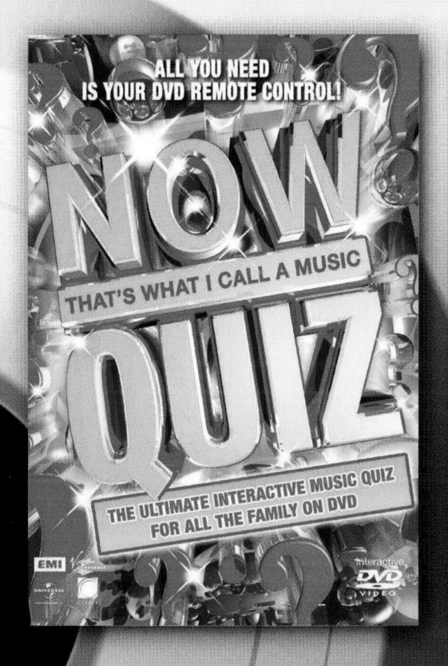

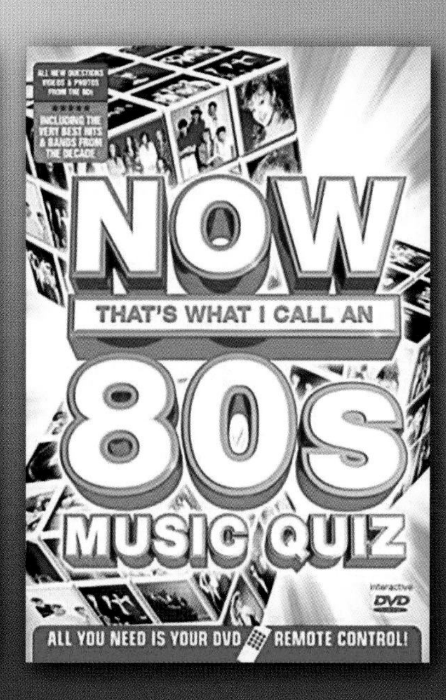

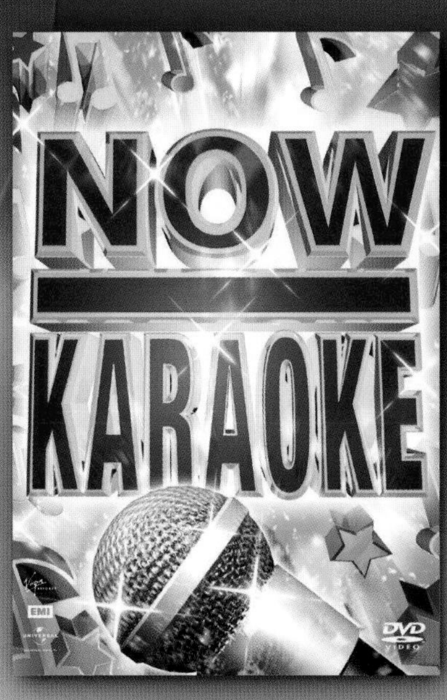

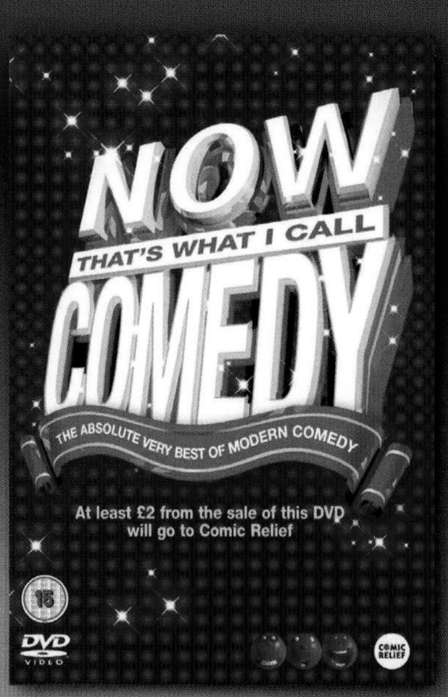

ALSO HAPPENING IN APRIL 2003

- A statue of Saddam Hussein was toppled in Iraq, marking the end of his rule
- At the Oscars, *Chicago* won Best Picture. Catherine Zeta-Jones was named Best Actress
- In the cinema: *Johnny English*, *S Club Seeing Double*, *Jackass: the Movie*
- The iTunes music store opened. Over 1 million downloads were purchased in the first week
- Albums released included *Elephant* **(The White Stripes)**, *American Life* **(Madonna)**, *Black Cherry* **(Goldfrapp)**
- The final episode of *Cold Feet* was broadcast

TRACKLISTING NOW 54

CD1

1 *All The Things She Said* t.A.T.u.
2 *Like I Love You* Justin Timberlake
3 *Dilemma* Nelly feat. Kelly Rowland
4 *Being Nobody* Richard X vs Liberty X
5 *Make Luv* Room 5 feat. Oliver Cheatham
6 *Move Your Feet* Junior Senior
7 *Sound Of The Underground* Girls Aloud
8 *Year 3000* Busted
9 *Here It Comes Again* Melanie C
10 *I Can't Break Down* Sinéad Quinn
11 *Rushes* Darius
12 *Don't Worry* Appleton
13 *Love Doesn't Have To Hurt* Atomic Kitten
14 *U Make Me Wanna* Blue
15 *'03 Bonnie & Clyde* Jay-Z feat. Beyoncé Knowles
16 *True* Jaimeson feat. Angel Blu
17 *Treat Me Like A Lady* Zoe Birkett
18 *Alive* S Club
19 *Sacred Trust* One True Voice
20 *Cry* Kym Marsh
21 *Keep Me A Secret* Ainslie Henderson

CD2

1 *If You're Not The One* Daniel Bedingfield
2 *Stop Living The Lie* David Sneddon
3 *Feel* Robbie Williams
4 *Songbird* Oasis
5 *Pain Killer* Turin Brakes
6 *Clocks* Coldplay
7 *We've Got Tonight* Ronan Keating & Lulu
8 *Stronger* Sugababes
9 *Street Life* Beenie Man
10 *Hey Ma* Cam'Ron feat. Juelz Santana, Freekey Zeekey, Toya
11 *Work It* Nelly feat. Justin Timberlake
12 *Mundian To Bach Ke* Panjabi MC
13 *Weekend!* Scooter
14 *The Boys Of Summer* DJ Sammy
15 *The Way (Put Your Hand In My Hand)* Divine Inspiration
16 *Flash* Queen & Vanguard
17 *Solsbury Hill* Erasure
18 *Can You Dig It?* The Mock Turtles
19 *Big Yellow Taxi* Counting Crows feat. Vanessa Carlton
20 *Science of Silence* Richard Ashcroft
21 *Special Cases* Massive Attack

▶ The longest consecutive run in *NOW* history started here! *Popstars: The Rivals* victors **Girls Aloud** wouldn't miss a *NOW* until volume *67* over four years later. Vanquished opponents **One True Voice** managed two appearances before fading into obscurity.

▶ The **Richard X vs Liberty X** single featured elements of The **Human League**'s 'Being Boiled'. This extended the band's *NOW* career into a third decade having appeared on the very first volume.

▶ The first series of the BBC talent show *Fame Academy* contributed three new performers to the series: winner **David Sneddon**, runner-up **Sinead Quinn**, and fourth-placed **Ainslie Henderson**. Third-placed **Lemar** would appear on later *NOW*s.

ALSO HAPPENING IN JULY 2003

- Roman Abramovich bought Chelsea FC for £150 million
- At the cinema: *Bruce Almighty*, *Charlie's Angels: Full Throttle*, *Daddy Day Care*, *Hulk*, *2 Fast 2 Furious*
- Albums launched this summer included *Permission to Land* (**The Darkness**) and *Final Straw* (**Snow Patrol**). **Beyoncé** released her debut album *Dangerously in Love*, which went on to win five Grammy Awards
- Bestsellers published in 2003 included *The Da Vinci Code* (Dan Brown), *The Time Traveler's Wife* (Audrey Niffenegger) and *Eats, Shoots & Leaves* (Lynne Truss)

TRACKLISTING NOW 55

CD1

1 *Ignition (Remix)* R. Kelly
2 *In Da Club* 50 Cent
3 *Cry Me A River* Justin Timberlake
4 *No Letting Go* Wayne Wonder
5 *Real Things* Javine
6 *Come On Over* Kym Marsh
7 *No Good Advice* Girls Aloud
8 *Not Gonna Get Us* t.A.T.u.
9 *Fool No More* S Club 8
10 *Fast Food Song* Fast Food Rockers
11 *Fly On The Wings Of Love* XTM & DJ Chucky presents Annia
12 *Lately* Lisa Scott-Lee
13 *Shakespeare's (Way With) Words* One True Voice
14 *Husan* Bhangra Knights vs Husan
15 *Loneliness* Tomcraft
16 *Hot In Herre* Tiga feat. Jake Shears
17 *All Over* Lisa Maffia
18 *Satisfaction* Benny Benassi presents The Biz
19 *Deepest Blue* Deepest Blue
20 *Sunlight* DJ Sammy
21 *Damaged* Plummet
22 *Nothing But You* Paul van Dyk feat. Hemstock and Jennings
23 *The Night* Scooter

CD2

1 *Come Undone* Robbie Williams
2 *You Said No* Busted
3 *I Can't Read You* Daniel Bedingfield
4 *Misfit* Amy Studt
5 *Big Sur* The Thrills
6 *God Put A Smile Upon Your Face* Coldplay
7 *Everything Eventually* Appleton
8 *Don't Let Go* David Sneddon
9 *The Long Goodbye* Ronan Keating
10 *Incredible (What I Meant To Say)* Darius
11 *Just The Way I'm Feeling* Feeder
12 *What You Need Is...* Sinéad Quinn
13 *On The Horizon* Melanie C
14 *Free Me* Emma
15 *Say Goodbye* S Club
16 *Shape* Sugababes
17 *Excuse Me Miss* Jay-Z feat. Pharrell Williams
18 *Boy (I Need You)* Mariah Carey feat. Cam'Ron
19 *Mesmerize* Ja Rule feat. Ashanti

▶ **50 Cent** made his first of three showings with 'In Da Club'. In currency terms the rapper, born Curtis James Jackson III, is precisely half of *NOW 11* 'Oh L'Amour' singers **Dollar** and 'Rock This Party (Everybody Dance Now)' hitmaker **Dollarman** (*NOW 65*).

▶ Having previously appeared twice with **Alisha's Attic** (*NOW 36* and *NOW 41*), Karen Poole took a song writing credit here on **Amy Studt**'s 'Misfit'. Karen returned on *NOW*s *57*, *58* and *69* writing songs for **Kylie Minogue**.

▶ Mike Stock's *NOW* ubiquity continued having written the 'Fast Food Song'. He first appeared on *NOW 5* having produced **Dead or Alive**'s 'In Too Deep' alongside Aitken and Waterman. S/A/W was the team behind thirteen inclusions between *NOW*s *7* and *19*.

ALSO HAPPENING IN NOVEMBER 2003

- England became Rugby world champions, beating Australia 20–17 after extra time
- The final *Concorde* flight took place
- The last episode of *Brookside* was broadcast on Channel 4 after twenty-one years on screen
- At the cinema: *Kill Bill Vol. 1*, *The Matrix: Revolutions*
- Albums released included *Being Somebody* (**Liberty X**), *Try This* (**Pink**), *Body Language* (**Kylie Minogue**), *In the Zone* (**Britney Spears**) and *Call Off the Search* (**Katie Melua**). The Christmas No.1 was 'Mad World' (**Michael Andrew & Gary Jules**)

TRACKLISTING NOW 56

CD1

1 *Where Is The Love?* **The Black Eyed Peas**
2 *Sweet Dreams My LA Ex* **Rachel Stevens**
3 *Slow* **Kylie Minogue**
4 *Guilty* **Blue**
5 *Be Faithful* **Fatman Scoop feat. The Crooklyn Clan**
6 *Crazy In Love* **Beyoncé feat. Jay-Z**
7 *Hole In The Head* **Sugababes**
8 *Jumpin'* **Liberty X**
9 *Superstar* **Jamelia**
10 *Never Leave You (Uh Oooh, Uh Oooh)* **Lumidee**
11 *Stuck* **Stacie Orrico**
12 *Dance (With U)* **Lemar**
13 *Surrender (Your Love)* **Javine**
14 *Maybe* **Emma Bunton**
15 *Sundown* **S Club 8**
16 *Pretty Green Eyes* **Ultrabeat**
17 *Mixed Up World* **Sophie Ellis-Bextor**
18 *Hold On Me* **Phixx**
19 *Invisible* **D-Side**
20 *Pandora's Kiss* **Louise**
21 *Life Got Cold* **Girls Aloud**
22 *If You Come To Me* **Atomic Kitten**

CD2

1 *Are You Ready For Love* **Elton John**
2 *Rock Your Body* **Justin Timberlake**
3 *Something Beautiful* **Robbie Williams**
4 *Someday* **Nickelback**
5 *Sleeping With The Light On* **Busted**
6 *Four Minute Warning* **Mark Owen**
7 *Under The Thumb* **Amy Studt**
8 *Carnival Girl* **Texas feat. Kardinal Offishall**
9 *21 Questions* **50 Cent feat. Nate Dogg**
10 *Rock Wit U (Awww Baby)* **Ashanti**
11 *Pump It Up* **Joe Budden**
12 *Complete* **Jaimeson**
13 *Too Far Gone* **Lisa Scott-Lee**
14 *Love Me Right (Oh Sheila)* **Angel City feat. Lara McAllen**
15 *Finest Dreams* **Richard X feat. Kelis**
16 *Dance With You* **Rishi Rich Project feat. Jay Sean & Juggy D**
17 *Swing Low* **UB40 feat. The United Colours Of Sound**
18 *Silence Is Easy* **Starsailor**
19 *Maybe Tomorrow* **Stereophonics**
20 *Never Gonna Leave Your Side* **Daniel Bedingfield**
21 *Mad World* **Michael Andrews feat. Gary Jules**

▶ Occasionally tracks are edited before being included on *NOW* albums. **Mark Owen** must have been disappointed, though, when he cleverly planned his 'Four Minute Warning' single to last exactly four minutes – only for it to be shorn of thirty seconds on *NOW 56*.

▶ 'Where Is The Love?' was the biggest-selling single of 2003, the first **Black Eyed Peas** single to reach the Top 10 singles chart, and their first showing on a *NOW*. They can boast fifteen appearances as a band, with **will.i.am** clocking up thirteen more solo.

▶ Two recordings of the American spiritual song 'Swing Low Sweet Chariot' have appeared on *NOW* albums after becoming hit singles tied in with Rugby World Cups. Veterans of the first *NOW*, our old friends **UB40** bowed out with their version.

ALSO HAPPENING IN APRIL 2004

- Outrage ensued after photographs were released of American troops mistreating Iraqi detainees at Abu Ghraib prison
- Facebook was founded by a group of students at Harvard University
- ITV revealed details of its new talent show, *The X Factor.* The first episode of *Strictly Come Dancing* was broadcast in May
- At the cinema: *Starsky and Hutch*, *Dawn of the Dead*, *21 Grams*, *Monster*
- Albums released included **Franz Ferdinand**'s self-titled debut album, *Musicology* (**Prince**) and *Hopes and Fears* (**Keane**)

TRACKLISTING NOW 57

CD1

1 *Toxic* Britney Spears
2 *Milkshake* Kelis
3 *Thank You* Jamelia
4 *Red Blooded Woman* Kylie Minogue
5 *Buleria* David Bisbal
6 *Not In Love* Enrique Iglesias feat. Kelis
7 *Shut Up* The Black Eyed Peas
8 *So Confused* 2 Play feat. Raghav & Jucxi
9 *Dude* Beenie Man feat. Ms. Thing and Shawnna
10 *Mysterious Girl* Peter Andre feat. Bubbler Ranx
11 *Cha Cha Slide* DJ Casper
12 *Jump* Girls Aloud
13 *Somebody To Love* Boogie Pimps
14 *Ladies Night* Atomic Kitten feat. Kool & The Gang
15 *I'll Be There* Emma
16 *I Won't Change You* Sophie Ellis-Bextor
17 *Comfortably Numb* Scissor Sisters
18 *Give It Away* Deepest Blue
19 *Take Me To The Clouds Above* LMC vs U2
20 *Come With Me* Special D
21 *Feelin' Fine* Ultrabeat
22 *As The Rush Comes* Motorcycle
23 *Rock Your Body Rock* Ferry Corsten

CD2

1 *Leave Right Now* Will Young
2 *The Closest Thing To Crazy* Katie Melua
3 *Sunrise* Norah Jones
4 *Breathe Easy* Blue
5 *Changes* Kelly Osbourne feat. Ozzy Osbourne
6 *I Miss You* Blink-182
7 *Who's David* Busted
8 *Stacy's Mom* Fountains of Wayne
9 *Take Me Out* Franz Ferdinand
10 *Bring It On* Alistair Griffin
11 *Too Lost In You* Sugababes
12 *Love You Like Mad* VS
13 *Fell In Love With A Boy* Joss Stone
14 *Must Be Love* FYA feat. Smujji
15 *She Wants To Move* N.E.R.D.
16 *Frontin' (Live)* Jamie Cullum
17 *Somewhere Only We Know* Keane
18 *Run* Snow Patrol
19 *Maybe That's What It Takes* Alex Parks
20 *She Believes (In Me)* Ronan Keating
21 *All This Time* Michelle

▶ Upon release, propelled by eight No.1 singles, *NOW 57* was the fastest selling album of the 21st Century.

▶ 'Michelle' is **Michelle McManus**, winner of the second and final series of *Pop Idol*. This was her sole *NOW* entry but one of numerous writing credits for Steve Mac. **Will Young**, who won the first series, also featured here and has appeared a total of six times to date.

▶ It was hello *and* goodbye to **Ozzy Osbourne** and daughter **Kelly** who both appeared for the first and last time – either together or alone – with their No.1 single 'Changes'.

ALSO HAPPENING IN JULY 2004

- As the *9/11 Commission Report* was published, construction began on the new One World Trade Center in New York City
- Maria Sharapova became the Wimbledon champion, beating Serena Williams
- Greece won the Euro 2004 football tournament
- At the cinema: *Around the World in 80 Days*, *Walking Tall*, *Farenheit 9/11*, *The Notebook*, *Shrek 2*
- **McFly**'s debut album, *Room on the 3rd Floor*, went straight to No.1. Other albums released that summer included *Hot Fuss* (**The Killers**) and *Trouble* (**Akon**)

TRACKLISTING NOW 58

CD1

1 *Some Girls* Rachel Stevens
2 *Lola's Theme* The Shapeshifters
3 *Left Outside Alone* Anastacia
4 *Trick Me* Kelis
5 *See It In A Boy's Eyes* Jamelia
6 *F**k It (I Don't Want You Back)* Eamon
7 *F.U.R.B. (F U Right Back)* Frankee
8 *Dip It Low* Christina Milian
9 *Hey Ya!* Outkast
10 *Hey Mama* The Black Eyed Peas
11 *Laura* Scissor Sisters
12 *Flawless (Go To The City)* George Michael
13 *I Like It* Narcotic Thrust
14 *Come As You Are* Beverley Knight
15 *Super Duper Love* Joss Stone
16 *Everybody's Changing* Keane
17 *Matinée* Franz Ferdinand
18 *Golden Touch* Razorlight
19 *In The Shadows* The Rasmus
20 *Now We Are Free* Gladiator feat. Izzy

CD2

1 *Everytime* Britney Spears
2 *Chocolate* Kylie Minogue
3 *The Show* Girls Aloud
4 *5 Colours In Her Hair* McFly
5 *In The Middle* Sugababes
6 *Air Hostess* Busted
7 *Dragostea Din Tei* O-Zone
8 *Bubblin'* Blue
9 *Blood Sweat And Tears* V
10 *It Can't Be Right* 2 Play feat. Raghav & Naila Boss
11 *Move Ya Body* Nina Sky feat. Jabba
12 *It Takes Scoop* Fatman Scoop feat. The Crooklyn Clan
13 *Through The Wire* Kanye West
14 *Maybe* N*E*R*D
15 *1980* Estelle
16 *Eyes On You* Jay Sean feat. The Rishi Rich Project
17 *Call U Sexy* VS
18 *Ride Wit U* Joe
19 *Stay The Same* Gabrielle
20 *Last Thing On My Mind* Ronan Keating feat. LeAnn Rimes
21 *Story Of My Life* Kristian Leontiou
22 *Someone Like Me* Atomic Kitten

There was an outbreak of obscenity on Disc 1 as **Eamon**'s ribald ditty was followed by **Frankee**'s similarly smutty answer record, as happened at the top of the charts. Neither artist made the Top 20 again.

McFly introduced themselves with '5 Colours In Her Hair', the first of eleven consecutive *NOW* appearances. This is the joint-second-longest run in *NOW* history and overlaps **Girls Aloud**'s record-setting run.

'Lola's Theme' by **The Shapeshifters** was the fourth No.1 single for EMI's Positiva label. All four singles appeared on *NOW*s: 'Tocas Miracle' by **Fragma** kicked off the run in 2000 (*NOW 45*). In total, this was the fifteenth appearance to date for the illustrious dance label.

ALSO HAPPENING IN NOVEMBER 2004

- George W. Bush was re-elected as US President
- Smoking in enclosed public places was banned
- Bestsellers published this year included *Cloud Atlas* (David Mitchell) and *The Shadow of the Wind* (Carlos Ruiz Zafón)
- New albums included *Second First Impression* (**Daniel Bedingfield**), *Encore* (**Eminem**), *Destiny Fulfilled* (**Destiny's Child**) and *How to Dismantle an Atomic Bomb* (U2). Christmas No.1 was 'Do They know it's Christmas?' (**Band Aid 20**)
- At the cinema: *Finding Neverland*, *Bridget Jones: the Edge of Reason*

TRACKLISTING NOW 59

CD1

1 *Curtain Falls* Blue
2 *She Will Be Loved* Maroon 5
3 *These Words* Natasha Bedingfield
4 *Radio* Robbie Williams
5 *Thunderbirds Are Go* Busted
6 *Call On Me* Eric Prydz
7 *Love Machine* Girls Aloud
8 *Obviously* McFly
9 *More, More, More* Rachel Stevens
10 *Kinda Love* Darius
11 *Hip To Hip* V
12 *Leave (Get Out)* JoJo
13 *Stolen* Jay Sean
14 *Mary* Scissor Sisters
15 *Bedshaped* Keane
16 *Can't Stand Me Now* The Libertines
17 *The Reason* Hoobastank
18 *Gravity* Embrace
19 *What You're Made Of* Lucie Silvas
20 *I Hope You Dance* Ronan Keating
21 *I Believe My Heart* Duncan James & Keedie

CD2

1 *Nothing Hurts Like Love* Daniel Bedingfield
2 *Stop* Jamelia
3 *Happy People* R. Kelly
4 *My Place* Nelly feat. Jaheim
5 *Let's Get It Started* The Black Eyed Peas
6 *Millionaire* Kelis feat. André 3000
7 *Babycakes* 3 of a Kind
8 *My Neck My Back (Lick It)* Khia
9 *You Can Do It (2004)* Ice Cube feat. Mack 10 and Ms. Toi
10 *You Had Me* Joss Stone
11 *Whatever U Want* Christina Milian feat. Joe Budden
12 *Caught In A Moment* Sugababes
13 *You Should Really Know* The Pirates Feat. Enya, Shola Ama, Naila Boss and Ishani
14 *I Like That* Houston feat. Chingy, Nate Dogg & 1-20
15 *Is It 'Cos I'm Cool?* Mousse T feat. Emma Lanford
16 *Flashdance* Deep Dish
17 *Do You Know (I Go Crazy)* Angel City feat. Lara McAllen
18 *The Weekend* Michael Gray
19 *Get It On* Intenso Project feat. Lisa Scott-Lee
20 *You Won't Forget About Me* Dannii Minogue vs Flower Power
21 *Pump It Up* Danzel
22 *Hungry Eyes* Eyeopener

The inclusion of **Bedingfield, N** and **Bedingfield, D** marked the only time brother and sister have appeared on the same *NOW* with two different songs.

'Call On Me' by **Eric Prydz** is based on a sample from **Steve Winwood**'s song 'Valerie'. Winwood re-recorded the vocal for the Prydz single, thus marking his first appearance on a *NOW* since 'Higher Love' (*NOW 8*).

Enya's credit alongside **The Pirates** on 'You Should Really Know' was the second time the haunting sample from her song 'Boudicea' had been heard on a 2003 hit – **Mario Winans** had had a No.1 three months beforehand. Both followed the example set by **The Fugees** on 'Ready Or Not' who were the first to use the excerpt six years previously.

ALSO HAPPENING IN MARCH 2005

- The first YouTube video was uploaded
- *Doctor Who* returned to television starring Christopher Ecclestone in the title role, and also featured Billie Piper
- At the Academy Awards, *Million Dollar Baby* won four Oscars including Best Film and Best Actress for Hilary Swank. Jamie Foxx won Best Actor for *Ray*
- At the cinema: *Hitch*, *Fever Pitch*, *Coach Carter*, *Hotel Rwanda*
- Albums released included the **Kaiser Chiefs'** debut *Employment*, *Rebirth* (**Jennifer Lopez**) and *The Emancipation of Mimi* (**Mariah Carey**)

TRACKLISTING NOW 60

CD1

1 *What You Waiting For?* Gwen Stefani
2 *Falling Stars* Sunset Strippers
3 *I Believe In You* Kylie Minogue
4 *All About You* McFly
5 *Over And Over* Nelly feat. Tim McGraw
6 *If There's Any Justice* Lemar
7 *I'll Stand By You* Girls Aloud
8 *Out Of Touch* Uniting Nations
9 *Filthy/Gorgeous* Scissor Sisters
10 *Galvanize* The Chemical Brothers feat. Q-Tip
11 *Hush* LL Cool J feat. 7 Aurelius
12 *Only U* Ashanti
13 *Goodies* Ciara feat. Petey Pablo
14 *Locked Up* Akon feat. Styles P.
15 *Spoiled* Joss Stone
16 *Don't Play Nice* Verbalicious
17 *Back To Basics* The Shapeshifters
18 *Ride It* Geri
19 *Shine* The Lovefreekz
20 *Need To Feel Loved* Reflekt feat. Delline Bass
21 *Strings Of Life* Soul Central feat. Kathy Brown
22 *Heartbeatz* Styles & Breeze

CD2

1 *Vertigo* U2
2 *Somebody Told Me* The Killers
3 *Dakota* Stereophonics
4 *This Is The Last Time* Keane
5 *So Here We Are* Bloc Party
6 *Wires* Athlete
7 *Misunderstood* Robbie Williams
8 *Father And Son* Ronan Keating feat. Yusuf Islam
9 *Live Twice* Darius
10 *Wrap My Words Around You* Daniel Bedingfield
11 *Breathe In* Lucie Silvas
12 *Black And White Town* Doves
13 *An Honest Mistake* The Bravery
14 *Do This! Do That!* Freefaller
15 *Thru The Glass* Thirteen Senses
16 *Tumble And Fall* Feeder
17 *Angel Eyes* Raghav feat. Frankey Maxx & Jucxi D
18 *Baby It's You* Jojo
19 *Cradle* Atomic Kitten
20 *Almost Here* Brian McFadden & Delta Goodrem
21 *(Is This The Way To) Amarillo* Tony Christie feat. Peter Kay

▶ Duetting with **Ronan Keating** here, Yusuf Islam found fame in the late 60s as **Cat Stevens.** Keating's band **Boyzone** had already appeared on *NOW 33* with 'Father And Son', so while Keating repeated himself, songwriter Yusuf got paid twice.

▶ **The Bravery**'s vocalist Sam Endicott later co-wrote 'She Wolf', a *NOW 74* inclusion for three-time *NOW* contributor, Colombian chanteuse **Shakira.**

▶ *Pop Idol* graduate **Darius** made the last of five appearances with 'Live Twice'. From the same series **Rik Waller** (*NOW 51,* singing 'I Will Always Love You') and **Zoe Birkett** (*NOW 54*) also made the grade, alongside winner **Will Young**. Despite four No.1 singles *Pop Idol* runner-up **Gareth Gates** has never appeared.

ALSO HAPPENING IN JULY 2005

- Ten Live 8 concerts took place across the world in aid of Make Poverty History campaign. Over 1000 musicians took part, including **Madonna, Pink Floyd and Elton John**
- The 2012 Summer Olympic Games were awarded to London by the International Olympic Committee
- At the cinema: *Batman Begins*, *Sin City*, *Madagascar*, *Wedding Crashers*, *Fantastic Four*, *Mr and Mrs Smith*, *War of the Worlds*
- Albums released this summer included *Stars of CCTV* (**Hard-Fi**), *Tissues and Issues* (**Charlotte Church**) and *Unwritten* (**Natasha Bedingfield**)

TRACKLISTING NOW 61

CD1

1 *You're Beautiful* James Blunt
2 *Ghetto Gospel* 2Pac feat. Elton John
3 *Speed Of Sound* Coldplay
4 *Feel Good Inc.* Gorillaz
5 *Don't Phunk With My Heart* The Black Eyed Peas
6 *Shot You Down* Audio Bullys feat. Nancy Sinatra
7 *They* Jem
8 *Shiver* Natalie Imbruglia
9 *Other Side Of The World* KT Tunstall
10 *Lyla* Oasis
11 *Somewhere Else* Razorlight
12 *I Like The Way* Bodyrockers
13 *Everyday I Love You Less And Less* Kaiser Chiefs
14 *Jerk It Out* Caesars
15 *Smile Like You Mean It* The Killers
16 *Hard To Beat* Hard-Fi
17 *Beverly Hills* Weezer
18 *Lonely No More* Rob Thomas
19 *Forever Lost* The Magic Numbers
20 *Good People* Jack Johnson
21 *Sometimes You Can't Make It On Your Own* U2

CD2

1 *Lonely* Akon
2 *Let Me Love You* Mario
3 *Rich Girl* Gwen Stefani feat. Eve
4 *Switch* Will Smith
5 *Roc Ya Body (Mic Check 1, 2)* M.V.P.
6 *It's Like That* Mariah Carey
7 *N Dey Say* Nelly
8 *Slow Down* Bobby Valentino
9 *Again* Faith Evans
10 *Don't Cha Wanna Ride* Joss Stone
11 *The Avenue* Roll Deep
12 *Crazy Chick* Charlotte Church
13 *So Good* Rachel Stevens
14 *Nasty Girl* Inaya Day
15 *Say Hello* Deep Dish
16 *So Much Love To Give* Freeloaders feat. The Real Thing
17 *Giving You Up* Kylie Minogue
18 *Wake Me Up* Girls Aloud
19 *Axel F* Crazy Frog
20 *Avenues And Alleyways* Tony Christie
21 *You've Got A Friend* McFly
22 *Proud* Heather Small

▶ After six weeks in the Top 15, 'You're Beautiful' by **James Blunt** finally hit the top spot in July. It was the first single to debut outside of the Top 10 and climb to No.1 since 'Boom Boom Boom' by the **Outhere Brothers** (*NOW 31*).

▶ *NOW 61* marked the only appearance from a Sinatra (here alongside **Audio Bullys**). However, Nancy's catalogue has been plundered twice before, both times by **Robbie Williams:** 'Something Stupid' (*NOW 51*) and the strings from 'You Only Live Twice' sampled on 'Millenium' (*NOW 41*).

▶ Lawlessness forecasters **Kaiser Chiefs** put in an introductory appearance on *NOW 61*. Lead singer Ricky Wilson has recently returned to the public eye via his stint on *The Voice;* his band's *NOW* score of five is equal to that of **The Script** (lead singer Danny was a judge), but is exceeded by fellow panellists Kylie Minogue (twenty-three), **will.i.am** (thirteen), **Jessie J** (ten) and **Tom Jones** (seven).

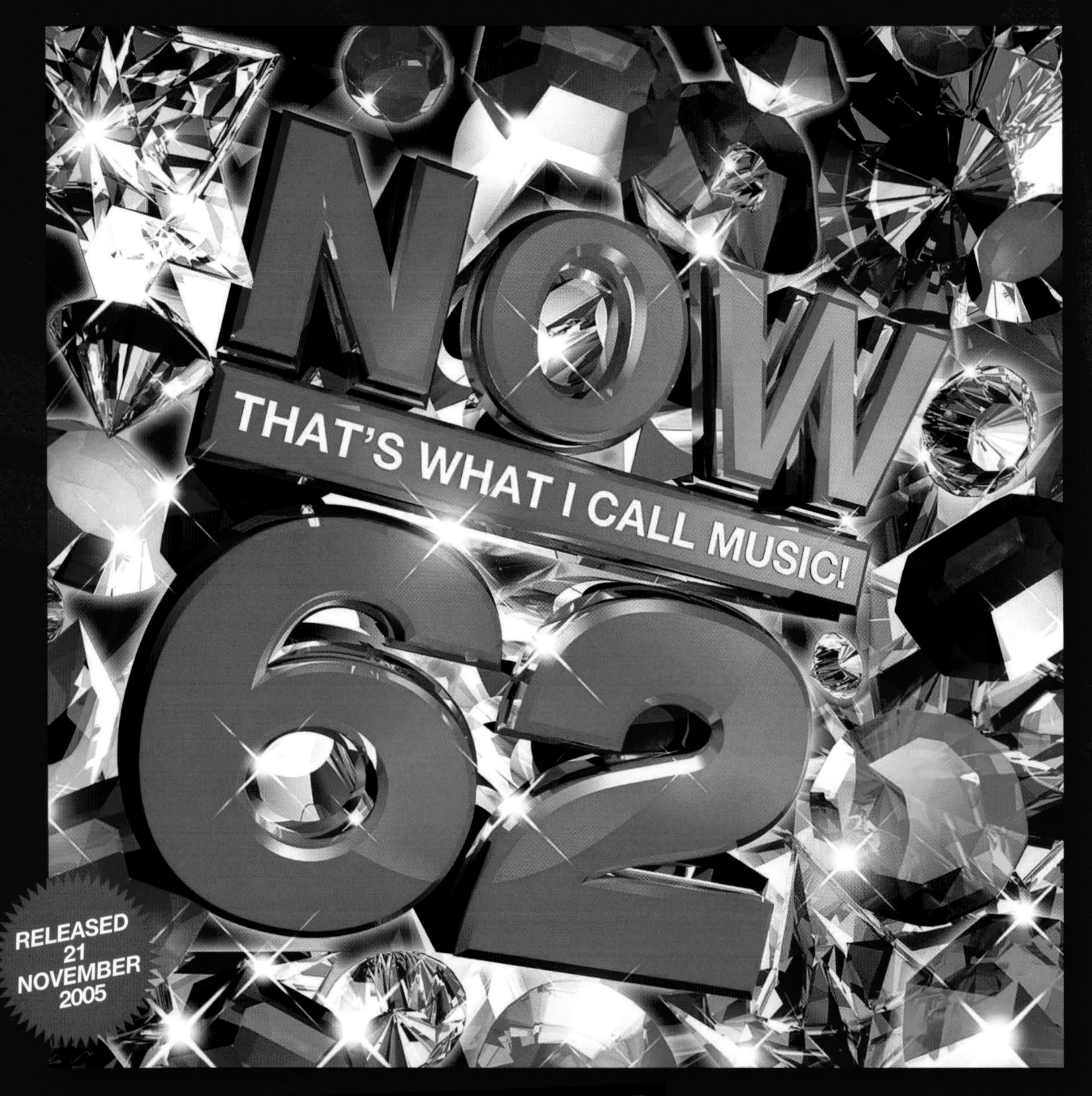

ALSO HAPPENING IN NOVEMBER 2005

- Pubs in England and Wales were allowed to open around the clock
- Microsoft released the Xbox 360 console
- In the cinema: *Harry Potter and the Goblet of Fire, Godzilla, Saw II*
- New albums included *Confessions on a Dance Floor* (**Madonna**) and *Oral Fixation Vol. 2* (**Shakira**). Christmas No.1 was 'That's My Goal' (**Shayne Ward**)
- Bestselling books published in 2005 included *The Girl with the Dragon Tattoo* (Stieg Larsson), *Twilight* (Stephenie Meyer) and *Marley & Me* (John Grogan)

TRACKLISTING NOW 62

CD1

1 *Push The Button* Sugababes
2 *Tripping* Robbie Williams
3 *Don't Cha* Pussycat Dolls feat. Busta Rhymes
4 *Bad Day* Daniel Powter
5 *The One I Love* David Gray
6 *Since U Been Gone* Kelly Clarkson
7 *Switch It On* Will Young
8 *Biology* Girls Aloud
9 *I'll Be OK* McFly
10 *I Predict A Riot* Kaiser Chiefs
11 *Do You Want To* Franz Ferdinand
12 *Suddenly I See* KT Tunstall
13 *All About Us* t.A.T.u.
14 *Wake Up* Hilary Duff
15 *I Said Never Again (But Here We Are)* Rachel Stevens
16 *Song 4 Lovers* Liberty X
17 *Baby Goodbye* Friday Hill
18 *Lay Your Hands* Simon Webbe
19 *We Belong Together* Mariah Carey
20 *Electricity* Elton John
21 *Nine Million Bicycles* Katie Melua
22 *You Raise Me Up* Westlife

CD2

1 *DARE* Gorillaz
2 *Hollaback Girl* Gwen Stefani
3 *Diamonds From Sierra Leone* Kanye West
4 *Fix You* Coldplay
5 *The Importance Of Being Idle* Oasis
6 *Don't Lie* The Black Eyed Peas
7 *Can I Have It Like That* Pharrell feat. Gwen Stefani
8 *Ooh La La* Goldfrapp
9 *Doctor Pressure* Mylo vs Miami Sound Machine
10 *Love Generation* Bob Sinclar feat. Gary 'Nesta' Pine
11 *Gasolina* Daddy Yankee
12 *Pon De Replay* Rihanna
13 *1 Thing* Amerie
14 *Belly Dancer (Bananza)* Akon
15 *Big City Life* Mattafix
16 *Welcome To Jamrock* Damian 'Jr. Gong' Marley
17 *Precious* Depeche Mode
18 *City Of Blinding Lights* U2
19 *Love Me Like You* The Magic Numbers
20 *Getaway* Texas
21 *Have A Nice Day* Bon Jovi

It's remarkable to think of it now, but up to and including *NOW 61* you couldn't purchase the latest edition as a digital download. *62* was the first to be released as a bundle of MP3s.

Rihanna crammed twenty-five appearances into twenty-three *NOW*s (*62* to *84*). 'Pon De Replay' means 'play it again' in Bajan Creole, one of the two official languages of Barbados.

Kanye West's 'Diamonds From Sierra Leone' was the third *NOW* track to feature the full name of a nation state as part of its title, the others being 'French Kissing In The USA' and 'China In Your Hand'. 'Princess Of China' came later.

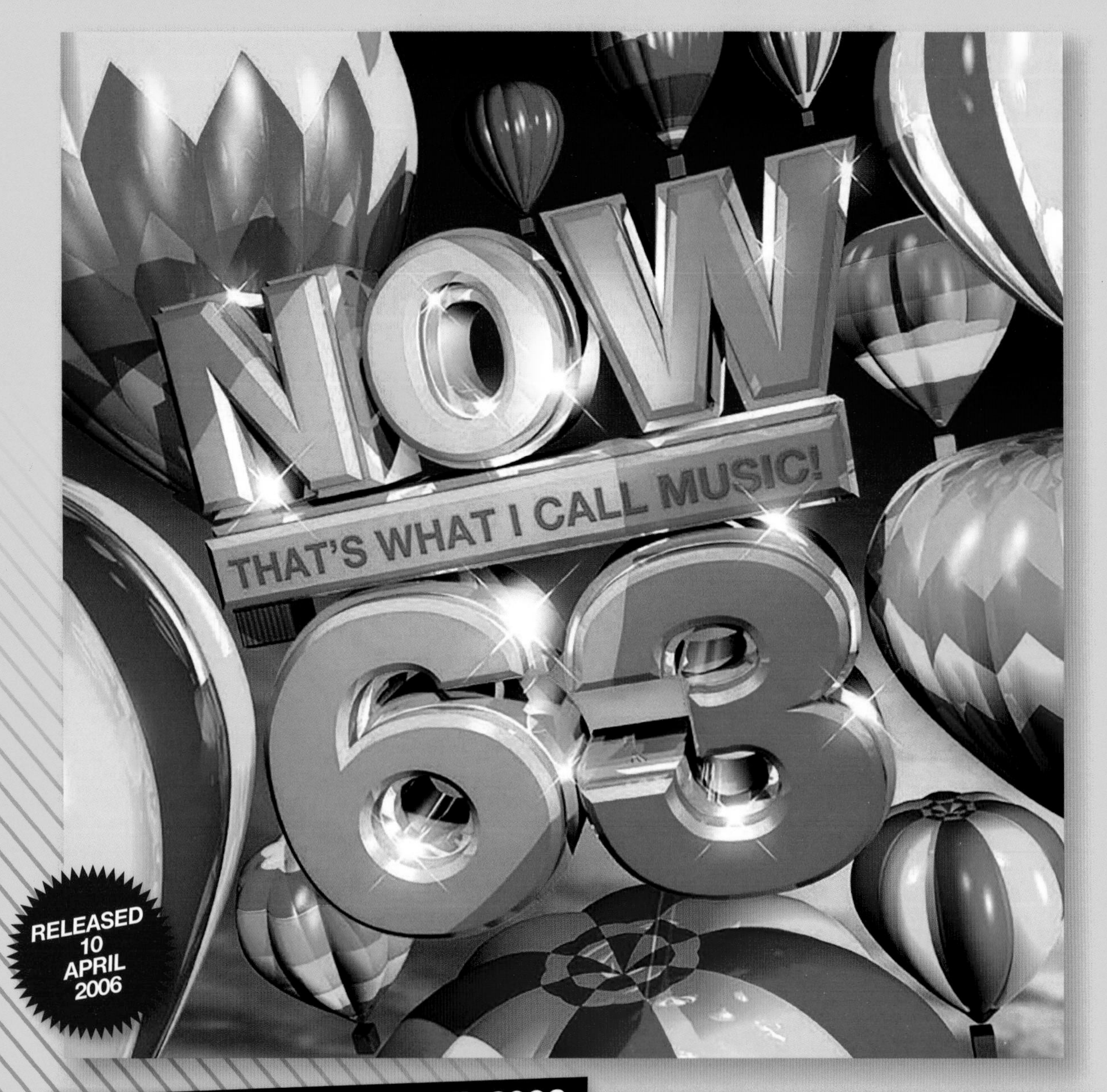

ALSO HAPPENING IN APRIL 2006

- At the Academy Awards, *Crash* won Best Picture and Reese Witherspoon was named Best Actress for *Walk the Line*
- The BBC announced that *Grandstand* would end next year, after nearly fifty years on television
- *Waterloo Road* began on BBC1
- At the cinema: *Ice Age: the Meltdown*, *V for Vendetta*, *Basic Instinct 2*. Ant and Dec made their film debut in *Alien Autopsy*
- Albums released included *I'm Not Dead* (**Pink**), *St Elsewhere* (**Gnarls Barkley**) and *A Girl Like Me* (**Rihanna**)

TRACKLISTING NOW 63

CD1

1 *Put Your Records On* **Corinne Bailey Rae**
2 *Beep* **The Pussycat Dolls feat. will.i.am**
3 *My Humps* **The Black Eyed Peas**
4 *No Tomorrow* **Orson**
5 *Boys Will Be Boys* **The Ordinary Boys**
6 *Thunder In My Heart Again* **Meck feat. Leo Sayer**
7 *Say Say Say (Waiting 4 U)* **Hi_Tack**
8 *You Spin Me Round (Like A Record)* **Dead Or Alive**
9 *It's Chico Time* **Chico**
10 *That's My Goal* **Shayne Ward**
11 *Ugly* **Sugababes**
12 *No Worries* **Simon Webbe**
13 *All Time Love* **Will Young**
14 *Because Of You* **Kelly Clarkson**
15 *Amazing* **Westlife**
16 *Hang Up* **Andy Abraham**
17 *I Wanna Hold You* **McFly**
18 *Ticket Outta Loserville* **Son Of Dork**
19 *One More Night Alone* **Friday Hill**
20 *A Night To Remember* **Liberty X**
21 *If It's Lovin' That You Want* **Rihanna**
22 *Woman In Love* **Liz McClarnon**
23 *See The Day* **Girls Aloud**

CD2

1 *JCB Song* **Nizlopi**
2 *Nature's Law* **Embrace**
3 *Advertising Space* **Robbie Williams**
4 *Talk* **Coldplay**
5 *Analogue (All I Want)* **A-ha**
6 *Sewn* **The Feeling**
7 *Break The Night With Colour* **Richard Ashcroft**
8 *Sleep* **Texas**
9 *Modern Way* **Kaiser Chiefs**
10 *All Because Of You* **U2**
11 *Sugar, We're Goin Down* **Fall Out Boy**
12 *Ride A White Horse* **Goldfrapp**
13 *Dirty Harry* **Gorillaz**
14 *Bounce, Shake, Move, Stop!* **M.V.P.**
15 *I'll Be Ready* **Sunblock**
16 *Incredible* **The Shapeshifters**
17 *You Got The Love* **The Source feat. Candi Staton**
18 *Grow* **Kubb**
19 *Heartbeats* **José González**

▶ *NOW 63* holds the dubious distinction of featuring the lowest-selling No.1 single of all time. Take a bow **Orson**, 17,694 copies sold in the second week of March 2006.

▶ This is currently the last appearance on a *NOW* release for polymath pop genius Damon Albarn who has appeared fourteen times since *NOW 28* in 1994 (nine with **Blur**, five with **Gorillaz**).

▶ **Son Of Dork** were formed by guitarist James Bourne after the seven times *NOW* veterans **Busted** had split. Fellow émigré **Matt Willis** managed to place two solo singles in the series (*NOW*s *64* and *65*). The third **Busted** bloke, Charlie Simpson, is yet to feature as a solo artist or with his other band **Fightstar**.

BESTSELLING UK SINGLES TO FEATURE ON *NOW*

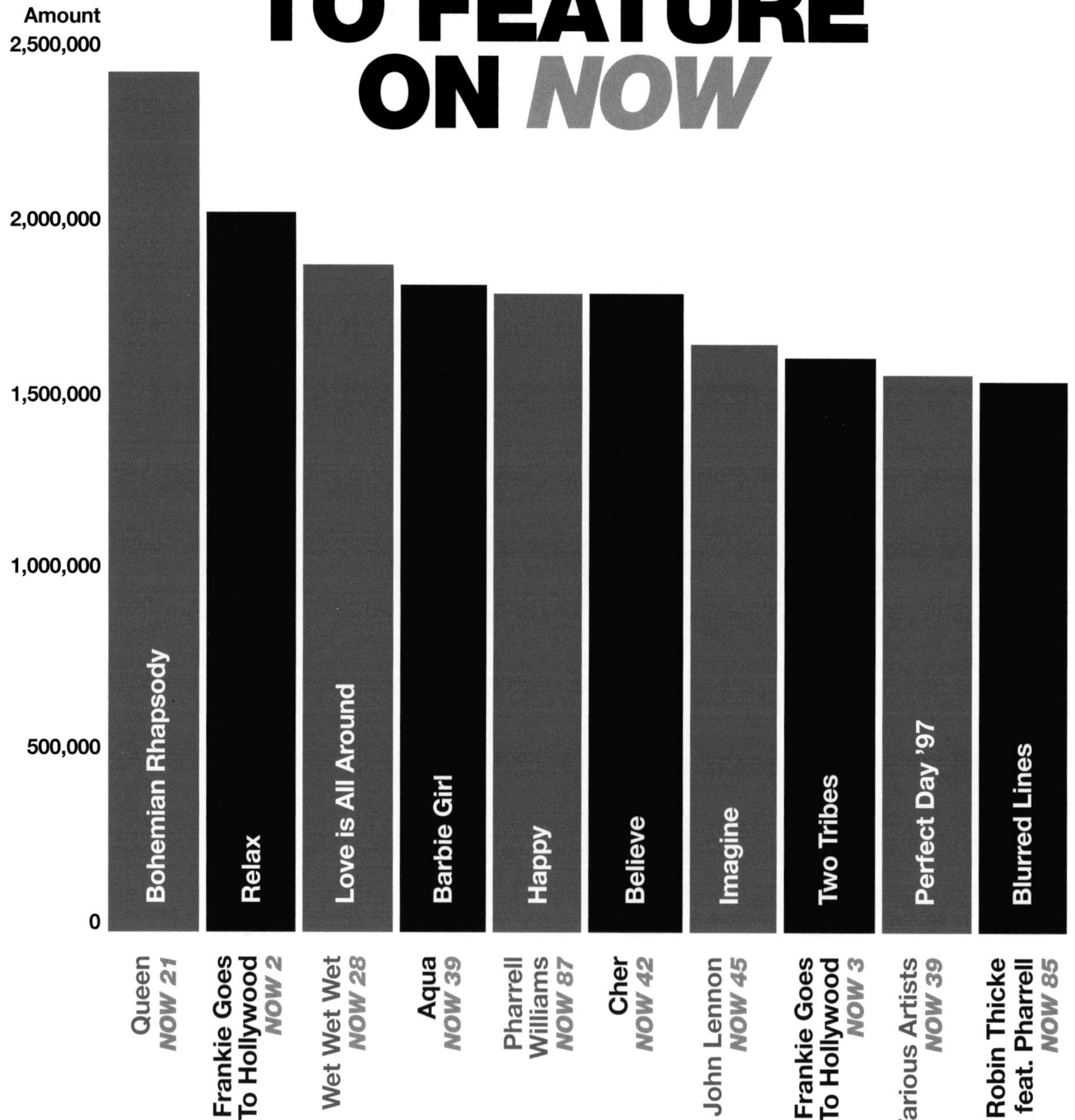

Amount
2,500,000
2,000,000
1,500,000
1,000,000
500,000
0

Bohemian Rhapsody
Relax
Love is All Around
Barbie Girl
Happy
Believe
Imagine
Two Tribes
Perfect Day '97
Blurred Lines

Queen *NOW 21*
Frankie Goes To Hollywood *NOW 2*
Wet Wet Wet *NOW 28*
Aqua *NOW 39*
Pharrell Williams *NOW 87*
Cher *NOW 42*
John Lennon *NOW 45*
Frankie Goes To Hollywood *NOW 3*
Various Artists *NOW 39*
Robin Thicke feat. Pharrell *NOW 85*

SIDE ONE, TRACK ONE

Five artists have opened *NOW* proceedings three or more times.

NOW 2	*NOW* 6	*NOW* 15	*NOW* 21	*NOW* 25	*NOW* 32	*NOW* 33	Queen
NOW 3	*NOW* 5	*NOW* 8					Duran Duran
NOW 12	*NOW* 28	*NOW* 31					Wet Wet Wet
NOW 34	*NOW* 35	*NOW* 36					Spice Girls
NOW 44	*NOW* 46	*NOW* 57					Britney Spears

Some artists have missed out on canonisation in *NOW* history. We tip a hat to these acts and note their number of Top 75 singles released since 1983.

MADONNA 70

MICHAEL BOLTON 17

METALLICA 19

BRUCE SPRINGSTEEN 18

GREEN DAY 22

GUNS N' ROSES 15

LINKIN PARK 17

SUPER FURRY ANIMALS 17

RED HOT CHILI PEPPERS 22

GLORIA ESTEFAN 27

SHAKIN' STEVENS 19

THE WEDDING PRESENT 17

ELVIS PRESLEY 40

NOW AND THE

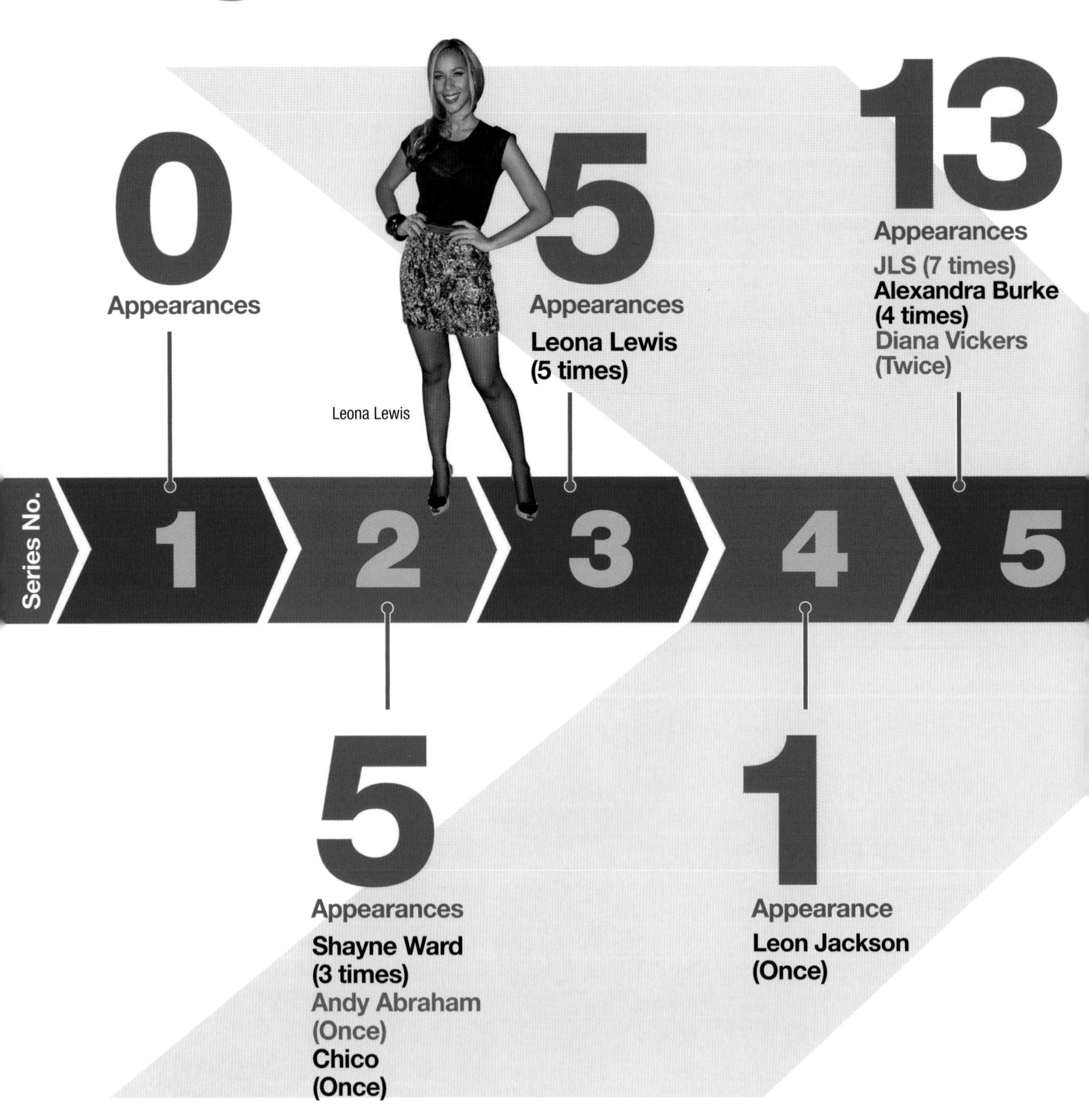
0
Appearances
Leona Lewis
5
Appearances
Leona Lewis
(5 times)
13
Appearances
JLS (7 times)
Alexandra Burke
(4 times)
Diana Vickers
(Twice)
Series No.
1
2
3
4
5
5
Appearances
Shayne Ward
(3 times)
Andy Abraham
(Once)
Chico
(Once)
1
Appearance
Leon Jackson
(Once)

X FACTOR

NOW appearances from former contestants. **Steve Brookstein** is the only winner absent.

One Direction

Jedward

Little Mix

EBENEEZER GOODE

- The main geezer ☑
- A real crowd pleaser ☑
- Refined ☑
- Sublime ☑
- Ever so good ☑
- Mischievous ☑
- Mysterious ☑
- Devious ☑
- Fun ☑
- Something of a genius ☑
- The love you could lose ☑
- The kind of geezer who must never be abused ☑
- A gentleman of leisure ☑
- There for your pleasure ☑
- The geezer who loves to muscle in ☑
- Kotcheled in the corner laughing by the bass bin ☑

The Shamen,
NOW 23, 1992

Kayleigh

Do you remember...

...chalk hearts melting
on a playground wall...
dawn escapes from moon
washed college halls...
the cherry blossom in
the market square...
I thought it was
confetti in our hair
...barefoot on the lawn
with shooting stars...
loving on the floor in
Belsize Park...dancing in
stilettoes in the snow...
you never understood I
had to go.

Marillion,
NOW 5, 1985

ONE better day **Madness** *NOW 3*

TWO princes **Spin Doctors** *NOW 26*

THREE lions '94 **Baddiel, Skinner, Lightning Seeds** *NOW 40*

FOUR letter word **Kim Wilde** *NOW 14*

FIVE colours in her hair **Mcfly** *NOW 64*

5, **SIX**, 7, 8 **Steps** *NOW 39*

Sailing on the **SEVEN** seas **OMD** *NOW 20*

Sexcrime (nineteen **EIGHT**y four) **Eurythmics** *NOW 4*

Cloud number **NINE** **Bryan Adams** *NOW 43*

TEN years asleep **Kingmaker** *NOW 25*

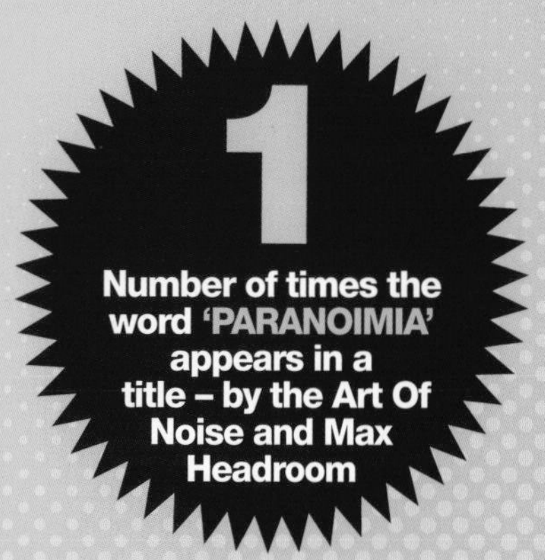

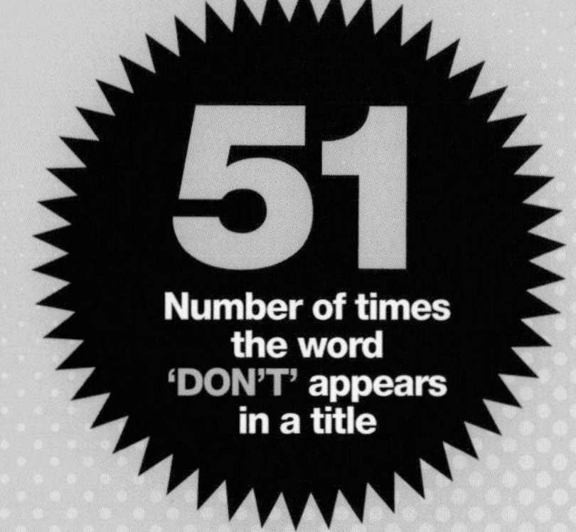

ALSO HAPPENING IN JULY 2006

- Twitter was launched
- A survey revealed that UK young people spend more time on the Internet than watching television
- The last weekly edition of *Top of the Pops* was broadcast after forty-two years on air
- At the cinema: *Pirates of the Caribbean: Dead Man's Chest*, *United 93*, *District 13*, *Superman Returns*, *The Break-Up*
- Albums released this summer included *Black Holes and Revelations* (**Muse**), *Alright, Still* (**Lily Allen**), *These Streets* (**Paolo Nutini**) and **Razorlight**'s self-titled debut album

TRACKLISTING NOW 64

CD1

1 *Crazy* Gnarls Barkley
2 *Maneater* Nelly Furtado
3 *From Paris To Berlin* Infernal
4 *Voodoo Child* Rogue Traders
5 *Don't Stop Me Now* McFly
6 *Who Knew* P!nk
7 *I Wish I Was A Punk Rocker (With Flowers In My Hair)* Sandi Thom
8 *She Moves In Her Own Way* The Kooks
9 *Fill My Little World* The Feeling
10 *Is It Any Wonder?* Keane
11 *You're All I Have* Snow Patrol
12 *In The Morning* Razorlight
13 *Bright Idea* Orson
14 *Valerie* The Zutons
15 *Bang Bang You're Dead* Dirty Pretty Things
16 *Monster* The Automatic
17 *Faster Kill Pussycat* Oakenfold feat. Brittany Murphy
18 *Stoned In Love* Chicane feat. Tom Jones
19 *Country Girl* Primal Scream
20 *Who Says You Can't Go Home* Bon Jovi
21 *Up All Night* Matt Willis
22 *Dance, Dance* Fall Out Boy

CD2

1 *Smile* Lily Allen
2 *SOS* Rihanna
3 *Pump It* The Black Eyed Peas
4 *Buttons* The Pussycat Dolls feat. Snoop Dogg
5 *So Sick* Ne-Yo
6 *Touch It* Busta Rhymes
7 *Say I* Christina Milian feat. Young Jeezy
8 *Mas Que Nada* Sérgio Mendes feat. The Black Eyed Peas
9 *Nine2five* The Ordinary Boys vs Lady Sovereign
10 *Red Dress* Sugababes
11 *Somebody's Watching Me* BeatFreakz
12 *First Time* Sunblock feat. Robin Beck
13 *World, Hold On (Children Of The Sky)* Bob Sinclar feat. Steve Edwards
14 *Tell Me Why* Supermode
15 *Horny As A Dandy* Mousse T. vs The Dandy Warhols
16 *Sensitivity* The Shapeshifters & Chic
17 *Piece Of My Heart* Beverley Knight
18 *You Give Me Something* James Morrison
19 *Who Am I* Will Young
20 *All Over Again* Ronan Keating and Kate Rusby
21 *Whole Lotta History* Girls Aloud

There's the tiniest of overlaps between MP3 and cassette in the history of *NOW* – this was the last to be released on tape, and only a very limited number were made available. CD remains the largest-selling format to this day.

Robin Beck holds the distinction of being the only chart-topping one-hit wonder to appear on *NOW* albums twice! Once with her original of 'First Time' on *NOW 14*, and again as a featured vocalist on *NOW 64* with **Sunblock**.

Ne-Yo, the former Shaffer Smith, has had five No.1 singles in the UK – the first of which, 'So Sick', is on *NOW 64*. Later in the series he appears on singles alongside **Kanye West**, **Pitbull**, **Calvin Harris** and **David Guetta** amongst others.

ALSO HAPPENING IN NOVEMBER 2006

- Nintendo released the Wii console
- At the cinema: *Borat*, *The History Boys*. Daniel Craig made his James Bond debut in *Casino Royale*
- Albums released in late 2006 included *9* (**Damien Rice**), *The Love Album* (**Westlife**) and *Beautiful World* (**Take That**). The Christmas No.1 was 'A Moment Like This' (**Leona Lewis**)
- Bestselling books published in 2006 included *Half of a Yellow Sun* (Chimamanda Ngozi Adichie), *The Boy in the Striped Pyjamas* (John Boyne), *New Moon* (Stephenie Meyer), and *The Road* (Cormac McCarthy)

TRACKLISTING NOW 65

CD1

1 *I Don't Feel Like Dancin'* **Scissor Sisters**
2 *Hips Don't Lie* **Shakira feat. Wyclef Jean**
3 *Something Kinda Ooooh* **Girls Aloud**
4 *Chelsea Dagger* **The Fratellis**
5 *Rehab* **Amy Winehouse**
6 *Wonderful World* **James Morrison**
7 *Lovelight* **Robbie Williams**
8 *Ain't No Other Man* **Christina Aguilera**
9 *SexyBack* **Justin Timberlake**
10 *Promiscuous* **Nelly Furtado feat. Timbaland**
11 *Déja Vu* **Beyoncé**
12 *Ridin'* **Chamillionaire feat. Krayzie Bone**
13 *Rock This Party (Everybody Dance Now)* **Bob Sinclar & Cutee B feat. Dollarman & Big Ali & Makedah**
14 *Put Your Hands Up For Detroit* **Fedde Le Grand**
15 *London Bridge* **Fergie**
16 *I Don't Need A Man* **The Pussycat Dolls**
17 *Sexy Love* **Ne-Yo**
18 *Me & U* **Cassie**
19 *It's Not That Easy* **Lemar**
20 *Unfaithful* **Rihanna**
21 *The Rose* **Westlife**
22 *Breaking Free* **Gabriella & Troy**

CD2

1 *America* **Razorlight**
2 *Chasing Cars* **Snow Patrol**
3 *Last Request* **Paolo Nutini**
4 *Nothing In My Way* **Keane**
5 *Never Be Lonely* **The Feeling**
6 *Empire* **Kasabian**
7 *When You Were Young* **The Killers**
8 *U + Ur Hand* **P!nk**
9 *LDN* **Lily Allen**
10 *Rock Steady* **All Saints**
11 *Coming Around Again* **Simon Webbe**
12 *Something About You* **Jamelia**
13 *Yeah Yeah* **Bodyrox feat. Luciana**
14 *Love Don't Let Me Go (Walking Away)* **David Guetta vs The Egg**
15 *Everytime We Touch* **Cascada**
16 *Borderline* **Michael Gray feat. Shelly Poole**
17 *Superfreak* **Beatfreakz**
18 *Chacarron* **El Chombo**
19 *Smiley Faces* **Gnarls Barkley**
20 *Star Girl* **McFly**
21 *Hey Kid* **Matt Willis**
22 *Jump In My Car* **David Hasselhoff**
23 *It's All Coming Back To Me Now* **Meat Loaf**

▶ **Snow Patrol**'s 'Chasing Cars' peaked at No.6 in the singles chart but has sold over a million copies to date. It currently holds the record for the most weeks within the Top 100.

▶ It was the first of six consecutive appearances for the late **Amy Winehouse** – including two entries on *NOW 68* where she also appeared as a featured vocalist on **Mark Ronson**'s 'Valerie'. The original **Zutons** version appeared first on *NOW 64*.

▶ 'Every Time We Touch' by Euro dance trio **Cascada** (four *NOW* appearances) was co-written by Maggie Reilly. Maggie provided the vocal on **Mike Oldfield**'s 'Moonlight Shadow' on the very first *NOW*.

ALSO HAPPENING IN APRIL 2007

- The Playstation 3 console was released in Europe
- At the Academy Awards, *The Departed* won four Oscars, including Best Film and Best Director. Helen Mirren was named as Best Actress for her role in *The Queen*
- At the cinema: *Hot Fuzz*, *Ghost Rider*, *300*, *The Hills Have Eyes II*
- Albums released in early 2007 included *Favourite Worst Nightmare* (Arctic Monkeys), *Introducing...Joss Stone* (**Joss Stone**), *The Best Damn Thing* (**Avril Lavigne**) and *Call Me Irresponsible* (**Michael Bublé**)
- *Deal or No Deal* began on television

TRACKLISTING NOW 66

CD1

1 *Grace Kelly* **MIKA**
2 *Ruby* **Kaiser Chiefs**
3 *Walk This Way* **Sugababes vs Girls Aloud**
4 *Patience* **Take That**
5 *What Goes Around... Comes Around* **Justin Timberlake**
6 *Say It Right* **Nelly Furtado**
7 *Irreplaceable* **Beyoncé**
8 *Lil Star* **Kelis feat. CeeLo**
9 *Smack That* **Akon feat. Eminem**
10 *Starz In Their Eyes* **Just Jack**
11 *Acceptable In The 80s* **Calvin Harris**
12 *Perfect (Exceeder)* **Mason vs Princess Superstar**
13 *Boogie 2Nite* **Booty Luv**
14 *Proper Education* **Eric Prydz vs Floyd**
15 *P.A.T.T. (Party All The Time)* **Sharam**
16 *Truly Madly Deeply* **Cascada**
17 *I Think We're Alone Now* **Girls Aloud**
18 *Last Night A DJ Saved My Life* **Seamus Haji feat. KayJay**
19 *The Creeps* **Camille Jones vs Fedde Le Grand**
20 *Beware Of The Dog* **Jamelia**
21 *Wind It Up* **Gwen Stefani**
22 *Too Little Too Late* **JoJo**
23 *A Moment Like This* **Leona Lewis**

CD2

1 *How To Save A Life* **The Fray**
2 *Same Jeans* **The View**
3 *Standing In The Way Of Control* **Gossip**
4 *Catch You* **Sophie Ellis-Bextor**
5 *Golden Skans* **Klaxons**
6 *This Ain't A Scene, It's An Arms Race* **Fall Out Boy**
7 *Read My Mind* **The Killers**
8 *Window In The Skies* **U2**
9 *She's Madonna* **Robbie Williams with Pet Shop Boys**
10 *Whistle For The Choir* **The Fratellis**
11 *I Luv U* **The Ordinary Boys**
12 *Open Your Eyes* **Snow Patrol**
13 *Before I Fall To Pieces* **Razorlight**
14 *She's My Man* **Scissor Sisters**
15 *Love It When You Call* **The Feeling**
16 *Sorry's Not Good Enough* **McFly**
17 *Alfie* **Lily Allen**
18 *Calm Down Dearest* **Jamie T**
19 *Easy* **Sugababes**
20 *You Know I'm No Good* **Amy Winehouse**
21 *I'm Gonna Be (500 Miles)* **The Proclaimers feat. Brian Potter & Andy Pipkin**

▶ The nearest **Pink Floyd** come to appearing on a *NOW* is here, where 'Another Brick In The Wall' was heavily sampled on 'Proper Education' by the coyly named **Eric Prydz vs Floyd. Scissor Sisters** covered 'Comfortably Numb' on *NOW 57.*

▶ Busy Dumfries-derived dance devotee **Calvin Harris** had to wait until *NOW 66* before opening his account but has already racked up seventeen appearances to date. If he keeps up that rate he'll overtake **Robbie Williams** by *NOW 106.*

▶ Despite only being released on December 20th, 'A Moment Like This' by **Leona Lewis** ended up as the best selling single of 2006, selling 50,000 downloads in its first half hour on sale. Leona appeared on five *NOW*s in total.

ALSO HAPPENING IN JULY 2007

- *Harry Potter and the Deathly Hallows* was published, the final book in the series. It became the fastest-selling book in history, selling more than 11 million copies on the day of release
- The UK smoking ban came into effect on 1 July
- The Concert for Diana was held at Wembley Stadium, featuring **Elton John** and **Tom Jones**, and hosted by Princes William and Harry
- At the cinema: *Harry Potter and the Order of the Phoenix*, *Die Hard 4.0*, *Shrek the Third*

TRACKLISTING NOW 67

CD1

1 *Umbrella* Rihanna feat. Jay-Z
2 *The Sweet Escape* Gwen Stefani feat. Akon
3 *Cupid's Chokehold/Breakfast In America* Gym Class Heroes
4 *Foundations* Kate Nash
5 *Girlfriend* Avril Lavigne
6 *Shine* Take That
7 *Do You Know? (The Ping Pong Song)* Enrique Iglesias
8 *Love Today* MIKA
9 *Real Girl* Mutya Buena
10 *Beautiful Liar* Beyoncé & Shakira
11 *Give It To Me* Timbaland feat. Justin Timberlake & Nelly Furtado
12 *Take Control* Amerie
13 *Candyman* Christina Aguilera
14 *Never Again* Kelly Clarkson
15 *Baby's Coming Back* McFly
16 *I Wanna Have Your Babies* Natasha Bedingfield
17 *Glamorous* Fergie feat. Ludacris
18 *LoveStoned/I Think She Knows* Justin Timberlake
19 *Because Of You* Ne-Yo
20 *I Wanna Love You* Akon Feat. Snoop Dogg
21 *Lost Without U* Robin Thicke

CD2

1 *Signal Fire* Snow Patrol
2 *Makes Me Wonder* Maroon 5
3 *Stop Me* Mark Ronson feat. Daniel Merriweather
4 *Here (In Your Arms)* Hellogoodbye
5 *Destination Calabria* Alex Gaudino feat. Crystal Waters
6 *Shine* Booty Luv
7 *The Girls* Calvin Harris
8 *Heavyweight Champion Of The World* Reverend and The Makers
9 *New Shoes* Paolo Nutini
10 *Dance Tonight* Paul McCartney
11 *Back To Black* Amy Winehouse
12 *Over My Head (Cable Car)* The Fray
13 *Either Way* The Twang
14 *Smokers Outside The Hospital Doors* Editors
15 *Your Love Alone Is Not Enough* Manic Street Preachers feat. Nina Persson
16 *Thnks Fr Th Mmrs* Fall Out Boy
17 *It's Not Over Yet* Klaxons
18 *Bigger Than Big* Super Mal feat. Luciana
19 *Get Down* Groove Armada feat. Stush and Red Rat
20 *What Am I Fighting For?* Unklejam
21 *Do It Again* The Chemical Brothers
22 *Sheila* Jamie T

▶ 'Beautiful Liar' co-writer Ian Dench also helped pen 'Tattoo' by **Jordin Sparks** on *NOW 71*. Dench however had appeared twice before (*NOW 19* and *NOW 31*) as guitarist and songwriter for west country indie ravers **E.M.F.**

▶ 'Lost Without You' by **Robin Thicke** reached No.11 in 2007. It would be another six years before Robin charted – and featured on *NOW* – again. However, he did so in some style – 'Blurred Lines' on *NOW 85* would become the biggest-selling single of 2013.

▶ Its 1–1 in the Nelly vs Kelly Name-Off on *NOW 67*. In total, the 'Kellys' are victorious with twenty-five appearances across the series, whereas the 'Nellys' still deliver a notable seventeen. **Kele Le Roc** is disqualified on a spelling technicality.

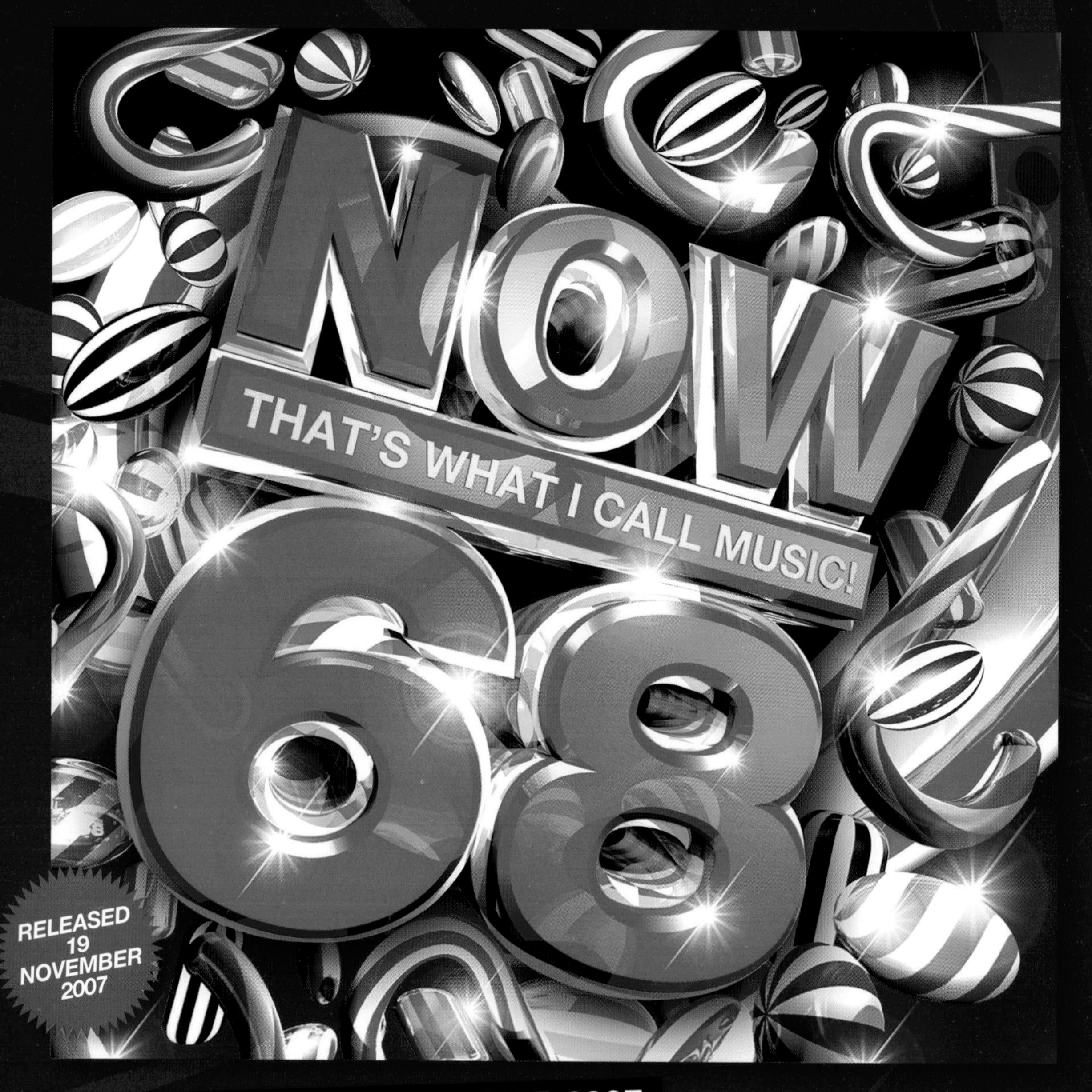

ALSO HAPPENING IN NOVEMBER 2007

- The iPhone became available in the UK
- The first Kindle e-reader were on sale in the US
- The High Speed 1 railway link opened between London and the Channel Tunnel
- Albums released in late 2007 included *Back Home* (**Westlife**), *Spirit* (**Leona Lewis**), *As I Am* (**Alicia Keys**), *X* (**Kylie Minogue**) and *Tangled Up* (**Girls Aloud**). The Christmas No.1 was 'When You Believe' (**Leon Jackson**)
- Bestselling books published in 2007 included *A Thousand Splendid Suns* (Khaled Hosseini) and *Eclipse* (Stephenie Meyer)

TRACKLISTING NOW 68

CD1

1 *Bleeding Love* Leona Lewis
2 *Rule The World* Take That
3 *2 Hearts* Kylie Minogue
4 *Valerie* Mark Ronson feat. Amy Winehouse
5 *About You Now* Sugababes
6 *Stronger* Kanye West
7 *Hot Stuff (Let's Dance)* Craig David
8 *Beautiful Girls* Sean Kingston
9 *No U Hang Up* Shayne Ward
10 *The Way I Are* Timbaland feat. Keri Hilson & D.O.E.
11 *Gimme More* Britney Spears
12 *Shut Up and Drive* Rihanna
13 *Sexy! No No No...* Girls Aloud
14 *With Every Heartbeat* Robyn And Kleerup
15 *Tired Of Being Sorry* Enrique Iglesias
16 *Song 4 Mutya (Out Of Control)* Groove Armada
17 *Like This Like That* Se:Sa feat. Sharon Phillips
18 *Let Me Think About It* Ida Corr vs Fedde Le Grand
19 *I Found U* Axwell feat. Max'C
20 *The Creeps (Get On The Dancefloor)* Freaks
21 *Waiting 4* Peter Gelderblom
22 *Love Is Gone* David Guetta and Chris Willis

CD2

1 *Hey There Delilah* Plain White T's
2 *1973* James Blunt
3 *Dream Catch Me* Newton Faulkner
4 *Worried About Ray* The Hoosiers
5 *She's So Lovely* Scouting For Girls
6 *1234* Feist
7 *In The Air Tonight* Phil Collins
8 *When You're Gone* Avril Lavigne
9 *The Heart Never Lies* McFly
10 *Mr Rock & Roll* Amy MacDonald
11 *Hold On* KT Tunstall
12 *Tranquilize* The Killers feat. Lou Reed
13 *It Means Nothing* Stereophonics
14 *Young Folks* Peter Bjorn And John feat. Victoria Bergsman
15 *Uninvited* Freemasons feat. Bailey Tzuke
16 *Big Girl (You Are Beautiful)* MIKA
17 *Tears Dry On Their Own* Amy Winehouse
18 *Do It Well* Jennifer Lopez
19 *Big Girls Don't Cry (Personal)* Fergie
20 *Don't Matter* Akon
21 *Baby Love* Nicole Scherzinger feat. will.i.am
22 *Home* Westlife

▶ **Lou Reed**'s most fondly remembered songs date from before the scope of the *NOW* series, but he did make a belated entrance as a credited artist on *NOW 68* alongside **The Killers**. *NOW 39*'s 'Perfect Day' was written and originally recorded by the former **Velvet Underground** vocalist.

▶ Farewell to daily activity describer **Craig David**, who appeared twice on *NOW 45*: solo with 'Fill Me In' and with **Artful Dodger** on 'Re-Rewind (The Crowd Say Bo Selecta)'.

▶ Incoming were piano-pummelling praise poets **Scouting For Girls** and future *X Factor* judge **Nicole Scherzinger**, who has clocked up eleven *NOW*s as a solo artist and leader of the **The Pussycat Dolls**.

ALSO HAPPENING IN MARCH 2008

- Heathrow Terminal 5 was opened by the Queen. Due to chaos with IT and baggage systems, over 500 flights were cancelled on the first day
- *No Country for Old Men* won four Oscars at the Academy Awards, including Best Picture and Best Director
- At the cinema: *Cloverfield*, *Rambo*
- Albums released in early 2008 included *11* (**Bryan Adams**) and *19*, the debut album from **Adele**. 2008 marked the 25th anniversary of **Michael Jackson**'s *Thriller*, which was re-released as *Thriller 25* with additional content

TRACKLISTING NOW 69

CD1

1 *Mercy* Duffy
2 *Don't Stop The Music* Rihanna
3 *Now You're Gone* Basshunter feat. DJ Mental Theo's Bazzheadz
4 *Call The Shots* Girls Aloud
5 *Rockstar* Nickelback
6 *Stop And Stare* OneRepublic
7 *Sun Goes Down* David Jordan
8 *Work* Kelly Rowland
9 *Crank That* Soulja Boy Tell'em
10 *Piece Of Me* Britney Spears
11 *Heartbroken* T2 feat. Jodie Aysha
12 *What's It Gonna Be* H "two" O feat. Platnum
13 *Come On Girl* Taio Cruz feat. Luciana
14 *Wow* Kylie Minogue
15 *Be Mine!* Robyn
16 *What Hurts The Most* Cascada
17 *Some Kinda Rush* Booty Luv
18 *Heater* Samim
19 *Just Fine* Mary J. Blige
20 *Ride It* Jay Sean
21 *Breathless* Shayne Ward
22 *When You Believe* Leon Jackson

CD2

1 *Chasing Pavements* Adele
2 *Apologize* Timbaland presents OneRepublic
3 *No One* Alicia Keys
4 *Happy Ending* MIKA
5 *Homecoming* Kanye West feat. Chris Martin
6 *Goodbye Mr A* The Hoosiers
7 *I Thought It Was Over* The Feeling
8 *Fascination* Alphabeat
9 *Elvis Ain't Dead* Scouting For Girls
10 *Just For Tonight* One Night Only
11 *Ready For The Floor* Hot Chip
12 *Flux* Bloc Party
13 *Something Good '08* Utah Saints
14 *The Journey Continues* Mark Brown feat. Sarah Cracknell
15 *This Is The Life* Amy MacDonald
16 *Pumpkin Soup* Kate Nash
17 *Change* Sugababes
18 *A&E* Goldfrapp
19 *Love Is A Losing Game* Amy Winehouse
20 *What A Wonderful World* Eva Cassidy & Katie Melua

▶ The first of four consecutive appearances for **Duffy**. 'Mercy' was co-written by Steve Booker who would help pen two more *NOW* entries with her in addition to **John Newman**'s 'Love Me Again' smash on *NOW 85*.

▶ It was **Katie Melua**'s final *NOW* appearance to date, with her (and **Eva Cassidy**'s) only No.1 single. The single holds the record for fewest weeks in the Top 40 for a chart topper, a record it shares with **Blur** ('Beetlebum', *NOW 36*) and **McFly** ('Baby's Coming Back', *NOW 67*).

▶ A *NOW* debut for **OneRepublic**. The band's Ryan Tedder however had already contributed to *NOW 68*, having written 'Bleeding Love' for **Leona Lewis**. He also returns later in the series writing for **Beyoncé** (*NOW 73*) **Ellie Goulding** (*NOW 86*) and **Ella Henderson** (*NOW 88*).

ALSO HAPPENING IN JULY 2008

- The Summer Olympics were held in Beijing. Great Britain won a total of forty-seven medals, with Chris Hoy winning three gold medals, and Bradley Wiggins and Rebecca Adlington winning two each. It was the most successful Olympics for Great Britain since 1908
- At the cinema: *The Incredible Hulk*, *Wall-E*, *Mamma Mia!*, *Kung Fu Panda*, *Hancock*
- Albums released in the summer of 2008 included *Breakout* (**Miley Cyrus**), *The Fame* (**Lady Gaga**), *One of the Boys* (**Katy Perry**) and *Viva la Vida* (**Coldplay**)

TRACKLISTING NOW 70

CD1

1 *American Boy* Estelle feat. Kanye West
2 *Dance Wiv Me* Dizzee Rascal feat. Calvin Harris & Chrome
3 *Singin' In The Rain* Mint Royale
4 *Black & Gold* Sam Sparro
5 *Warwick Avenue* Duffy
6 *Love Song* Sara Bareilles
7 *Sweet About Me* Gabriella Cilmi
8 *Closer* Ne-Yo
9 *Can't Speak French* Girls Aloud
10 *In My Arms* Kylie Minogue
11 *Denial* Sugababes
12 *S.O.S.* Jonas Brothers
13 *10,000 Nights* Alphabeat
14 *That's Not My Name* The Ting Tings
15 *Always Where I Need To Be* The Kooks
16 *Propane Nightmares* Pendulum
17 *I'm Not Gonna Teach Your Boyfriend How To Dance With You* Black Kids
18 *Heartbeat* Scouting For Girls
19 *Turn It Up* The Feeling
20 *Cops And Robbers* The Hoosiers
21 *Have You Made Up Your Mind* Paul Weller
22 *Violet Hill* Coldplay

CD2

1 *Take A Bow* Rihanna
2 *No Air* Jordin Sparks with Chris Brown
3 *Heartbreaker* will.i.am feat. Cheryl Cole
4 *Love In This Club* Usher feat. Young Jeezy
5 *Touch My Body* Mariah Carey
6 *Better In Time* Leona Lewis
7 *With You* Chris Brown
8 *Stay With Me (Everybody's Free)* Ironik
9 *I Can Be* Taio Cruz
10 *We Cry* The Script
11 *Break The Ice* Britney Spears
12 *Scream* Timbaland feat. Keri Hilson & Nicole Scherzinger
13 *Low* Flo Rida feat. T-Pain
14 *Wearing My Rolex* Wiley
15 *You Wot!* DJ Q feat. MC Bonez
16 *All I Ever Wanted* Basshunter
17 *Jumping All Over The World* Scooter
18 *Discolights* Ultrabeat vs Darren Styles
19 *Watch Out* Alex Gaudino feat. Shena
20 *Cry For You* September
21 *Toca's Miracle* Fragma

▶ *NOW 70* was the fastest-selling volume in the series to date, having sold over 380,000 copies in its first week in the shops.

▶ A new wave of R&B, hip hop and grime artists swept in, with first *NOW* representations for **Chris Brown, Wiley, Flo Rida, Dizzee Rascal** and **Usher**, all of whom have subsequently appeared on at least five editions and have forty-four entries between them.

▶ Having already scored nineteen Top 10 hits in the UK, multi-octaved throat warbler **Mariah Carey** came late to the *NOW* party, appearing for the first time on *NOW 55* with '(Boy) I Need You'. 'Touch My Body' is her last appearance to date.

ALSO HAPPENING IN NOVEMBER 2008

- Barack Obama was elected as US President
- Lewis Hamilton became the youngest-ever Formula One world champion
- Woolworths went into administration in the UK
- Albums released in late 2008 included *Out of Control* (**Girls Aloud**), *Fearless* (**Taylor Swift**) and *I Am... Sasha Fierce* (**Beyoncé**). The Christmas No.1 was 'Hallelujah' (**Alexandra Burke**)
- At the cinema: *Quantum of Solace*, *High School Musical 3*, *Saw V*
- Bestselling books published in 2008 included *Breaking Dawn* (Stephenie Meyer) and *The Hunger Games* (Suzanne Collins)

TRACKLISTING NOW 71

CD1

1 *The Promise* Girls Aloud
2 *I Kissed A Girl* Katy Perry
3 *So What* P!nk
4 *Sex On Fire* Kings of Leon
5 *All Summer Long* Kid Rock
6 *Disturbia* Rihanna
7 *Miss Independent* Ne-Yo
8 *When I Grow Up* The Pussycat Dolls
9 *Beggin'* Madcon
10 *Forever* Chris Brown
11 *Spotlight* Jennifer Hudson
12 *You Make It Real* James Morrison
13 *Changes* Will Young
14 *Tattoo* Jordin Sparks
15 *The Winner's Song* Geraldine McQueen
16 *Girls* Sugababes
17 *Up* The Saturdays
18 *Love You Anyway* Boyzone
19 *Hot N Cold* Katy Perry
20 *Raindrops (Encore Une Fois)* Sash! feat. Stunt
21 *Angel In The Night* Basshunter
22 *Pjanoo* Eric Prydz
23 *Paddy's Revenge* Steve Mac

CD2

1 *Viva La Vida* Coldplay
2 *The Man Who Can't Be Moved* The Script
3 *Wire To Wire* Razorlight
4 *5 Years Time* Noah and the Whale
5 *In This City* Iglu & Hartly
6 *Shut Up And Let Me Go* The Ting Tings
7 *Never Miss A Beat* Kaiser Chiefs
8 *Take Back The City* Snow Patrol
9 *Love Is Noise* The Verve
10 *Infinity 2008* Guru Josh Project
11 *Dream On* Christian Falk feat. Robyn
12 *Stepping Stone* Duffy
13 *Handlebars* Flobots
14 *Spiralling* Keane
15 *Lies* McFly
16 *Boyfriend* Alphabeat
17 *Mountains* Biffy Clyro
18 *I Like You So Much Better When You're Naked* Ida Maria
19 *The World Should Revolve Around Me* Little Jackie
20 *Cookie Jar* Gym Class Heroes feat. The-Dream
21 *She's Like A Star* Taio Cruz
22 *Love Shy (Thinking About You)* Platnum

▶ **Coldplay**'s 'Viva La Vida' became the first single to reach the top of the chart without a physical format. Download sales alone gave the band their first No.1 single.

▶ **Katy Perry** got up and running on *NOW 71* with her first two entries. Alongside **Robbie Williams** and **Emeli Sandé** she has appeared twice, twice. **Rihanna** however holds the multiple appearance record with two entries on five separate volumes.

▶ It was the last appearance to date for **Boyzone**, giving **Ronan Keating** a total of twenty-eight entries either solo or with the group, second only to **Robbie Williams.** Between 1995 and 2008 there was only one year when Ronan did not appear (2007, having a little rest).

ALSO HAPPENING IN APRIL 2009

- The BBC was fined £150,000 over 'Sachsgate', where Russell Brand and Jonathan Ross left offensive messages on the answering machine of actor Andrew Sachs
- At the cinema: *Marley & Me*, *The Boat That Rocked*
- Albums released in early 2009 included *It's Not Me, It's You* (**Lily Allen**) and *No Line on the Horizon* (**U2**)
- **Susan Boyle**'s performance of 'I Dreamed a Dream' from *Les Miserables* on *Britain's Got Talent* caused a sensation. The YouTube video of her performance has been viewed over 200 million times

TRACKLISTING NOW 72

CD1

1 *The Fear* **Lily Allen**
2 *Just Dance* **Lady Gaga feat. Colby O'Donis**
3 *Right Round* **Flo Rida feat. Ke$ha**
4 *The Boy Does Nothing* **Alesha Dixon**
5 *Just Can't Get Enough* **The Saturdays**
6 *My Life Would Suck Without You* **Kelly Clarkson**
7 *Take Me Back* **Tinchy Stryder feat. Taio Cruz**
8 *Day 'N' Nite* **Kid Cudi vs Crookers**
9 *Womanizer* **Britney Spears**
10 *Live Your Life* **T.I. feat. Rihanna**
11 *Right Now (Na Na Na)* **Akon**
12 *T-Shirt* **Shontelle**
13 *Mad* **Ne-Yo**
14 *Issues* **The Saturdays**
15 *Forgive Me* **Leona Lewis**
16 *The Loving Kind* **Girls Aloud**
17 *Can't Get Over* **September**
18 *Show Me Love* **Steve Angello & Laidback Luke feat. Robin S**
19 *Strong Again* **N-Dubz**
20 *Thinking Of You* **Katy Perry**
21 *Hallelujah* **Alexandra Burke**
22 *Hero* **X Factor Finalists 2008**

CD2

1 *Greatest Day* **Take That**
2 *Breathe Slow* **Alesha Dixon**
3 *Broken Strings* **James Morrison feat. Nelly Furtado**
4 *Love Story* **Taylor Swift**
5 *Sober* **P!nk**
6 *Human* **The Killers**
7 *Breakeven* **The Script**
8 *I'm Yours* **Jason Mraz**
9 *Don't Upset The Rhythm (Go Baby Go)* **Noisettes**
10 *Shake It* **Metro Station**
11 *Get On Your Boots* **U2**
12 *Kids* **MGMT**
13 *Omen* **The Prodigy**
14 *Let It Rock* **Kevin Rudolf feat. Lil Wayne**
15 *Cash In My Pocket* **Wiley feat. Daniel Merriweather**
16 *Heartless* **Kanye West**
17 *Dead And Gone* **T.I. feat. Justin Timberlake**
18 *Change* **Daniel Merriweather feat. Wale**
19 *Love etc.* **Pet Shop Boys**
20 *Rain On Your Parade* **Duffy**
21 *Islands In The Stream* **Vanessa Jenkins, Bryn West and Sir Tom Jones feat. Robin Gibb**

▶ 'Show Me Love' was a hit for **Robin S** all the way back in 1992 (*NOW* 24) and went on to hit the Top 75 in various remixed forms in 1997, 2002, 2006 and again here in 2009 in tandem with **Swedish House Mafia** don Steve Angello.

▶ 'Get On Your Boots' was at the time of writing the last appearance **U2** made on a *NOW* album. It was the first lead single from a **U2** album to miss No.1 since 1993. To date they have featured on nineteen *NOW*s since their debut on the fourth edition – no band containing a male musician has more credits.

▶ *NOW 72* was also the final edition **Pet Shop Boys** contributed to, and they did so as performers (with 'Love etc.') and songwriters: they co-wrote the **Girls Aloud** track 'The Loving Kind'.

ALSO HAPPENING IN JULY 2009

- **Michael Jackson**'s memorial service was watched by an estimated 1 billion people around the world
- Windows 7 was released by Microsoft
- It was announced that Teletext would cease broadcasting within six months after being available since the 1970s
- At the cinema: *Harry Potter and the Half-Blood Prince*, *Bruno*, *Ice Age 3*
- Albums released in summer 2009 included *Lungs* (**Florence + the Machine**), *Ocean Eyes* (**Owl City**), *Ready for the Weekend* (**Calvin Harris**) and *I Look to You* (**Whitney Houston**)

TRACKLISTING NOW 73

CD1

1 *Poker Face* Lady Gaga
2 *Evacuate The Dancefloor* Cascada
3 *When Love Takes Over* David Guetta feat. Kelly Rowland
4 *I'm Not Alone* Calvin Harris
5 *In For The Kill* La Roux
6 *Number 1* Tinchy Stryder feat. N-Dubz
7 *Jai Ho! (You Are My Destiny)* A.R. Rahman & The Pussycat Dolls feat. Nicole Scherzinger
8 *Diamond Rings* Chipmunk feat. Emeli Sandé
9 *Not Fair* Lily Allen
10 *Mama Do (Uh Oh, Uh Oh)* Pixie Lott
11 *Please Don't Leave Me* P!nk
12 *Untouched* The Veronicas
13 *Waking Up In Vegas* Katy Perry
14 *Untouchable* Girls Aloud
15 *Release Me* Agnes
16 *Heartbreak (Make Me A Dancer)* Freemasons feat. Sophie Ellis-Bextor
17 *Let's Get Excited* Alesha Dixon
18 *Work* The Saturdays
19 *Up All Night* Take That
20 *If U Seek Amy* Britney Spears
21 *Battlefield* Jordin Sparks
22 *Stuck With Each Other* Shontelle feat. Akon

CD2

1 *Halo* Beyoncé
2 *Red* Daniel Merriweather
3 *Knock You Down* Keri Hilson feat. Kanye West and Ne-Yo
4 *Love Sex Magic* Ciara feat. Justin Timberlake
5 *Boom Boom Pow* The Black Eyed Peas
6 *Kiss Me Thru The Phone* Soulja Boy Tell'Em feat. Sammie
7 *Beautiful* Akon feat. Kardinal Offishall and Colby O'Donis
8 *Sugar* Flo Rida feat. Wynter
9 *Tiny Dancer (Hold Me Closer)* Ironik feat. Chipmunk and Elton John
10 *I Know You Want Me (Calle Ocho)* Pitbull
11 *Bonkers* Dizzee Rascal & Armand Van Helden
12 *Warrior's Dance* The Prodigy
13 *Don't Trust Me* 3OH!3
14 *Fire* Kasabian
15 *Rabbit Heart (Raise It Up)* Florence + the Machine
16 *Never Forget You* Noisettes
17 *New In Town* Little Boots
18 *Please Don't Stop The Rain* James Morrison
19 *Candy* Paolo Nutini
20 *We Are The People* Empire of the Sun
21 *I Remember* deadmau5 & Kaskade
22 *Poppiholla* Chicane

▶ Two years and seven volumes before her breakout hits on *NOW 80* ('Read All About It' and 'Heaven'), **Emeli Sandé** made her first *NOW* appearance supporting **Chipmunk** and co-writing 'Diamond Rings'.

▶ *NOW 73* marks the only appearance to date for a song called 'Bonkers' (**Dizzee Rascal**, nine entries thus far). However, we have also had two 'Crazy's, one 'Mad', one 'Insane' and an 'Out Of My Head' (**John Newman**, *NOW 87*).

▶ **Pixie Lott**'s debut single 'Mama Do' started a run of five consecutive entries. Co-writer Phil Thornally played bass on **The Cure**'s 'Love Cats' taking us right back to the very first volume in 1983. He also co-wrote 'Torn' by **Natalie Imbruglia** on *NOW 39*.

ALSO HAPPENING IN NOVEMBER 2009

- At the cinema: *The Men who Stare at Goats*, *2012*, *The Twilight Saga: New Moon*
- **Lady Gaga** began her Monster's Ball tour
- Albums released included *Reality Killed the Video Star* (**Robbie Williams**), *Against All Odds* (**N-Dubz**), *My World* (**Justin Bieber**), *The Fame Monster* (**Lady Gaga**) and *Rated R* (**Rihanna**). Christmas No.1 was 'Killing in the Name of' (**Rage Against the Machine**)
- Bestsellers published in 2009 included *The Lost Symbol* (Dan Brown) and *The Girl Who Played With Fire* (Stieg Larsson)

TRACKLISTING NOW 74

CD1

1 *Fight For This Love* Cheryl Cole
2 *Haven't Met You Yet* Michael Bublé
3 *I Gotta Feeling* The Black Eyed Peas
4 *Sexy Chick* David Guetta feat. Akon
5 *Bulletproof* La Roux
6 *Break Your Heart* Taio Cruz
7 *I Need You* N-Dubz
8 *Whatcha Say* Jason Derülo
9 *Down* Jay Sean feat. Lil Wayne
10 *To Love Again* Alesha Dixon
11 *Oopsy Daisy* Chipmunk feat. Dayo Olatunji
12 *Never Leave You* Tinchy Stryder feat. Amelle
13 *Remedy* Little Boots
14 *Boys And Girls* Pixie Lott
15 *Left My Heart In Tokyo* Mini Viva
16 *Fire Burning* Sean Kingston
17 *Hotel Room Service* Pitbull feat. Nicole Scherzinger
18 *Get Sexy* Sugababes
19 *Forever Is Over* The Saturdays
20 *I Got Soul* Young Soul Rebels
21 *I Need You Now* Agnes
22 *Beat Again* JLS

CD2

1 *Paparazzi* Lady Gaga
2 *Sweet Dreams* Beyoncé
3 *She Wolf* Shakira
4 *Run This Town* Jay-Z feat. Rihanna and Kanye West
5 *Supernova* Mr Hudson feat. Kanye West
6 *Bodies* Robbie Williams
7 *Holiday* Dizzee Rascal
8 *Ready For The Weekend* Calvin Harris
9 *Million Dollar Bill* Whitney Houston
10 *Get Shaky* The Ian Carey Project
11 *End Credits* Chase & Status feat. Plan B
12 *Sweet Disposition* The Temper Trap
13 *Uprising* Muse
14 *Just Say Yes* Snow Patrol
15 *You've Got The Love* Florence + the Machine
16 *22* Lily Allen
17 *Pencil Full Of Lead* Paolo Nutini
18 *We Are Golden* MIKA
19 *Good Girls Go Bad* Cobra Starship feat. Leighton Meester
20 *Little Lion Man* Mumford & Sons
21 *The Day I Died* Just Jack
22 *Outta Here* Esmée Denters
23 *Ghosts 'n' Stuff* deadmau5 feat. Rob Swire

▶ Canadian charmer **Michael Bublé** reached the Top 10 of the singles chart for the first time with 'Haven't Met You Yet'. The parent album, *Crazy Love*, has now sold over 3 million copies and as of early 2014 was declared the 25th bestselling album of all time in the UK.

▶ **Whitney Houston**'s last Top 10 hit was 'Million Dollar Bill', and perhaps surprisingly it was the only time one of her singles would appear on a *NOW*.

▶ Hailing from Teignmouth in Devon, **Muse**'s only inclusion on a *NOW* came with their eighteenth Top 40 hit. Other Devonians to feature over the years include **Military Wives**, **Ben Howard**, Chris Martin of **Coldplay**, **Snowy White**, Beth Gibbons of **Portishead** and Dave Hill from **Slade**.

ALSO HAPPENING IN MARCH 2010

- *The Hurt Locker* won 6 Academy Awards, including Best Picture. Sandra Bullock was awarded the Best Actress Oscar for *The Blind Side*
- Actor Corey Haim, best known for his role in *The Lost Boys*, died at the age of thirty-eight
- At the cinema: *Tim Burton's Alice in Wonderland*, *The Girl with the Dragon Tattoo*, *Green Zone*, *Shutter Island*

TRACKLISTING NOW 75

CD1

1 *Bad Romance* Lady Gaga
2 *Starstrukk* 3OH!3 feat. Katy Perry
3 *Meet Me Halfway* The Black Eyed Peas
4 *Everybody In Love* JLS
5 *Replay* Iyaz
6 *Pass Out* Tinie Tempah
7 *TiK ToK* Ke$ha
8 *If We Ever Meet Again* Timbaland feat. Katy Perry
9 *In My Head* Jason Derülo
10 *Rude Boy* Rihanna
11 *Look For Me* Chipmunk feat. Talay Riley
12 *Don't Stop Believin'* Glee Cast
13 *On A Mission* Gabriella Cilmi
14 *Broken Heels* Alexandra Burke
15 *About A Girl* Sugababes
16 *Ego* The Saturdays
17 *Under Pressure (Ice Ice Baby)* Jedward feat. Vanilla Ice
18 *One Time* Justin Bieber
19 *Do You Remember* Jay Sean feat. Sean Paul & Lil Jon
20 *Cry Me Out* Pixie Lott
21 *The Climb* Joe McElderry
22 *Everybody Hurts* Helping Haiti

CD2

1 *Empire State Of Mind (Part II) Broken Down* Alicia Keys
2 *Fireflies* Owl City
3 *Young Forever* Jay-Z feat. Mr Hudson
4 *3 Words* Cheryl Cole feat. will.i.am
5 *You Know Me* Robbie Williams
6 *Don't Stop Believin'* Journey
7 *Dog Days Are Over* Florence + the Machine
8 *Hollywood* Marina & The Diamonds
9 *Starry Eyed* Ellie Goulding
10 *Many Of Horror* Biffy Clyro
11 *Stay Too Long* Plan B
12 *Never Be Your Woman* Naughty Boy presents Wiley feat. Emeli Sandé
13 *Won't Go Quietly* Example
14 *Riverside (Let's Go)* Sidney Samson feat. Wizard Sleeve
15 *Why Don't You* Gramophonedzie
16 *The Way Love Goes* Lemar
17 *Playing With Fire* N-Dubz feat. Mr Hudson
18 *Opposite Of Adults* Chiddy Bang
19 *BedRock* Young Money feat. Lloyd
20 *My Name* McLean
21 *Russian Roulette* Rihanna

▶ 'The inclusion of 'Don't Stop Believin' marked the only occasion an original and cover version of the same song have appeared on the same edition.

▶ **Marina and the Diamonds** 'Hollywood' was another successful single from Richard Stannard's Biffco production team. They have been responsible for over twenty entries since *NOW 31*, including five hits by the **Spice Girls** alone.

▶ The **Sugababes** take a long bath after nineteen appearances and three line-up changes (with only Heidi Range surviving since their very first entry on *NOW 52*). They are second only to **Girls Aloud** as the group with most entries.

NOW GEOGRAPHY

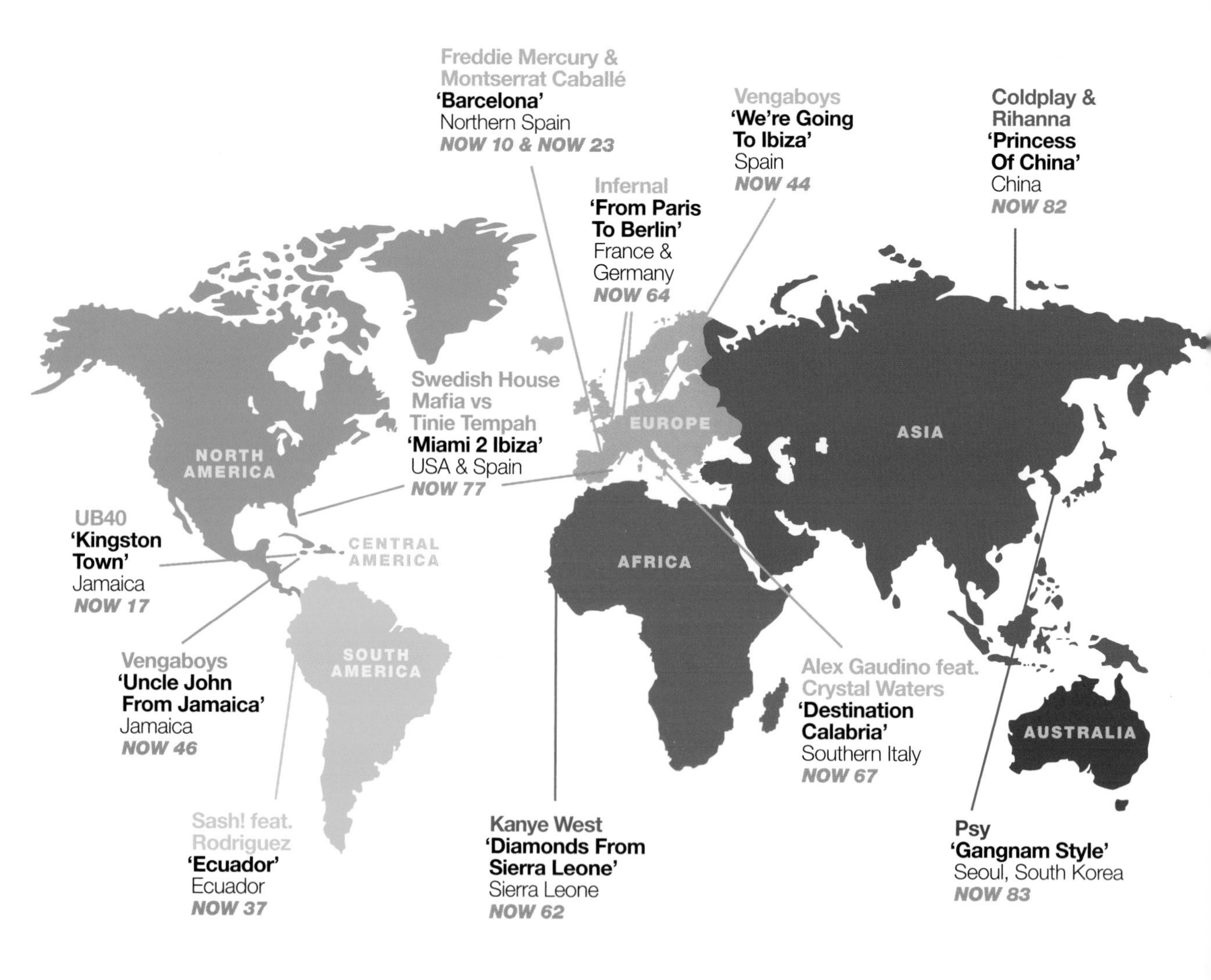

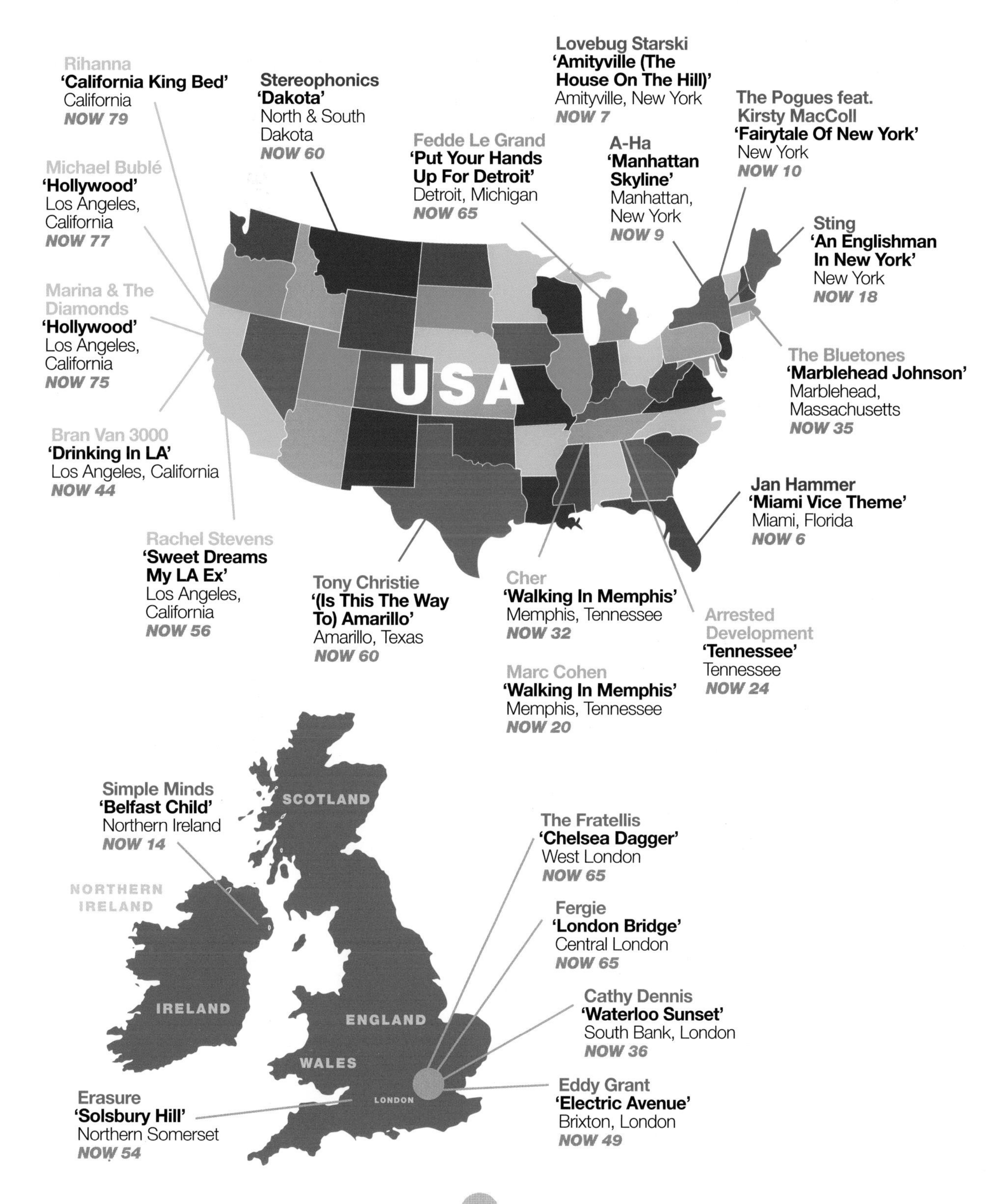
Rihanna
'California King Bed'
California
NOW 79
Stereophonics
'Dakota'
North & South Dakota
NOW 60
Lovebug Starski
'Amityville (The House On The Hill)'
Amityville, New York
NOW 7
The Pogues feat. Kirsty MacColl
'Fairytale Of New York'
New York
NOW 10
Fedde Le Grand
'Put Your Hands Up For Detroit'
Detroit, Michigan
NOW 65
A-Ha
'Manhattan Skyline'
Manhattan, New York
NOW 9
Michael Bublé
'Hollywood'
Los Angeles, California
NOW 77
Sting
'An Englishman In New York'
New York
NOW 18
Marina & The Diamonds
'Hollywood'
Los Angeles, California
NOW 75
USA
The Bluetones
'Marblehead Johnson'
Marblehead, Massachusetts
NOW 35
Bran Van 3000
'Drinking In LA'
Los Angeles, California
NOW 44
Jan Hammer
'Miami Vice Theme'
Miami, Florida
NOW 6
Rachel Stevens
'Sweet Dreams My LA Ex'
Los Angeles, California
NOW 56
Tony Christie
'(Is This The Way To) Amarillo'
Amarillo, Texas
NOW 60
Cher
'Walking In Memphis'
Memphis, Tennessee
NOW 32
Arrested Development
'Tennessee'
Tennessee
NOW 24
Marc Cohen
'Walking In Memphis'
Memphis, Tennessee
NOW 20
Simple Minds
'Belfast Child'
Northern Ireland
NOW 14
SCOTLAND
NORTHERN IRELAND
The Fratellis
'Chelsea Dagger'
West London
NOW 65
Fergie
'London Bridge'
Central London
NOW 65
IRELAND
ENGLAND
Cathy Dennis
'Waterloo Sunset'
South Bank, London
NOW 36
WALES
LONDON
Erasure
'Solsbury Hill'
Northern Somerset
NOW 54
Eddy Grant
'Electric Avenue'
Brixton, London
NOW 49

THE BACKROOM BOYS

A hearty pat on the back and firm handshakes to the songwriter/producer teams behind the hits.

'Michael Caine'
Madness
NOW 2

'Nelson Mandela'
Special AKA
NOW 3

'Robert De Niro's Waiting'
Bananarama
NOW 3

'Brimful of Asha (Norman Cook Mix)'
Cornershop
NOW 39

'The Ballad of Tom Jones'
Space with Cerys Matthews
NOW 39

'Clint Eastwood'
Gorillaz
NOW 48

CELEBRITY SQUARES

'James Dean'
Daniel Bedingfield
NOW 53

'Grace Kelly'
Mika
NOW 66

'She's Madonna'
Robbie Williams with Pet Shop Boys
NOW 66

'Barbra Streisand'
Duck Sauce
NOW 77

'Moves Like Jagger'
Maroon 5 with Christina Aguilera
NOW 80

'Walks Like Rihanna'
The Wanted
NOW 85

PHARRELL WILLIAMS:

As a songwriter, producer and performer Pharrell has bee

NOW 22

A twenty-year-old Pharrell's vocals were heard on SWV's 'Right Here'. He also had a hand in the song's production.

NOW 45

Wrote and produced 'Caught Out There' by Kelis with Chad Hugo as part of The Neptunes team. 'Milkshake' later appeared on *NOW 57* from the same grouping.

NOW 57 & 58

Having formed N.E.R.D. with Shay Haley, Pharrell and Hugo appeared on *NOW*s as performers with 'She Wants To Move' and 'Maybe'.

A 'HAPPY' ENDING

uietly racking up *NOW* appearances for longer than you might have thought.

NOW 50

The Neptunes wrote and produced 'I'm A Slave 4 U' for Britney Spears.

NOWs 52, 54 & 56

The Neptunes were behind *NSYNC's 'Girlfriend' and solo singles by band member Justin Timberlake, 'Like I Love You' and 'Rock Your Body'.

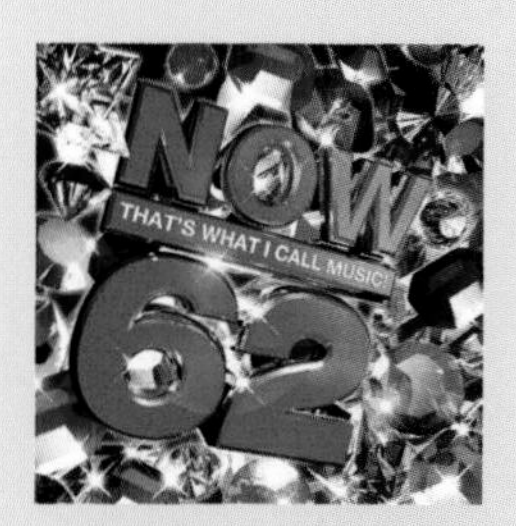

NOW 62

A first solo credit on a *NOW*. 'Can I Have It Like That' featured Gwen Stefani, whose solo single 'Wind It Up' on *NOW 66* was produced by Williams.

NOW 76

Pharrell contributed vocals to Swedish House Mafia's 'One'.

NOW 87

'Happy' topped the UK chart on a record three separate occasions.

ALSO HAPPENING IN JULY 2010

- The Wikileaks website published over 90,000 documents on the United States' role in the war in Afghanistan
- Apple launched the iPad in the UK
- Albums released in summer 2010 included *Can't Be Tamed* (**Miley Cyrus**), *Night Work* (**Scissor Sisters**), *Recovery* (**Eminem**) and *Aphrodite* (**Kylie Minogue**)
- At the cinema: *Inception*, *Toy Story 3*, *The Twilight Saga: Eclipse*, *Shrek Forever After*
- The final episode of *The Bill* was broadcast after twenty-six years on television

TRACKLISTING NOW 76

CD1

1 *California Gurls* Katy Perry feat. Snoop Dogg
2 *I Like It* Enrique Iglesias feat. Pitbull
3 *The Club Is Alive* JLS
4 *OMG* Usher feat. will.i.am
5 *Gettin' Over You* David Guetta
6 *All The Lovers* Kylie Minogue
7 *Just Be Good To Green* Professor Green feat. Lily Allen
8 *Nothin' On You* B.o.B feat. Bruno Mars
9 *Alejandro* Lady Gaga
10 *Parachute* Cheryl Cole
11 *Te Amo* Rihanna
12 *Good Times* Roll Deep
13 *Commander* Kelly Rowland feat. David Guetta
14 *Dirtee Disco* Dizzee Rascal
15 *We No Speak Americano* Yolanda Be Cool & DCUP
16 *Hot* Inna
17 *Stereo Love* Edward Maya feat. Vika Jigulina
18 *Eenie Meenie* Sean Kingston and Justin Bieber
19 *Can't Be Tamed* Miley Cyrus
20 *Turn It Up* Pixie Lott
21 *Baby* Justin Bieber feat. Ludacris
22 *Solo* Iyaz
23 *Carry Out* Timbaland feat. Justin Timberlake

CD2

1 *She Said* Plan B
2 *This Ain't A Love Song* Scouting for Girls
3 *Wavin' Flag* K'NAAN
4 *Ridin' Solo* Jason Derülo
5 *Try Sleeping With A Broken Heart* Alicia Keys
6 *She's Always A Woman* Fyfe Dangerfield
7 *Hey, Soul Sister* Train
8 *Fire With Fire* Scissor Sisters
9 *Once* Diana Vickers
10 *Kickstarts* Example
11 *One (Your Name)* Swedish House Mafia feat. Pharrell
12 *Rock That Body* The Black Eyed Peas
13 *All Night Long* Alexandra Burke feat. Pitbull
14 *Candy* Aggro Santos feat. Kimberly Wyatt
15 *Dirty Picture* Taio Cruz feat. Ke$ha
16 *Until You Were Gone* Chipmunk feat. Esmee Denters
17 *Rescue Me* Skepta
18 *We Dance On* N-Dubz feat. Bodyrox
19 *Dancing On My Own* Robyn
20 *You Got The Dirtee Love* Florence + the Machine & Dizzee Rascal
21 *Acapella* Kelis
22 *Frisky* Tinie Tempah
23 *Watercolour* Pendulum

▶ **Bruno Mars** is a prolific songwriter as well as a performer – he had a hand in 'Get Sexy' by **Sugababes** (*NOW 74*), **Cee Lo Green**'s 'Forget You' (*NOW 77*) and **The Vamps**' 'Can We Dance' (*NOW 86*) in addition to tracks where he is credited as an artist.

▶ **Timbaland** made his name as a producer but appeared seven times on *NOW*s as a performer, each time featuring a different guest – joining him at various times have been **Nelly Furtado** (*NOW 65*), **OneRepublic** (*NOW 69*), **Katy Perry** (*NOW 75*) and **Justin Timberlake** (*NOW 76*).

▶ **Vika Jigulina** is the only credited Moldovan in the entire series. Her 'Stereo Love' partner **Edward Maya** was born in Romania, as was Michael Cretu of **Enigma** (*NOW*s *19* and *27*).

ALSO HAPPENING IN NOVEMBER 2010

- Prince William and Catherine Middleton announced their engagement
- At the cinema: *Despicable Me*, *Harry Potter and the Deathly Hallows Part 1*, *Due Date*, *The Social Network*
- Albums released included *Messy Little Raindrops* (**Cheryl Cole**), *Some Kind of Trouble* (**James Blunt**), *Loud* (**Rihanna**) and *Progress* (**Take That**). The Christmas No.1 was 'When We Collide' (**Matt Cardle**)
- Bestselling books published in 2010 included *The Girl Who Kicked the Hornets' Nest* (Stieg Larsson) and *Our Kind of Traitor* (John le Carré)

TRACKLISTING NOW 77

CD1

1 *Only Girl (In The World)* Rihanna
2 *Firework* Katy Perry
3 *Promise This* Cheryl Cole
4 *Club Can't Handle Me* Flo Rida feat. David Guetta
5 *Forget You* Cee Lo Green
6 *Dynamite* Taio Cruz
7 *Written In The Stars* Tinie Tempah feat. Eric Turner
8 *Cooler Than Me* Mike Posner
9 *Heartbeat* Enrique Iglesias feat. Nicole Scherzinger
10 *DJ Got Us Fallin' In Love* Usher feat. Pitbull
11 *All Time Low* The Wanted
12 *Please Don't Let Me Go* Olly Murs
13 *Pack Up* Eliza Doolittle
14 *Hollywood* Michael Bublé
15 *Get Outta My Way* Kylie Minogue
16 *Higher* The Saturdays feat. Flo Rida
17 *Green Light* Roll Deep
18 *Beautiful Monster* Ne-Yo
19 *Barbra Streisand* Duck Sauce
20 *Miami 2 Ibiza* Swedish House Mafia vs Tinie Tempah
21 *In My System* Tinchy Stryder
22 *My Wicked Heart* Diana Vickers

CD2

1 *Just The Way You Are* Bruno Mars
2 *Airplanes* B.o.B feat. Hayley Williams of Paramore
3 *For The First Time* The Script
4 *Shame* Robbie Williams and Gary Barlow
5 *Make You Feel My Love* Adele
6 *Slow* Rumer
7 *Impossible* Shontelle
8 *Just A Dream* Nelly
9 *Let The Sun Shine* Labrinth
10 *Billionaire* Travie McCoy feat. Bruno Mars
11 *Drummer Boy* Alesha Dixon
12 *Bang Bang Bang* Mark Ronson & The Business Intl
13 *Crossfire* Brandon Flowers
14 *The Cave* Mumford & Sons
15 *Prayin'* Plan B
16 *2012 (It Ain't The End)* Jay Sean feat. Nicki Minaj
17 *Best Behaviour* N-Dubz
18 *What If* Jason Derülo
19 *Broken Arrow* Pixie Lott
20 *Ambitions* Joe McElderry
21 *Party Girl* McFly
22 *Katy On A Mission* Katy B

▶ *NOW 77* was the highest selling release since *NOW 56* in 2003 and featured twelve No.1 singles, a record it held until the release of *NOW 88*.

▶ Über producer Trevor Horn's credits span almost the entire series, starting off with 'Double Dutch' by **Malcolm McLaren** on the very first *NOW*, right up to this Robbie and Gary duet on *NOW 77*.

▶ **Adele** delivered the second of only two **Bob Dylan** covers across the entire series (and he never appears in person). The first? Our old friends **UB40** performing 'I'll Be Your Baby Tonight' with **Robert Palmer** on *NOW 18*.

ALSO HAPPENING IN APRIL 2011

- Prince William and Catherine Middleton were married, watched by an estimated 2 billion people around the world (24.5 million in the UK alone). The wedding day was a public holiday in the UK
- At the Academy Awards, *The King's Speech* won four Oscars including Best Picture and Best Actor for Colin Firth
- At the cinema: *Rio*, *Fast and Furious Five*, *Oranges and Sunshine*, *Sucker Punch*
- Albums released in early 2011 included *21* (**Adele**), *Let England Shake* (**PJ Harvey**) and *Femme Fatale* (**Britney Spears**)

TRACKLISTING NOW 78

CD1

1 *Grenade* Bruno Mars
2 *Rolling In The Deep* Adele
3 *Do It Like A Dude* Jessie J
4 *S&M* Rihanna
5 *We R Who We R* Ke$ha
6 *Gold Forever* The Wanted
7 *When We Collide* Matt Cardle
8 *The Flood* Take That
9 *Your Song* Ellie Goulding
10 *Eyes Wide Shut* JLS feat. Tinie Tempah
11 *Who's That Chick?* David Guetta
12 *Higher* Taio Cruz feat. Travie McCoy
13 *Yeah 3X* Chris Brown
14 *Hold It Against Me* Britney Spears
15 *Happiness* Alexis Jordan
16 *Louder* Parade
17 *Thinking Of Me* Olly Murs
18 *What The Hell* Avril Lavigne
19 *Shine A Light* McFly feat. Taio Cruz
20 *L.I.F.E.G.O.E.S.O.N.* Noah and the Whale
21 *I Know Him So Well* Peter Kay and Comic Relief presents Susan Boyle and Geraldine McQueen

CD2

1 *Price Tag* Jessie J
2 *Champion* Chipmunk feat. Chris Brown
3 *Black And Yellow* Wiz Khalifa
4 *What's My Name?* Rihanna feat. Drake
5 *The Time (Dirty Bit)* The Black Eyed Peas
6 *Poison* Nicole Scherzinger
7 *Tonight (I'm Lovin' You)* Enrique Iglesias feat. Ludacris and DJ Frank E
8 *Bright Lights Bigger City* Cee Lo Green feat. Wiz Khalifa
8 *E.T.* Katy Perry feat. Kanye West
9 *F**kin' Perfect* P!nk
10 *Wonderman* Tinie Tempah
11 *Whip My Hair* Willow
12 *Lights On* Katy B feat. Ms Dynamite
13 *Hello* Martin Solveig feat. Dragonette
14 *Who Dat Girl* Flo Rida feat. Akon
15 *Like A G6* Far East Movement feat. The Cataracs & Dev
16 *Traktor* Wretch 32 feat. L
17 *Like U Like* Aggro Santos feat. Kimberley Walsh
18 *Runaway* Devlin feat. Yasmin
19 *Let It Rain* Tinchy Stryder feat. Melanie Fiona
20 *Blind Faith* Chase & Status feat. Liam Bailey

▶ **Jessie J** is one of eight female artists who has appeared twice on the same volume, a trend that started with **Tina Turner** on *NOW 6*. These were her first two hit singles.
▶ **Willow Smith** – daughter of *NOW* veteran Will – is the youngest credited performer in the series. She was nine years old when 'Whip My Hair' was a hit.
▶ **Susan Boyle** holds the record for the fastest-selling debut album in history, having chalked up over 411,000 sales of *I Dreamed A Dream* in the first week on sale. Her sole credited *NOW* appearance was here with 'I Know Him So Well' but she did also feature on **Helping Haiti**'s 'Everybody Hurts'.

ALSO HAPPENING IN JULY 2011

- After 168 years in existence, the final edition of the *News of the World* was published in the wake of the phone-hacking scandal
- Singer **Amy Winehouse** died at the age of twenty-seven
- At the cinema: *Harry Potter and the Deathly Hallows Part 2*, *Captain America: the First Avenger*, *Horrible Bosses*, *Cars 2*
- Albums released in summer 2011 included *Killer Sounds* (**Hard-Fi**), *I'm With You* (**Red Hot Chili Peppers**), *Love?* (**Jennifer Lopez**) and *Born This Way* (**Lady Gaga**)

TRACKLISTING NOW 79

CD1

1 *Someone Like You* Adele
2 *I Need A Dollar* Aloe Blacc
3 *The Lazy Song* Bruno Mars
4 *Don't Wanna Go Home* Jason Derülo
5 *Born This Way* Lady Gaga
6 *On The Floor* Jennifer Lopez
7 *Mr. Saxobeat* Alexandra Stan
8 *Last Friday Night (T.G.I.F.)* Katy Perry
9 *Glad You Came* The Wanted
10 *Don't Hold Your Breath* Nicole Scherzinger
11 *Just Can't Get Enough* The Black Eyed Peas
12 *Love Love* Take That
13 *Nobody's Perfect* Jessie J
14 *Notorious* The Saturdays
15 *California King Bed* Rihanna
16 *Love How It Hurts* Scouting for Girls
17 *Every Teardrop Is A Waterfall* Coldplay
18 *I Want You (Hold On To Love)* Cee Lo Green
19 *Finish Line* Yasmin
20 *The A Team* Ed Sheeran
21 *Skinny Love* Birdy
22 *One Big Family* Templecloud

CD2

1 *Give Me Everything* Pitbull feat. Ne-Yo, Afrojack & Nayer
2 *Party Rock Anthem* LMFAO feat. Lauren Bennett & GoonRock
3 *Louder* DJ Fresh feat. Sian Evans
4 *Changed The Way You Kiss Me* Example
5 *Where Them Girls At* David Guetta feat. Nicki Minaj & Flo Rida
6 *Beautiful People* Chris Brown feat. Benny Benassi
7 *Bounce* Calvin Harris feat. Kelis
8 *How We Roll* Loick Essien feat. Tanya Lacey
9 *Super Bass* Nicki Minaj
10 *Spaceship* Tinchy Stryder feat. Dappy
11 *Unorthodox* Wretch 32 feat. Example
12 *Badman Riddim (Jump)* Vato Gonzalez feat. Foreign Beggars
13 *Sweat* Snoop Dogg vs David Guetta
14 *Save The World* Swedish House Mafia
15 *Bass Down Low* DEV feat. The Cataracs
16 *Buzzin'* Mann feat. 50 Cent
17 *Hitz* Chase & Status feat. Tinie Tempah
18 *Broken Record* Katy B
19 *Guilt* Nero
20 *What A Feeling* Alex Gaudino feat. Kelly Rowland
21 *Dirty Talk* Wynter Gordon
22 *Sun Is Up* Inna

▶ In the U.S, **Katy Perry**'s 'Last Friday Night' became the 5th track to hit No.1 from one album, a record previously held by **Michael Jackson.** In the UK, Perry has appeared fifteen times across the last seventeen editions of *NOW.*

▶ **Coldplay**'s lead track from their fifth album featured elements of the song 'I Go To Rio' by Peter Allen and Adrienne Anderson. Anderson was better known for writing **Barry Manilow**'s 'Could It Be Magic', a series entrant in its own right courtesy of **Take That** (*NOW 24*).

▶ Despite a Top 3 hit with **Professor Green,** Ed Drewett found greater success as a songwriter, here co-authoring his second of three *NOW* entries for **The Wanted.** 'Best Song Ever' by **One Direction** (*NOW 86*) and 'Dear Darlin'' by **Olly Murs** (*NOW 85*) are also to his credit.

ALSO HAPPENING IN NOVEMBER 2011

- The year's most wanted toys were Moshi Monsters
- At the cinema: *Twilight Saga: Breaking Dawn Part I*, *My Week with Marilyn*, *The Ides of March*, *The Help*
- Albums released included **One Direction**'s debut, *Up All Night*, *On Your Radar* (**The Saturdays**) and *Talk That Talk* (**Rihanna**). Christmas No.1 was 'Wherever You Are' (**Military Wives with Gareth Malone**)
- Bestsellers published in 2011 included *A Dance With Dragons* (George R.R. Martin) and *Before I Go To Sleep* (S.J. Watson)

TRACKLISTING NOW 80

CD1

1 *Moves Like Jagger* Maroon 5 feat. Christina Aguilera
2 *We Found Love* Rihanna feat. Calvin Harris
3 *What Makes You Beautiful* One Direction
4 *Marry You* Bruno Mars
5 *Take A Chance On Me* JLS
6 *Jar Of Hearts* Christina Perri
7 *Mr. Know It All* Kelly Clarkson
8 *Heart Skips A Beat* Olly Murs feat. Rizzle Kicks
9 *Lightning* The Wanted
10 *All About Tonight* Pixie Lott
11 *All Fired Up* The Saturdays
12 *The Edge Of Glory* Lady Gaga
13 *Jealousy* Will Young
14 *I Won't Let You Go* James Morrison
15 *You Need Me, I Don't Need You* Ed Sheeran
16 *Cannonball* Damien Rice
17 *Video Games* Lana Del Rey
18 *Wherever You Will Go* Charlene Soraia
19 *Iris* Goo Goo Dolls
20 *Run For Your Life* Matt Cardle
21 *Lighthouse* Westlife

CD2

1 *Set Fire To The Rain* Adele
2 *Read All About It* Professor Green feat. Emeli Sandé
3 *Stereo Hearts* Gym Class Heroes feat. Adam Levine
4 *Earthquake* Labrinth feat. Tinie Tempah
5 *It Girl* Jason Derülo
6 *No Regrets* Dappy
7 *Without You* David Guetta feat. Usher
8 *Feel So Close* Calvin Harris
9 *Collide* Leona Lewis feat. Avicii
10 *Stay Awake* Example
11 *Party All Night (Sleep All Day)* Sean Kingston
12 *Off The Record* Tinchy Stryder feat. Calvin Harris & BURNS
13 *Loca People* Sak Noel
14 *Down With The Trumpets* Rizzle Kicks
15 *With Ur Love* Cher Lloyd feat. Mike Posner
16 *Who's Laughing Now* Jessie J
17 *Cheers (Drink To That)* Rihanna
18 *Got 2 Luv U* Sean Paul feat. Alexis Jordan
19 *Heaven* Emeli Sandé
20 *I Need* Maverick Sabre
21 *Don't Go* Wretch 32 feat. Josh Kumra
22 *Teardrop* The Collective

▶ 2011's *Children In Need* telethon benefited from 'Teardrop' by **The Collective**, whose massed ranks included *NOW* regulars **Chipmunk**, **Tulisa**, **Ed Sheeran**, **Tinchy Stryder**, **Wretch 32** and **Rizzle Kicks**. **Gary Barlow** organised the project. **Massive Attack**'s original version of the song was on *NOW 40*.

▶ **Damien Rice**'s 'Cannonball' was a hit in 2003 and 2004, and returned to the chart in late 2011 after an *X Factor* auditionee performed it. Eventual winners **Little Mix** then covered the song as their first single three months later.

▶ Debut appearance for the reigning 'Biggest Group in the World', **One Direction**. The boys have placed seven songs over the last nine editions. To date, they have chalked up over 20 million single sales globally.

ALSO HAPPENING IN APRIL 2012

- The Oxford and Cambridge Boat Race descended into chaos due to a swimmer in the water
- Facebook purchased Instagram for $1 billion
- *The Artist* won five Academy Awards including Best Picture. Meryl Streep won the Best Actress Oscar for her role in *The Iron Lady*
- At the cinema: *Headhunters*, 21 Jump Street, The Hunger Games, Mirror Mirror
- Albums released in early 2012 included *Pink Friday* (Nicki Minaj) and *Born to Die* (Lana Del Rey)

TRACKLISTING NOW 81

CD1

1 *Somebody That I Used To Know* Gotye feat. Kimbra
2 *Paradise* Coldplay
3 *Lego House* Ed Sheeran
4 *Levels* Avicii
5 *Stronger (What Doesn't Kill You)* Kelly Clarkson
6 *Domino* Jessie J
7 *Titanium* David Guetta feat. Sia
8 *Good Feeling* Flo Rida
9 *Elephant* Alexandra Burke feat. Erick Morillo
10 *Last Time* Labrinth
11 *Mama Do The Hump* Rizzle Kicks
12 *Dance With Me Tonight* Olly Murs
13 *Get Yourself Back Home* Gym Class Heroes feat. Neon Hitch
14 *One Thing* One Direction
15 *Seven Nation Army* Marcus Collins
16 *Twilight* Cover Drive
17 *Alone Again* Alyssa Reid feat. Jump Smokers
18 *Who You Are* Jessie J
19 *Ray Charles* Chiddy Bang
20 *Proud* JLS
21 *Wherever You Are* Military Wives, Gareth Malone & The London Metropolitan Orchestra

CD2

1 *Sexy And I Know It* LMFAO
2 *Wild Ones* Flo Rida feat. Sia
3 *Marry The Night* Lady Gaga
4 *Next To Me* Emeli Sandé
5 *International Love* Pitbull feat. Chris Brown
6 *Dedication To My Ex (Miss That)* Lloyd feat. André 3000 & Lil Wayne
7 *She Doesn't Mind* Sean Paul
8 *Troublemaker* Taio Cruz
9 *The One That Got Away* Katy Perry
10 *Antidote* Swedish House Mafia vs Knife Party
11 *When I Was A Youngster* Rizzle Kicks
12 *Love Me* Stooshe feat. Travie McCoy
13 *Kiss The Stars* Pixie Lott
14 *You Da One* Rihanna
15 *Bright Lights (Good Life)* Tinchy Stryder feat. Pixie Lott
16 *Shake It Out* Florence + The Machine
17 *Take Care* Drake feat Rihanna
18 *Born To Die* Lana Del Rey
19 *Cannonball* Little Mix
20 *T.H.E. (The Hardest Ever)* will.i.am feat. Mick Jagger and Jennifer Lopez
21 *Rockstar* Dappy feat. Brian May

A doff of the cap to the man behind the scenes: *NOW 81* was the last in the series to be compiled by Ashley Abram who had helmed every album since the second edition in 1984.

Making his *NOW* debut as a featured solo artist, twenty-eight years after his band made their first appearance on *NOW 2*: ladies and gentlemen, opportunity knocks for **Sir Michael Philip Jagger**.

Also coming in from the cold and clocking up a fourth consecutive decade in twiddly guitared appearances, Mr Brian May CBE – guesting here alongside unlikely bedfellow, Dappy.

ALSO HAPPENING IN JULY 2012

- At the London Olympics, Great Britain won 29 gold medals. On 'Super Saturday' alone there were six golds, including wins for Jessica Ennis in the Heptathlon and Mo Farah in the 10,000 metres
- *Fifty Shades of Grey* by E.L. James became the fastest-selling paperback of all time – the trilogy has now sold over 100 million copies
- At the cinema: *The Amazing Spider-man*, *The Dark Knight Rises*
- Albums released in summer 2012 included *Fall to Grace* (**Paloma Faith**) and *Ora* (**Rita Ora**)

TRACKLISTING NOW 82

CD1

1 *We Are Young* Fun feat. Janelle Monáe
2 *Call Me Maybe* Carly Rae Jepsen
3 *Payphone* Maroon 5 feat. Wiz Khalifa
4 *Whistle* Flo Rida
5 *Princess Of China* Coldplay & Rihanna
6 *Feel The Love* Rudimental feat. John Newman
7 *Starships* Nicki Minaj
8 *Where Have You Been* Rihanna
9 *R.I.P.* Rita Ora feat. Tinie Tempah
10 *Can't Say No* Conor Maynard
11 *Boyfriend* Justin Bieber
12 *Small Bump* Ed Sheeran
13 *Oliver Twist* D'Banj
14 *Black Heart* Stooshe
15 *Part Of Me* Katy Perry
16 *Primadonna* Marina & The Diamonds
17 *Picking Up The Pieces* Paloma Faith
18 *Drive By* Train
19 *Sparks* Cover Drive
20 *I Won't Give Up* Jason Mraz
21 *Too Close* Alex Clare
22 *My Kind Of Love* Emeli Sandé

CD2

1 *This Is Love* will.i.am feat. Eva Simons
2 *Call My Name* Cheryl Cole
3 *Hot Right Now* DJ Fresh feat. Rita Ora
4 *Young* Tulisa
5 *Turn Me On* David Guetta feat. Nicki Minaj
6 *Let's Go* Calvin Harris feat. Ne-Yo
7 *Scream* Usher
8 *LaserLight* Jessie J feat. David Guetta
9 *Turn Up The Music* Chris Brown
10 *Chasing The Sun* The Wanted
11 *30 Days* The Saturdays
12 *Euphoria* Loreen
13 *GreyHound* Swedish House Mafia
14 *212* Azealia Banks feat. Lazy Jay
15 *iLL Manors* Plan B
16 *So Good* B.o.B
17 *Level Up* Sway
18 *There She Goes* Taio Cruz
19 *Express Yourself* Labrinth
20 *Only The Horses* Scissor Sisters
21 *When She Was Mine* Lawson
22 *Sing* Gary Barlow & The Commonwealth Band

▶ *NOW 82* holds the record for the most weeks at No.1 on the compilation album chart – thirteen weeks, a quarter of a year.

▶ Exiting the series here, **Scissor Sisters** have yet to place a track on the Hot 100 singles chart in their native USA, a status which also applies to *NOW* hitmakers **The Dandy Warhols** and **Fun Lovin' Criminals.**

▶ **Loreen** won the 2012 Eurovision Song Contest with 'Euphoria'. Non-victorious UK entries from *NOW* history are **Love City Groove**'s 'Love City Groove' (*NOW 31*), **Gina G**'s 'Ooh Aah Just A Little Bit' (*NOW 34*), and **Precious**'s 'Say It Again' (*NOW 43*). The Eurovision-winning artists to be included on *NOW*s are **Abba, Celine Dion, Katrina & The Waves, Lulu** and **Bucks Fizz.**

ALSO HAPPENING IN NOVEMBER 2012

- **Psy's** *Gangnam Style* became the most-viewed YouTube video of all time
- Albums released in late 2012 included *Take the Crown* (**Robbie Williams**), *Take Me Home* (**One Direction**) and *DNA* (**Little Mix**). The Christmas No.1 was 'He Ain't Heavy, He's My Brother' (**The Justice Collective**)
- At the cinema: *Madagascar 3*, *Argo*, *Skyfall*, *Twilight: Breaking Dawn Part 2*, *Silver Linings Playbook*
- Bestsellers published in 2012 included *The Fault in Our Stars* (John Green), *Gone Girl* (Gillian Flynn) and *The Casual Vacancy* (J.K. Rowling)

TRACKLISTING NOW 83

CD1

1 *Gangnam Style* Psy
2 *Candy* Robbie Williams
3 *Don't You Worry Child* Swedish House Mafia feat. John Martin
4 *We Are Never Ever Getting Back Together* Taylor Swift
5 *I Found You* The Wanted
6 *Sweet Nothing* Calvin Harris feat. Florence Welch
7 *One More Night* Maroon 5
8 *Can You Hear Me? (Ayayaya)* Wiley feat. Skepta, JME & Ms D
9 *I Cry* Flo Rida
10 *Let Me Love You (Until You Learn To Love Yourself)* Ne-Yo
11 *Good Time* Owl City feat. Carly Rae Jepsen
12 *Wide Awake* Katy Perry
13 *Blow Me (One Last Kiss)* P!nk
14 *Wings* Little Mix
15 *Waterfalls* Stooshe
16 *Hottest Girl In The World* JLS
17 *Pound The Alarm* Nicki Minaj
18 *Lost In Your Love* Redlight
19 *How We Do (Party)* Rita Ora
20 *Under The Sun* Cheryl
21 *Heatwave* Wiley feat. Ms D
22 *Bom Bom* Sam and the Womp

CD2

1 *Beneath Your Beautiful* Labrinth feat. Emeli Sandé
2 *Hall Of Fame* The Script feat. will.i.am
3 *Spectrum (Say My Name)* Florence + the Machine
4 *She Wolf (Falling to Pieces)* David Guetta feat. Sia
5 *We'll Be Coming Back* Calvin Harris feat. Example
6 *Anything Could Happen* Ellie Goulding
7 *Wonder* Naughty Boy feat. Emeli Sandé
8 *Turn Around* Conor Maynard feat. Ne-Yo
9 *Live While We're Young* One Direction
10 *Don't Wake Me Up* Chris Brown
11 *You Bring Me Joy* Amelia Lily
12 *Some Nights* Fun
13 *Say Nothing* Example
14 *Taking Over Me* Lawson
15 *Brokenhearted* Karmin
16 *Simply Amazing* Trey Songz
17 *Summer Paradise* Simple Plan feat. Sean Paul
18 *Wonderful* Angel
19 *Watchtower* Devlin feat. Ed Sheeran
20 *I Will Wait* Mumford & Sons
21 *One Day Like This* Elbow

▷ YouTube phenomenon 'Gangnam Style' has been viewed over 2 billion times on the streaming platform. That's 28 per cent of the entire global population dancing like jockeys.

▷ Peaking initially at No.35, **Elbow**'s anthemic 'One Day Like This' rose to No.4, when the band played the Summer Olympics closing ceremony four years later. It remains their sole *NOW* entry to date.

▷ Born Alecia Moore, **P!nk** had been having hits since the year 2000 but it wasn't until *NOW 64* that she entered these annals. Making up for lost time, nine of her subsequent thirteen UK Top 40 singles have been included in the series.

ALSO HAPPENING IN MARCH 2013

- *Argo* was named Best Picture at the Academy Awards. Adele won the Oscar for Best Original Song for *Skyfall*
- Albums released in early 2013 included *The 20/20 Experience* (**Justin Timberlake**) and *The Next Day* (**David Bowie**)
- At the cinema: *Oz the Great and Powerful*, *GI Joe: Retaliation*, *The Croods*, *The Host*
- *The Cuckoo's Calling* by Robert Galbraith was published. It achieved modest sales until July when it was revealed that the author is actually J.K. Rowling and it became a No.1 bestseller

TRACKLISTING NOW 84

CD1

1 *One Way Or Another (Teenage Kicks)* One Direction
2 *Scream & Shout* will.i.am feat. Britney Spears
3 *I Knew You Were Trouble* Taylor Swift
4 *Just Give Me A Reason* P!nk feat. Nate Ruess
5 *Diamonds* Rihanna
6 *Pompeii* Bastille
7 *Impossible* James Arthur
8 *Troublemaker* Olly Murs feat. Flo Rida
9 *Locked Out Of Heaven* Bruno Mars
10 *Die Young* Ke$ha
11 *Ready Or Not* Bridgit Mendler
12 *DNA* Little Mix
13 *What About Us* The Saturdays feat. Sean Paul
14 *Something New* Girls Aloud
15 *Boomerang* Nicole Scherzinger
16 *Latch* Disclosure feat. Sam Smith
17 *Radioactive* Rita Ora
18 *Girl On Fire* Alicia Keys
19 *A Thousand Years* Christina Perri
20 *Clown* Emeli Sandé
21 *The Power Of Love* Gabrielle Aplin

CD2

1 *I Could Be The One* Avicii vs Nicky Romero
2 *Get Up (Rattle)* Bingo Players feat. Far East Movement
3 *Don't Stop The Party* Pitbull feat. TJR
4 *Drinking From The Bottle* Calvin Harris feat. Tinie Tempah
5 *Bassline Junkie* Dizzee Rascal
6 *Reload* Wiley feat. Chip
7 *Not Giving In* Rudimental feat. John Newman & Alex Clare
8 *Animal* Conor Maynard feat. Wiley
9 *White Noise* Disclosure feat. AlunaGeorge
10 *Rewind* Devlin feat. Diane Birch
11 *Standing In The Dark* Lawson
12 *Black Chandelier* Biffy Clyro
13 *My Songs Know What You Did In The Dark (Light Em Up)* Fall Out Boy
14 *Love Is Easy* McFly
15 *Only Love* Ben Howard
16 *Ho Hey* The Lumineers
17 *Little Things* One Direction
18 *Try* P!nk
19 *Please Don't Say You Love Me* Gabrielle Aplin
20 *Everywhere* Fleetwood Mac
21 *Explosions* Ellie Goulding
22 *He Ain't Heavy, He's My Brother* The Justice Collective

▷ **Girls Aloud**'s final hit single was featured to bring their tally up to twenty-one. All of their hits were produced by the Xenomania team, who have also helmed songs on *NOW*s for **Kylie Minogue, Sugababes, Gabriella Cilmi, Alesha Dixon, V, Mini Viva, Amelia Lily** and **Pet Shop Boys.**

▷ **Gabrielle Aplin**'s 'The Power Of Love' featured in a John Lewis advert. **Fyfe Dangerfield**'s 'She's Always A Woman' (2010, *NOW 76*), **Ellie Goulding**'s 'Your Song' (2010, *NOW 78*) and **Lily Allen**'s 'Somewhere Only We Know' (2013, *NOW 86*) gained prominence the same way.

▷ Released in aid of charities related to the Hillsborough disaster, **The Justice Collective** single featured several *NOW* regulars: **Robbie Williams, Melanie C, Paul McCartney, Paloma Faith** and **Holly Johnson** amongst them. Between them the vocalists involved have appeared on over 100 other *NOW* tracks.

ALSO HAPPENING IN JULY 2013

- Andy Murray became the first British man to win Wimbledon since 1936, beating Novak Djokovic in straight sets
- Prince George Alexander Louis was born to the Duke and Duchess of Cambridge. The new arrival became third in line to the throne
- At the cinema: *Pacific Rim*, *The Wolverine*, *Despicable Me 2*, *Monsters University*, *World War Z*, *The World's End*
- Albums released in summer 2013 included *Blurred Lines* (**Robin Thicke**), *Yeezus* (**Kanye West**) and *Magna Carta Holy Grail* (**Jay-Z**)

TRACKLISTING NOW 85

CD1

1 *Get Lucky* Daft Punk feat. Pharrell Williams
2 *Blurred Lines* Robin Thicke feat. Pharrell
3 *Let Her Go* Passenger
4 *Mirrors* Justin Timberlake
5 *La La La* Naughty Boy feat. Sam Smith
6 *I Love It* Icona Pop feat. Charli XCX
7 *Love Me Again* John Newman
8 *The Other Side* Jason Derülo
9 *True Love* P!nk feat. Lily Allen
10 *22* Taylor Swift
11 *Walks Like Rihanna* The Wanted
12 *Treasure* Bruno Mars
13 *Dear Darlin'* Olly Murs
14 *Heart attack* Demi Lovato
15 *Come & Get It* Selena Gomez
16 *Let's Get Ready To Rhumble* PJ & Duncan
17 *Bounce* Iggy Azalea
18 *Antenna* Fuse ODG
19 *Hey Porsche* Nelly
20 *Still Into You* Paramore
21 *Radioactive* Imagine Dragons
22 *Lighters (The One)* Gabz

CD2

1 *Waiting All Night* Rudimental feat. Ella Eyre
2 *Wild* Jessie J feat. Big Sean & Dizzee Rascal
3 *Need U (100%)* Duke Dumont feat. A*M*E
4 *#thatPOWER* will.i.am feat. Justin Bieber
5 *Play Hard* David Guetta feat. Ne-Yo & Akon
6 *I Need Your Love* Calvin Harris feat. Ellie Goulding
7 *Feel This Moment* Pitbull feat. Christina Aguilera
8 *Reload* Sebastian Ingrosso feat. Tommy Trash & John Martin
9 *This Is What It Feels Like* Armin van Buuren feat. Trevor Guthrie
10 *Lost & Not Found* Chase & Status feat. Louis M^ttrs
11 *So Good To Me* Chris Malinchak
12 *You & Me* Disclosure feat. Eliza Doolittle
13 *Jack* Breach
14 *Lights On* Wiley feat. Angel & Tinchy Stryder
15 *Goin' Crazy* Dizzee Rascal feat. Robbie Williams
16 *Gentleman* Psy
17 *Chocolate* The 1975
18 *Carry You* Union J
19 *Gentleman* The Saturdays
20 *On My Way* Charlie Brown
21 *Another Love* Tom Odell
22 *It's A Beautiful Day* Michael Bublé

▶ The 'feat' credit reaches overload as eighteen artists rope in others to help out. The first act to 'feature' this credit? 'I Got You Babe' by our old friends **UB40** featuring **Chrissie Hynde** (*NOW 6*).

▶ Despite uncredited support on **Kanye West**'s 'Stronger' (*NOW 68*), this is only **Daft Punk**'s second appearance (following 'Digital Love' on *NOW 50*). The group's Thomas Bangalter has also appeared previously with **Stardust** (*NOW 41*); his dad, who wrote 'D.I.S.C.O' for **Ottowan**, has not.

▶ **PJ & Duncan**'s TV-assisted surprise No.1 single in 2013 was written and produced by Nicky Graham. In 1972, Nicky played keyboards on **David Bowie**'s Ziggy Stardust tour. In 1987, he wrote the debut album by **Bros**.

ALSO HAPPENING IN NOVEMBER 2013

- *Doctor Who* celebrated its 50th anniversary
- Sony released the Playstation 4, selling 1 million on release day. Microsoft released the Xbox One
- At the cinema: *Philomena*, *Gravity*, *The Hunger Games: Catching Fire*, *Saving Mr Banks*
- Albums released in late 2013 included *The Marshall Mathers LP 2* **(Eminem)**, *ARTPOP* **(Lady Gaga)**, *Salute* **(Little Mix)** and *Midnight Memories* **(One Direction)**. The Christmas No.1 was 'Skyscraper' by X Factor winner **Sam Bailey**
- Bestsellers published in 2013 included *Inferno* (Dan Brown)

TRACKLISTING NOW 86

CD1

1 *Roar* Katy Perry
2 *Counting Stars* OneRepublic
3 *Talk Dirty* Jason Derulo feat. 2 Chain
4 *We Can't Stop* Miley Cyrus
5 *Wake Me Up* Avicii
6 *Look Right Through* Storm Queen
7 *Animals* Martin Garrix
8 *Burn* Ellie Goulding
9 *Hold On, We're Going Home* Drake feat. Majid Jordan
10 *You're Nobody 'Til Somebody Loves You* James Arthur
11 *Do I Wanna Know?* Arctic Monkeys
12 *Royals* Lorde
13 *Youth* Foxes
14 *Applause* Lady Gaga
15 *Gorilla* Bruno Mars
16 *Best Song Ever* One Direction
17 *It's My Party* Jessie J
18 *Can We Dance* The Vamps
19 *Juliet* Lawson
20 *Show Me Love (America)* The Wanted
21 *Bonfire Heart* James Blunt
22 *Somewhere Only We Know* Lily Allen

CD2

1 *Eat Sleep Rave Repeat* Fatboy Slim and Riva Starr feat. Beardyman
2 *Thinking About You* Calvin Harris feat. Ayah Marar
3 *You Make Me* Avicii
4 *Earthquake* DJ Fresh vs Diplo feat. Dominique Young Unique
5 *Sonnentanz (Sun Don't Shine)* Klangkarussell feat. Will Heard
6 *Summertime Sadness* Lana Del Rey vs Cedric Gervais
7 *Bang Bang* will.i.am
8 *What I Might Do* Ben Pearce
9 *Count On Me* Chase and Status feat. Moko
10 *Children Of The Sun* Tinie Tempah feat. John Martin
11 *Other Side Of Love* Sean Paul
12 *R U Crazy* Conor Maynard
13 *Lifted* Naughty Boy feat. Emeli Sandé
14 *Lost Generation* Rizzle Kicks
15 *Boom Boom (Heartbeat)* Ray Foxx feat. Rachel K Collier
16 *Cheating* John Newman
17 *Big When I Was Little* Eliza Doolittle
18 *Disco Love* The Saturdays
19 *Afterglow* Wilkinson
20 *Booyah* Showtek feat. We Are Loud & Sonny Wilson
21 *Something Really Bad* Dizzee Rascal feat. will.i.am
22 *The Fox (What Does The Fox Say?)* Ylvis

▶ **Fatboy Slim** returned as a credited artist fourteen years and forty-three editions after his previous appearance, and seventy-nine volumes after his first involvement: on 'Happy Hour' as the bassist with **The Housemartins**, *NOW 7*.
Mr Slim lent his remixing talents to 'Can You Dig It' by the **Mock Turtles** on *NOW 54*.

▶ Seven years after their initial breakthrough, with their first album amongst the ten fastest- selling of all time, **Arctic Monkeys** made their *NOW* debut with 'Do I Wanna Know?'.

▶ **Lorde** became the latest New Zealander to grace the *NOW* series, but she's by no means the first: Alannah Currie of **The Thompson Twins**, who is now married to Jimmy Cauty of the **KLF** (*NOW 19* and *21*), was with us all the way back on *NOW 2*.

ALSO HAPPENING IN APRIL 2014

- Same-sex marriage was legalised in England and Wales
- Malaysia Airlines Flight 370 went missing
- David Moyes was sacked as manager of Manchester United
- Bruce Forsyth stepped down as regular host of *Strictly Come Dancing*
- At the cinema: *The Amazing Spider-Man 2*, *Divergent*, *Half of a Yellow Sun*
- Albums released in early 2014 included *Little Red* (**Katy B**), *G I R L* (**Pharrell Williams**), *Kiss Me Once* (**Kylie Minogue**), *Shakira* (**Shakira**), *Meet the Vamps* (**The Vamps**) and *Sheezus* (**Lily Allen**)

TRACKLISTING NOW 87

CD1

1 *Happy* Pharrell Williams
2 *My Love* Route 94 feat. Jess Glynne
3 *I'm A Freak* Enrique Iglesias feat. Pitbull
4 *Hey Brother* Avicii
5 *Dark Horse* Katy Perry feat. Juicy J
6 *Money On My Mind* Sam Smith
7 *Word Up!* Little Mix
8 *She Looks So Perfect* 5 Seconds of Summer
9 *Wrecking Ball* Miley Cyrus
10 *Nasty* Pixie Lott
11 *Story Of My Life* One Direction
12 *Let Me Go* Gary Barlow
13 *If I Lose Myself* OneRepublic & Alesso
14 *Ready For Your Love* Gorgon City feat. MNEK
15 *Wild Heart* The Vamps
16 *Do What U Want* Lady Gaga feat. R. Kelly
17 *Do It All Over Again* Elyar Fox
18 *Crying For No Reason* Katy B
19 *All Of Me* John Legend
20 *Say Something* A Great Big World & Christina Aguilera
21 *How Long Will I Love You* Ellie Goulding
22 *Skyscraper* Sam Bailey

CD2

1 *#SELFIE* The Chainsmokers
2 *Timber* Pitbull feat. Ke$ha
3 *Tsunami (Jump)* DVBBS & Borgeous feat. Tinie Tempah
4 *Under Control* Calvin Harris & Alesso feat. Hurts
5 *Wizard* Martin Garrix & Jay Hardway
6 *Red Lights* Tiësto
7 *I Got U* Duke Dumont feat. Jax Jones
8 *Of The Night* Bastille
9 *Kids Again* Example
10 *Move* Little Mix
11 *Braveheart* Neon Jungle
12 *Dibby Dibby Sound* DJ Fresh vs Jay Fay feat. Ms Dynamite
13 *Dr. Who!* Tujamo & Plastik Funk feat. Sneakbo
14 *Thank You* Busta Rhymes feat. Q-Tip, Kanye & Lil Wayne
15 *Million Pound Girl (Badder Than Bad)* Fuse ODG
16 *Out Of My Head* John Newman
17 *Turn Back Time* Sub Focus
18 *Control* Matrix & Futurebound feat. Max Marshall
19 *Let Go For Tonight* Foxes
20 *Can't Rely On You* Paloma Faith
21 *Dance With Me* Le Youth feat. Dominique Young Unique
22 *Hey Now* London Grammar
23 *Riptide* Vance Joy
24 *Best Day Of My Life* American Authors

Having featured previously with **Naughty Boy** ('La, La, La', *NOW 85*), and sung with **Disclosure** ('Latch'), **Sam Smith** marks his solo debut in the *NOW* series with the first of two No.1 singles to date in 2014. 'Stay With Me' can be found on *NOW 88*.

With the release of his single 'Let Me Go', **Gary Barlow** pips Robbie to the post as the member of **Take That** with widest spread of appearances – both starting off on *NOW 22* with the boy band's 'It Only Takes A Minute'.

Lady Gaga and **R. Kelly** teamed up for 'Do What U Want'. The Lady rattled up her first ten *NOW* appearances in only sixteen editions (*NOW 72* to *87*) – it took Robert twice as long, from *NOW 28* to *59*, to hit the same mark.

ALSO HAPPENING IN JULY 2014

- The Commonwealth Games began in Glasgow
- At the cinema in summer 2014: *The Fault in Our Stars, How to Train Your Dragon 2, Transformers: Age of Extinction, Mrs. Brown's Boys D'Movie, Dawn of the Planet of the Apes, Boyhood, Hercules, Pudsey the Dog: the Movie*
- The summer's craze was the Rainbow Loom
- The Amazon Fire phone was due to become available in the US

TRACKLISTING NOW 88

CD1

1 *Ghost* Ella Henderson
2 *Sing* Ed Sheeran
3 *Stay With Me* Sam Smith
4 *Budapest* George Ezra
5 *Waves (Robin Schulz Radio Edit)* Mr Probz
6 *Problem* Ariana Grande feat. Iggy Azalea
7 *I Will Never Let You Down* Rita Ora
8 *A Sky Full Of Stars* Coldplay
9 *The Man* Aloe Blacc
10 *Love Never Felt So Good* Michael Jackson
11 *It's My Birthday* will.i.am feat. Cody Wise
12 *Fancy* Iggy Azalea feat. Charli XCX
13 *Loyal* Chris Brown feat. Lil Wayne & Tyga
14 *Extraordinary* Clean Bandit feat. Sharna Bass
15 *Right Here* Jess Glynne
16 *If I Go* Ella Eyre
17 *Classic* MKTO
18 *Don't Stop* 5 Seconds Of Summer
19 *Salute* Little Mix
20 *Me and My Broken Heart* Rixton
21 *Somebody To You* The Vamps feat. Demi Lovato
22 *Let It Go* Idina Menzel

CD2

1 *Rather Be* Clean Bandit feat. Jess Glynne
2 *Hideaway* Kiesza
3 *Gecko (Overdrive)* Oliver Heldens and Becky Hill
4 *Nobody To Love* Sigma
5 *Summer* Calvin Harris
6 *I Wanna Feel* SecondCity
7 *Jubel* Klingande
8 *Changes* Faul & Wad Ad vs Pnau
9 *Dangerous Love* Fuse ODG feat. Sean Paul
10 *Make U Bounce* DJ Fresh vs TC feat. Little Nikki
11 *Touch* Shift K3Y
12 *Always (Route 94 edit)* MK feat. Alana
13 *Wasted* Tiësto feat. Matthew Koma
14 *Anywhere For You* John Martin
15 *Take Me Home* Cash Cash feat. Bebe Rexha
16 *Don't Look Back* Matrix & Futurebound feat. Tanya Lacey
17 *Wiggle* Jason Derülo feat. Snoop Dogg
18 *Calling All Hearts* DJ Cassidy feat. Robin Thicke & Jessie J
19 *Welcome To The Jungle* Neon Jungle
20 *Chandelier* Sia
21 *Last Night* The Vamps
22 *Stay High (Habits Remix)* Tove Lo feat. Hippie Sabotage
23 *Only Love Can Hurt Like This* Paloma Faith

▶ 'Love Never Felt So Good' remained unreleased until after **Michael Jackson**'s death. With **Justin Timberlake** now on hand to add vocals, its inclusion on *NOW 88* marked the first representation for the King Of Pop since *NOW 4*. Jackson therefore holds record for the longest gap between appearances as well as the largest spread.

▶ **Aloe Blacc**'s 'The Man' contained a reinterpretation of part of the chorus of **Elton John**'s 'Your Song', originally a hit in 1971 but already in the *NOW* canon via **Ellie Goulding**'s version on *NOW 78*.

▶ At the time of writing, 'Let It Go' by **Idina Menzel** has been in the Top 40 for thirty-one consecutive weeks. The *Frozen* soundtrack – from where it is taken – is currently the best-selling album of the year.

Index

Page numbers in bold refer to *NOW* facts

A

B

C

G

I

J

K

L

N

T

V

W

X

Z

Pete Selby started working in the music industry in 1991 whilst avoiding higher education.

His favourite *NOW* album sleeve is *NOW 10* and he still misses *Smash Hits.*

Andy Healing has worked for an indie store, Our Price, Woolworths and Sainsbury's over a surprisingly long stretch dealing music to people. His first *NOW* was volume 7, on cassette. In his spare time he likes to leave writing micro-autobiographies to the last possible moment.

Louise Ward still has her first *NOW* album (volume 22, on tape). She has worked in the books buying team at Sainsbury's for 6 years and has read every *Sweet Valley High* book ever published.

The Authors would like to thank:
Scott Macrae, Pete Duckworth, Steve Pritchard, Jenny Fisher, Alex McCloy, Ashley Abram, Chris Shiels, Mavis Sarfo, Phil Carroll, Matt Newman.
At Simon and Schuster: Nick Venables, Rumana Haider, Olivia Morris, Abigail Bergstrom, Mike Jones.

A special thanks to Richard Branson.

Pete Selby would like to thank:
Our Price Class of '96. Dedicated to Jo, Esmé and Finn, with love.

Andy Healing would like to thank:
Classical Rock Records (don't look for it – it's not there anymore) and URB 963, where teeth were cut. Dedicated to Lucy, and all friends & family who have had to tolerate my stat-sourced balderdash. It was in the name of research, honest.

Louise Ward would like to thank:
The Sainsbury's Books team, my family & friends.
Dedicated to Mum, Dad, Grandma, Jacob & Jasmine.

All *NOW That's What I Call Music* cover art and *NOW* logos are trademarks.
© *NOW That's What I Call Music* LLP

First published in Great Britain by
Simon & Schuster UK Ltd, 2014
A CBS company
Copyright © 2014 by *NOW! That's What I Call Music* LLP and J Sainsbury PLC
This book is copyright under the Berne Convention.
No reproduction without permission.
All rights reserved.

The right of Andy Healing, Peter Selby and Louise Ward to be identified as the authors of this work has been asserted by them in accordance with sections 77 and 78 of the Copyright, Designs and Patents Act, 1988.

All *NOW* related stats and miscellany by Pete Selby and Andy Healing. 'Also happening...' entries by Louise Ward.

1 3 5 7 9 10 8 6 4 2

Simon & Schuster UK Ltd
1st Floor
222 Gray's Inn Road
London WC1X 8HB

www.simonandschuster.co.uk

Simon & Schuster Australia, Sydney

Simon & Schuster India, New Delhi

A CIP catalogue record for this book is available from the British Library.

ISBN: 978-1-47113-985-7

Design by Nick Venables.

Photo Credits: p18 Helga Esteb/Shutterstock.com, Featureflash/Shutterstock.com; p19 Featureflash/Shutterstock.com; p48 Featureflash/Shutterstock.com; p74 Featureflash/Shutterstock.com, Avis De Miranda/Shutterstock.com, J. Stone/Shutterstock.com, Helga Esteb/Shutterstock.com; p75 Everett Collection/Shutterstock.com; p104 Northfoto/Shutterstock.com; p105 Featureflash/Shutterstock.com; p164 S.Bukley/Shutterstock.com, Featureflash/Shutterstock.com, Jaguar PS/Shutterstock.com; p195 J. Stone/Shutterstock.com, Everett Collection/Shutterstock.com, Helga Esteb/Shutterstock.com, Featureflash/Shutterstock.com; p196 Jaguar PS/Shutterstock.com

The author and publishers have made all reasonable efforts to contact copyright-holders for permission, and apologise for any omissions or errors in the form of credits given.
Corrections may be made to future printings.

Printed in Spain.